Folk Culture
in the Digital Age

Folk Culture in the Digital Age

The Emergent Dynamics of Human Interaction

Edited by
Trevor J. Blank

UTAH STATE UNIVERSITY PRESS
❖
LOGAN

© 2012 by the University Press of Colorado

Published by Utah State University Press
An imprint of the University Press of Colorado
5589 Arapahoe Avenue, Suite 206C
Boulder, Colorado 80303

The University Press of Colorado is a proud member of

 The Association of American University Presses.

The University Press of Colorado is a cooperative publishing enterprise supported, in part, by Adams State University, Colorado State University, Fort Lewis College, Metropolitan State University of Denver, Regis University, University of Colorado, University of Northern Colorado, Utah State University, and Western State Colorado University.

ISBN: 978-0-87421-889-3 (paper)
ISBN: 978-0-87421-890-9 (e-book)

Cover design by Barbara Yale-Read

Cover illustration by Dominic "D.A." Tinio
Website: dominictinio.com
Tumblr: daofblackrock.tumblr.com/

Library of Congress Cataloging-in-Publication Data

Folk culture in the digital age : the emergent dynamics of human interaction / edited by Trevor J. Blank.
     p. cm.
  Includes bibliographical references and index.
  ISBN 978-0-87421-889-3 (pbk.) — ISBN 978-0-87421-890-9 (e-book)
  1. Folklore and the Internet. 2. Folklore—Computer network resources. I. Blank, Trevor J.
  GR44.E43F653 2012
  398.20285—dc23
                        2012032693

To John H. McDowell

Contents

     Look at a Virtual Community of Collectors
                         Bill Ellis   166

9   Face-to-Face with the Digital Folk: The Ethics of
     Fieldwork on Facebook
                     Montana Miller   212

     References   233
     About the Contributors   257
     Index   261

Acknowledgments

It has been a tremendous honor and privilege to work with the fantastic contributors of this volume, whose professionalism and dedication made my experience as an editor so incredibly fulfilling and enjoyable. In addition to the contributors, I wish to express my sincerest gratitude to everyone at Utah State University Press for their reliable enthusiasm and support throughout the book's production. In particular, I am indebted to John Alley and Michael Spooner for their steadfast guidance and encouragement, and for their amazing patience and tolerance of my many long e-mails packed with far too many questions. I would also like to thank the two anonymous reviewers of the book, whose suggestions greatly helped tighten and finalize the manuscript's contents.

Outside of this particular project, numerous individuals provided immeasurable support and/or intellectual stimulation. Above all, my wife, Angelina, and our dog, Penny, have helped make our home into a pleasant and loving retreat, full of good music and bad Nicolas Cage movies. My parents, Bruce and Anita, my sister, Natalie, and my in-laws Phil, Laura, and Christy Sanfilippo have all been pillars of loving support as well. Special thanks are due to my friends and colleagues Jade Alburo, Ron and Cathy Baker, Gabrielle Berlinger, Donald Allport Bird, Ian Brodie, Rebekah Burchfield, Charley Camp, Susan Eckelmann, Tim Evans, Gary Alan Fine, Russell Frank, Stephen Olbrys Gencarella, Joseph Goodwin, Spencer Lincoln Green, John Heflin, Suzanne Godby Ingalsbe, Jason Baird Jackson, Jeana Jorgensen, Merrill Kaplan, Julia Kelso, Andrea Kitta, Janet Langlois, Justin Levy, Tim Lloyd, Jay Mechling, Amy Milligan, Jodine Perkins, David Puglia, Kate Schramm, Jim Seaver, Steve Stanzak, Jeff Tolbert, Kristiana Willsey, and Adam Zolkover for all their support (in academic and non-academic ventures alike) over the years.

Finally, during my stint as a graduate student at Indiana University, John H. McDowell served as my advisor and frequent teacher. He was unusually supportive of my interest in studying folklore and the Internet, and, as I recall, he was one of the few faculty members at the time who also shared my interest in such research. John H. McDowell's early encouragement has had a profound impact on the trajectory of my career as a folklorist, and I dedicate this book to him.

A Brief Word on QR Codes

QR CODES ARE SMALL, SQUARE BARCODES THAT CONTAIN embedded information, such as a website, an e-mail address, or a phone number, among other possibilities. When scanned by a smartphone, tablet, or other capable computer device, QR codes can instantly transfer a reader directly to a website or a video clip on their device. Throughout the course of this volume, you may notice the occasional placement of QR codes in several chapters. In such instances, the QR codes have been intentionally placed in the margins alongside a paragraph that explicitly discusses the corresponding website or video clip that is embedded in the QR code. To enhance or supplement your reading of *Folk Culture in the Digital Age*, please feel free to scan a QR code and explore numerous additional, external dimensions of contributors' scholarship that strive to go well beyond the confines of this book and into the digital ether!

Folk Culture in the Digital Age

Introduction

Pattern in the Virtual Folk Culture of Computer-Mediated Communication

Trevor J. Blank

When historian Henry Adams stepped into the Paris Exhibition of 1900, a twirling, whizzing, bedazzling machine caught his eye.[1] Enamored with this "God-like creature" (in his words), Adams felt overwhelmed by the looming profundity of technology and its implications for the future. Later, in his autobiography, *The Education of Henry Adams* (1918), he recollects this moment and notes that the machine—"the dynamo"—appears to serve as a symbol for man's replacement of religion with technology. For Adams, the implication of this symbolic displacement was that man now worships machine; thus, people will henceforth stop at nothing to ensure the forward progress of technological innovation. Considering the context of Adams's time, a period of rapid labor mobilization and industrialization, he boldly predicts that someday man will serve machine.

It would be an understatement today to suggest that Henry Adams was correct in his prescient hypothesis. Indeed, one cannot enter a crowded movie theater, mall, or local teen hotspot (among numerous other places) in the United States without seeing technological minions devoutly using their cell phones or smartphones with mindboggling speed and dexterity as they text message others, play games, read and reply to e-mail, and/or sign into their profile on a social networking site.[2] Throughout the country, it is fairly common to encounter an individual carrying on a hands-free phone conversation through the use of a Bluetooth headset, located inconspicuously in one ear—which occasionally gives others in the user's proximity the false impression that they are talking to themselves![3] Meanwhile, the

DOI: 10.7330/9780874218909.c00   1

earlier means of wireless connectivity, like pagers/beepers and PalmPilots, have largely fallen into obscurity or morphed into something else altogether amid technological progress (see Selingo 2002).

Once a staple of on-the-go communication technology in America, pay phones are increasingly useless for many and are rapidly disappearing as Internet and new media technologies provide new opportunities for connectivity across geographical boundaries (Hanks 2010; Silverman 2007). According to the Pew Research Center's Internet & American Life Project (2011), approximately 85 percent of Americans over the age of eighteen now own a cell phone, with 90 percent of adults having at least one in their household (Zickuhr 2011); and roughly 35 percent of all American adults now own a smartphone (A. Smith 2011).[4] These mobile devices are often used in juxtaposition with stationary desktop computers at home or work, or with other smaller, more portable technological devices like laptop computers and tablets, which are also capable of facilitating the creation, adoption, and/or dissemination of folklore (see Horrigan 2009).[5]

In cases where users have limited access to these devices or a high-speed Internet connection, mobile devices provide an alternate route to the Internet, most notably for individuals from low-income households and other groups, such as teens and minorities, who have previously faced greater barriers to access and participation in computer-mediated communication (Brown, Campbell, and Ling 2011; Caverly, Ward, and Caverly 2009; see also Grameen Foundation 2009; Hargittai and Litt 2011). The key thing to note is that computer-mediated communication technology has clearly advanced beyond the need for physical tethering to a modem or electrical outlet. Wireless connection to the Internet or a cellular communication network is now possible throughout most of the United States and Canada (Howard, Busch, and Sheets 2010).[6] The times they are a-changin', and for folklorists, the inexorable advancement of computer-mediated communication technology has sparked important discussions, especially as new media devices have found more widespread adoption.

On the surface, it may appear that the identification of "folkness" via a technological medium (such as the Internet) is presumptuous, or worse, inherently "non-folk," since it requires some technical prowess with computer-mediated communication in order to be engaged. However, there is an inborn "folk" presence in cyberspace by virtue of the fact that people are behind nearly every symbolic interaction that takes place online and through new media technology. The technology is merely a conduit for expression—even if folklore scholars have been slow to fully acknowledge this in years past (see Blank 2009b). In truth, the permeation of technologically mediated folklore undoubtedly *does* mean that new and compounding research should be undertaken in order to complement (and possibly extend or amend) existing research on vernacular expression—it only makes sense considering that expressive behaviors are changing due to fundamental shifts in the ways that people go about construing meaning from their everyday lives. However, the study of technologically mediated folklore poses no threat of destroying or displacing more traditional folkloristic concepts and methodologies; it only presents the opportunity to revisit and recontextualize them en route to garnering new insights on contemporary folk culture.

It bears noting that the fear of cultural displacement via mass culture is nothing new.[7] Pundits predicted that radio technology would destroy traditions, but the medium instead helped reinforce some dynamics of storytelling and introduced listeners to folk music.[8] The introduction of the television only added further speculation that broadcast technology would spell doom for folk culture. Writing in 1961, historian Daniel Boorstin lamented that American society had "witnessed the decline of the 'folk' and the rise of the 'mass'," adding that "While the folk created heroes, the mass could only look and listen for them . . . The folk had a universe of its own creation . . . The mass lives in a very different fantasy world" (1987 [1961], 56). Fortunately, Boorstin's pessimism ultimately proved to be unfounded. As folklorist Linda Dégh notes, "mass media liberated folklore from its earlier confinement to the so-called lower layers of society and from the prejudice . . . that stigmatized it" (1994, 2).[9] So folk and mass culture not only coexist, they tend to intersect and influence each other in a productive way. After all, mass culture *uses* folk culture (see Blank 2009b, 12; Bronner 2004; Kirshenblatt-Gimblett 1998, 307). And as folklorist Robert Glenn Howard explains, when the folk "express meaning through new communication technologies, the distinction between folk and mass is . . . blurred by the vernacular deployment of institutionally produced commercial technologies," adding that with "online participatory media, the distinction is further blurred because the content that emerges intermingles vernacular, commercial, and institutional interests" (2008a, 194).

We must avoid the temptation to conceptualize the folk processes behind technologically mediated vernacular expression as separate or inherently different from correlative patterns of interaction found in face-to-face contexts. Instead, it is imperative that folklorists acknowledge and further contemplate the myriad ways that folk culture in the Digital Age is a product of hybridization (Blank 2013; de Souza e Silva 2006; Howard 2008a, 2008b). That is to say, new media technology has become so ubiquitous and integrated into users' communication practices that it is now a viable instrument and conduit of folkloric transmission; it works reciprocally with oral tradition, offering digital renderings of familiar interactive dynamics that allow users to advantageously communicate across face-to-face and digital settings in equally meaningful ways (see Larsen, Urry, and Axhausen 2008). One expressive venue is not separate from the other; users employ them cooperatively and interchangeably.

A barrier to demonstrating the presence of folk culture online comes from the fact that many antiquated arguments and factual misconceptions remain uncontested, such as the belief that Americans' access to the Internet is still disproportionately low among minorities and families with lower incomes (Yardi and Bruckman 2012).[10] At first glance, it may appear that the online venue *is* geared toward specific groups of people; however, this is not the case. Simply put, the Internet is *not* an elite medium. Beyond the home or work environment, it is readily available at schools, public libraries—even a tradition-centered folk group like the Amish use the Internet to occasionally communicate through e-mail and listserv![11]

While academics, computer enthusiasts, and the military primarily used the early days of the Internet for communication and information sharing (Abbate 1999; T. Friedman 2005; Hafner and Lyon 1998), today's participants come from all walks of life. Although it is true that early Internet users in America *were* predominantly white and middle class, current demographic data suggests that the medium attracts an increasingly diverse body of users, which serves to project a more accurate, inclusive culmination of dominant expressive motifs and values in American culture: 79 percent of adult men and women in the United States are regular Internet users. From a racial demographic perspective, 80 percent of white adults, 71 percent of black adults, and 82 percent of Hispanic adults use the Internet. Internet users comprise 95 percent of people aged 18–29, 87 percent of those 30–49, 78 percent of those 50–64, and 42 percent of those over 65. Families with a household income of under $30,000 yield a 64 percent Internet participation rate; $30,000–$49,999, 84 percent; $50,000–$74,999, 89 percent; and households earning over $75,000 have a 95 percent participation rate.[12] These percentages have risen dramatically since such data was regularly collected, beginning in 1995, and call attention to the penetration of new media technology into the social lives of the majority of Americans—rich and poor; young and old; male and female; black, white, and Hispanic.[13]

By early 2010, new research revealed that the average person spent up to thirty-one hours per week on the Internet; six out of every ten people received the news *digitally* every day, and at least one-third of Internet users posted updates about their status or personal goings-on at least once a week through social networking sites like Facebook and Twitter (Lardinois 2010; Rainie and Purcell 2010). Given the continual progression and cultural penetration of computer-mediated communication technologies (as well as their growing affordability and near-universal usability), subsequent calculations of these usage statistics will unquestionably yield significantly higher figures every year into the future.

If we accept the premise that folklore is capable of disseminating and meaningfully reaching individuals via technologically mediated communication, where do we begin? Is there a clear entry point for folklorists to identify examples of technologically mediated vernacular expression? And amid all of these rapid cultural changes and oscillating expressive modes, what can folklore scholars offer by documenting, analyzing, and presenting new research on folk culture in the Digital Age?

VIRTUALIZING FOLK CULTURE: EXPRESSIVE PATTERNS, EMERGENT CONCEPTS, AND CONSIDERATIONS

Traditionally, learning environments have been associated with corporeal interactive educational settings but now most certainly include digitally simulated/technologically mediated communicative venues as well.[14] The ways in which people learn, share, participate, or engage with others is changing, hybridizing, and adopting new media technologies in order to complement and supplement traditional means of vernacular expression. Many vetted and revered observations about folk culture now require reconsideration and, in some cases, updating via revision or new, compounding research. That said, there is no cause for alarm; folk culture has always been susceptible to change. And just because the most popular and far-reaching means of transmitting and receiving folklore today is often *computer-mediated* (as opposed to oral transmission or via face-to-face communication), the reality is that there is a lot of behavioral and structural overlap in many folkloric forms that exist both on- and offline. There is not only a clear hybridization of vernacular expression across lines of corporeality but altogether new (native) and emergent expressive phenomena ripe for folkloristic exploration and analysis.

Like all folklore, technologically mediated vernacular expression contains *patterns*: patterns of communicating or transmitting expression (in myriad forms—textual, visual, symbolic); patterns of discourse following an event (the protocols dictating social decorum); aesthetic patterns (in creating and/or designing a website or blog); or patterns of and within expressions themselves (narrative structure and organization, folk slang and jargon usage, and the influence of context).[15] Certainly, the collection and interpretation of expressive patterns is a hallmark of folkloristic inquiry (Charlot 1983; Glassie 1968; Halpert 1951; Kodish 1983; Paredes 1958; Schmaier 1963; Taylor 1964). Even as technology advances at an incredible rate, vernacular expression continues to emerge, adapt, and evolve across various forms of computer-mediated communication technology in lockstep. Within these cultural scenes and various enactments of symbolic expression, either individually or in conjunction with others in a group or community setting online, patterns naturally emerge. And without fail, they virtualize and mimic the dynamics or performative characteristics of many previously documented folkloric forms collected before the Internet was a pervasive expressive medium.[16]

Oxymoronically, many of the texts and performative dynamics that folklorists have traditionally identified in face-to-face contexts appear to be surfacing through technology in very similar meaningful ways as their oral and corporeal precedents (Baron 2010; Crystal 2006, 2011; Fernback 2003; Mason 1998; Soffer 2010; see also Ong 1988; Preston 1994).[17] Through communal reinforcement and user imitation, digital rhetoric purposely invokes familiar social or behavior customs, linguistic inflections, or symbolic gestures to convey correlating expressions from the "real world." In addition to textually simulating real-world emotions, this rhetoric also becomes inextricably linked with the real-world expressive patterns and strategies that it seeks to emulate. As rhetoric scholar Barbara Warnick points out,

> the emergence of the Web has brought with it a communication context that often is focused as much on the reader as on the message author; addresses dispersed audiences of users consuming modular, disaggregated texts; and conveys messages in a nonlinear mode that is differently consumed by various audiences. (2007, 121)

With regular online interaction and familiarity, users are eventually able to instantaneously identify and decode any expressive patterns or social dynamics online by cognitively linking them to a real-world correlate. Even so, the ways in which people actually express themselves and forge their identities online—whether anonymously, pseudonymously, openly, or something in between—also encompass distinct communicative practices that are not always entirely transferable or functionally replicable in face-to-face settings.[18] Wholly unique slang terms, concepts, and symbol gestures or emoticons abound.[19] Folk groups can be quickly identified online through websites and virtual communities that elicit ritualized participation and rhetorical discourse about matters of mutual interest. But even though these multifaceted means of identity presentation are most effective and authentically employed in their original, digital expressive contexts, there are many other forms of folklore originating online that are capable of influencing some forms of vernacular expression or folkloric transmission in the corporeal world. This is especially true in instances where individuals attempt to transpose digital forms of expression into correlating, symbolically equivalent face-to-face expressions, even if their delivery or composition do not fully align.

For example, in an online context, an individual's use of "LOL"—"laugh out loud"—typically conveys when that person finds something humorous, especially during the course of communicative exchanges with others via instant messaging or texting, or on a website containing a discussion forum or comments section. In person, however, someone might phonetically say aloud LOL [pronounced *lawl*] when trying to convey (often sarcastically) that they find something to be mildly humorous rather than just laughing or chuckling (see Frank 2009, 99–101; Mason 1998). Regardless of the expressive venue where someone uses LOL, the underlying fact remains that both corporeal and digital invocations of the term draw upon the same popularized, symbolic initialism that became widely adopted through its continual dissemination across numerous forms of computer-mediated interaction. The hybridization of folk culture is at work.

Even larger social dynamics underlying folk culture in the United States are clearly hybridizing in the Digital Age, especially as the long-standing traditions of folk protest grow to rely on participation through the collaborative use of mobile and other new media technologies in order to organize and sustain mass support.[20] This is particularly evident in the two most vivacious and enduring grassroots, populist political movements to appear in recent U.S. history: the Tea Party movement, which emerged in early

2009 with a conservative and libertarian agenda, and the Occupy movement, which burst onto the scene in September 2011. The Tea Party and Occupy movements have both used new media to maximize the reach and impact of their respective messages, distributing ideological literature, organizing and publicizing participatory events, and fund-raising through the medium while simultaneously facilitating digital and face-to-face forums for symbolic interaction, citizen journalism, and vernacular discourse that promote group cohesion and community.[21] But while computer-mediated communication has fueled these movements' growth and online presence, its greatest value has come from the ability to organize massive in-person participatory events where symbolic unity strengthens the resolve of protesters. Still, in-person gatherings and protests typically do not remain confined to their locus of enactment; video and audio clips, pictures, and blog postings about event happenings are circulated online, including through the news media, in an effort to further crystallize burgeoning narratives and public perceptions of the movements' message and/or its constituents, usually in a positive or at least sympathetic way.

In computer-mediated contexts, the folkloric process of repetition and variation is often identified by emergent patterns of widely disseminated, visually oriented vernacular expression; these constructs are emically referred to as *memes*, a term originally coined by evolutionary biologist Richard Dawkins (1976) to apply and explain evolutionary principles to cultural phenomena (see Foote 2007; McNeill 2009, 84–86, 96n2).[22] The visuality of the online medium has breathed life into various types of memes, such as image macros[23] and viral videos.[24] An especially colorful example of these kinds of creative expression, deriving from the interplay of the Occupy movement's online presence and general notoriety with the folk response to the heavy-handed actions of law enforcement during a nonvio-lent, in-person protest, can be seen in the wealth of clever "Photoshopped," or digitally manipulated, images depicting University of California–Davis police officer Lieutenant John Pike—better known as the "Casually Pepper Spray Everything Cop" (Figure 0.1).

Louise Macabitas, a 22-year-old psychobiology major at UC–Davis, photographed Pike pepper-spraying student protesters and posted it to her personal Facebook page on November 18, 2011. It was soon posted to the popular file-sharing social networking site Reddit before disseminating across the Internet and into the hands of numerous folk artists-in-waiting

Figure 0.1. The Casually Pepper Spray Everything Cop. Lieutenant John Pike of the UC–Davis Police pepper-sprays student protestors on November 18, 2011. This photograph (in addition to various accompanying videos of the event that were later posted online) set off a firestorm of controversy and provided the impetus for the "Pepper Spray Cop" meme.

(see O'Brien 2011). Within hours, the image went viral, and creative Internet users quickly began Photoshopping Pike into various historic paintings (such as John Trumbull's [1819] painting *Declaration of Independence* and Georges Seurat's [1884] *A Sunday Afternoon on the Island of La Grande Jatte*), symbolic figures and images in religious and popular culture (Figure 0.2), and actual photographs from modern history.

Perhaps most fittingly, one of the more popular Photoshopped historical images depicted Pike at another infamous event characterized by law enforcement's excessive force against unarmed college students: the shooting of four student protestors at Kent State University on May 4, 1970 (Figure 0.3). Unlike many of the other Photoshopped images of Pike, where he is seamlessly inserted as part of the scene, the image shows him bursting out of the original UC–Davis image (where he and the background are in color) and into the black and white past, stepping into the most famous image associated with the Kent State tragedy, originally captured by John Filo (who won a Pulitzer Prize for the photograph).

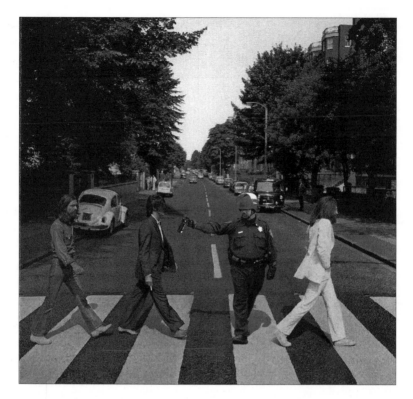

Figure 0.2. Lieutenant John Pike Pepper-Sprays the Beatles on Abbey Road. In this popularly circulated Photoshopped image, Lieutenant Pike replaces Ringo Starr in the Beatles' famous *Abbey Road* album cover and douses an unsuspecting Paul McCartney as he crosses the street. Note the attention to detail: even Pike's shadow is included!

The clever and often hilarious Photoshopped mockery of Pike's actions, captured in the hearty participation of numerous individuals (as creators, commentators, and disseminators), restored some symbolic control over the disheartening event back to the folk. Many individuals who were not interested and/or savvy with image-editing software still managed to contribute to the humorous dialogue, perhaps most notably by posting satirical "product reviews" on Amazon.com of *Defense Tech DT-56895 MK-9 Stream*—better known as Pike's pepper spray of choice for "watering [his] hippies," as one popular Photoshopped image read (see tinyurl.com/PepperSprayCopAmazonReview).

Clearly, the "Casually Pepper Spray Everything Cop" meme displays the hallmark characteristics of repetition and variation found in all genres of folklore. But it is only one salient example out of the thousands of digital

Figure 0.3. Four Dead in Ohio. Here, Lieutenant John Pike adds insult to historical injury by pepper-spraying Mary Ann Vecchio, who was famously photographed
by John Filo after she was shot by Ohio National Guardsmen at the "Kent State
Massacre" of May 4, 1970.

expressive threads in circulation, each reverberating through cyberspace,
repeating and varying along the way, while *also* gaining notoriety through
oral transmission.

Sticking to the principle observations and theories that ground folkloristics and applying them to contemporary computer-mediated vernacular
expression raises the potential (and underscores the need) for folklorists to
amend or reconsider earlier conclusions about how and why folklore perme-
ates in increasingly complex forms. In addition, pre-Internet folklore scholarship on vernacular expression can potentially serve as an excellent starting
point for comparative analysis or for further distinguishing the divergent
characteristics between corporeal and computer-mediated expressive venues
(both as facilitators of communication generally, and folklore, especially). At
the end of the day, it is crucial to remember that the overwhelming majority of vernacular expression online is initiated, prolonged, and transformed
through the actions of individual *people*, or by folks interacting in a group
or community setting online (see Baym 1993, 1994; Howard 2011; Jenkins

2008; Rheingold 2000). As such, it behooves folklorists to acknowledge that there is *significant* overlap in the distinguishing characteristics, contextual functions, and methods of dissemination between both face-to-face and virtualized venues of vernacular expression. If we accept that computer-mediated communication is fully capable of generating, transmitting, and archiving folklore and other symbolic communicative expression, then folklorists simply need to rely on their instincts and training in order to make sense of vernacular expression as it circulates via technology.[25]

It is imperative that folklorists revisit the scholarly conclusions forged before the Internet and new media technology fundamentally altered the ways in which people go about communicating with others. Concepts like "folk group" and "community" are more complicated in the context of the present day. Due to the influence of social networking, the ways in which individuals categorize and organize their hierarchy of friends continues to evolve as technology progresses; meanwhile, their changing definitions as to what constitutes a "stranger"—also brought on by the influence of social networking sites and complementary computer-mediated expression—clearly merits scrutiny as well. The informants of the online world can be ambiguous or enigmatic, but they often provide immense, underrated value to the study of contemporary vernacular expression. Even when folklore scholars cannot *physically* connect to such informants, numerous digitized creative outputs merit collection and analysis, such as avatars, video mashups, Photoshopped images, e-mailed humor, urban legend transmissions, virtual community discussion threads, real-time multiplayer games, and individually maintained websites.[26] In short, there remains a great deal of underexplored expressive material online that still merits folkloristic inquiry.

THE SCOPE OF *FOLK CULTURE IN THE DIGITAL AGE*

The reach of new media and the Internet—an incorporeal and liminal venue that perpetually simulates and virtualizes a meaningful construction of reality—is still expanding and maturing. Online or in-person, folklore is consumed, and as it is shared, it continues to undergo evolution, redefinition, and subsequent hybridized dissemination across various technological mediums and/or face-to-face interactions. In folkloristic terms: repetition and variation is clearly present and at a far greater and far-reaching rate than ever before.

With this in mind, it would be unrealistic to suggest that this volume—
or any volume, for that matter—presents an exhaustive, composite portrayal
of folk culture in the Digital Age. The Internet—and by extension, folklore
on and *from* the Internet—is simply far too dynamic and ever-changing to
be fully captured by a lone publication, especially as it exists in its latest, up-
to-the-minute iterations. So why try at all, then?

This volume's predecessor, *Folklore and the Internet: Vernacular
Expression in a Digital World* (Blank 2009a), was the first folkloristic anthology to examine the myriad ways in which folklore flourishes on the Internet
and how the online venue shapes, and is shaped by, the transmission of folklore. Producing the first book on any topic inherently requires the presentation of the subject matter's distinctive characteristics, thereby necessitating
an overview of salient examples that sufficiently demonstrate the need for its
greater scholarly examination. By following this protocol, *Folklore and the
Internet* endeavored to offer a theoretical grounding for the study of folklore
in the Digital Age[27] while also revealing the integration and cyclical, sym-
biotic influence of Internet and new media technologies on contemporary
folkloric forms of expression—especially those genres long documented by
scholars, including folk narratives (rumors, humor, etc.); folk groups; identity and community formation; religion and beliefs; memorialization; and
even the ways that digital technology and computer-mediated communication can and does impact folklorists who work in the public sector. In what
was largely underexplored scholastic territory for folklorists (at the time),[28]
Folklore and the Internet covered a lot of ground and helped to elucidate the
wide net cast by technologically mediated folklore and generated greater
attention and enthusiasm to the study of folklore and the Internet.[29]

Still, *Folklore and the Internet* had (and has) its limitations. One might
note the considerable wealth of expressive material falling into the book's
purview, yet the ambitious case studies presented therein only detail a handful of the mechanisms and venues for folkloric expression online. Why
aren't there *more*? The supporting rationale is simple: only so much can (or
should) be covered in a single, initial volume—especially given the relative
newness and vastness of the volume's subject matter at the time of publication. Indeed, a substantial portion of *Folklore and the Internet* was intentionally aimed at legitimizing the study of its very contents. And considering
the dearth of folkloristic scholarship on technologically mediated communication and expression preceding the volume's publication, the decision to
introduce its subject matter deliberately and conscientiously—taking time

to argue for its scholastic legitimacy while also exercising restraint and discretion in limiting its breadth so as not to overwhelm readers—is hopefully easier to understand now.

Thanks to these introductory efforts, as well as the growing interest and acceptability of studying technologically mediated folklore, *this* volume is free to dedicate more attention to direct examples of folkloric phenomena as it is transmitted, generated, and/or encountered through technologically mediated communication and expression. Moreover, instead of endeavoring to convince readers of the legitimacy of folklore generated on or by such technological mediums compared to more "traditional" source materials and/or methods of folkloristic inquiry, the contributing authors to this volume operate with the assumption that these contentions are fundamentally sound.

To complement (and supplement) its predecessor, *Folk Culture in the Digital Age* aims to document the emergent cultural scenes and expressive folkloric communications that are being made possible by digital new media technologies. Accordingly, this volume's scope is not limited to just computer technology and the Internet (although it is still the predominant area of inquiry) but also to cell phones, smartphones, tablets, and other such devices with Wi-Fi or 3G/4G capabilities, as well as social networking platforms like Facebook and Twitter, where so many now share their innermost thoughts and feelings. Above all, this volume aims to shed greater light on the folk processes that new media technologies facilitate or directly engage in order to thrive. Doing so reveals the fascinating ways in which people are transmitting folklore and construing meaning from daily interactions with technologically mediated communication devices.

Opening this volume is Robert Glenn Howard's essay, "How Counterculture Helped Put the 'Vernacular' in Vernacular Webs." Howard grounds our understanding of folk culture in the Digital Age by providing a historical overview of the important people and groups who facilitated the dawning of the computer revolution and managed to imbed a valuation of vernacularity into network communication. Beginning with an examination of Ted Nelson's *Computer Lib* (1974) and the popular hobbyist publication the Homebrew Computer Club newsletter, Howard explains how these types of publications inspired and united their readers to believe in the potential for computer technologies to be used primarily by *people* instead of institutions. In doing so, he details how this vernacular ethos shared between computer enthusiasts and hobbyists ultimately spurred the creation of the personal computer; emerged in the development of the basic computer code behind all Internet communication, despite being funded and overseen by institutions; and is now inextricably woven into the vernacular webs of contemporary digital culture as a result of hybridization between institutional and vernacular influences. Howard closes by underscoring the need for folklorists to embrace the study of technologically mediated communication—especially given the folklore discipline's unique insights and approaches to the study of expressive culture—and highlights how and why they can valuably contribute toward a more complete understanding of folk culture in the Digital Age.

The emergence of distinct, adaptive folk groups online has complicated the ways in which people now conceptualize and construct notions of identity, especially in digital contexts. Tok Thompson examines the proliferation of online folk groups in the Digital Age and the expressive cultures of several burgeoning folk groups that have coalesced online in chapter 2, "Netizens, Revolutionaries, and the Inalienable Right to the Internet." He chronicles the role of the Internet in helping citizens communicate and organize mass protests in Egypt—as well as the Egyptian government's attempts to shut down Internet access in fear of its unifying power—and how Egyptians managed to collaborate with others outside the nation's borders to keep the flow of information going while working to circumvent the government's imposed barriers to accessing the Internet. Indeed, access to the Internet has seemingly become a global right, and as its availability takes root in numerous developing countries across the globe, its powerful connectivity to information and the outside world has increasingly become an indispensible luxury for citizens in the Digital Age. The folk continue to adopt digital culture, and they are transitioning its use into their daily lives. From this vantage point, Thompson proceeds to explore the emergence of new cultural networks and social groups online and the ways in which they connect numerous groups of like-minded individuals through websites or other communicative forums that cater to their mutual interests. Ultimately, this chapter illustrates the emerging aesthetic choices in the new performative forms of Internet-based participatory culture while also distinguishing the adaptive characteristics of folk groups across historical, geographical, face-to-face, and online contexts.

Over the last decade, many cultural scholars have come to reject the contention (so commonly accepted in the 1990s) that digital environments operate as placeless and faceless venues of symbolic interaction. While the

increased acknowledgment of the similarities between digital and corporeal cultural spaces is a welcome innovation, a theory of performance—
one that specifically accounts for the aesthetic dynamics of expression that
emerge in digital performance settings—is still sorely needed. In chapter 3,
"Performance 2.0: Observations toward a Theory of the Digital Performance
of Folklore," Anthony Bak Buccitelli works to fill this theoretical void
within contemporary folkloristics. Employing a behavioral framework, he
underscores the need for the study of digital folklore performances on their
own terms, with deliberate attentiveness to the unique contexts that shape
and influence their identifying characteristics. After considering several elements of digital settings that are frequently operative in the process of performance, Buccitelli concludes by exploring the double-sided ambiguity of
performer and audience identities in digital environments and contemplates
the ways in which they give digital performances a distinctly different social
dynamic than those from face-to-face contexts.

Folk groups have been observed in global, national, regional, and local
contexts long before the Internet or other new media technology were facets
of everyday life; thus, their permanence and formation across corporeal and
virtualized expressive venues should not be surprising. Nevertheless, there is
still plenty of room for analysis in identifying the various ways that computer-
mediated communication technologies facilitate or directly influence the formation of folk groups. In chapter 4, "Real Virtuality: Enhancing Locality by
Enacting the Small World Theory," Lynne S. McNeill examines the social
interactions and behaviors of a relatively new type of folk group—one in
which members, usually strangers to one another, gather in-person (often
locally) for symbolic interaction or collaborative performances but choreo-
graph, coordinate, and organize the execution of these face-to-face gatherings through the cooperative use of Internet and new media technologies. In
particular, she analyzes flash mobs, alternate reality games, and small world
activities as representative examples of user-coordinated expressive forums
that utilize new media technology—from cell phones and text messages to
social networking sites like Facebook and Twitter—in order to cooperatively
plan events and subsequently enact them collectively, together, in the "real"
world. Coupled with the undeniable influence and penetration of new media
technology throughout mass culture, McNeill argues, these group interactions and their preceding collaborative preparation speak to the great unifying potential of computer-mediated communication technology for the creation, dissemination, and archiving of folkloric expression in the Digital Age.

In chapter 5, "Jokes on the Internet: Listing toward Lists," Elliott Oring examines the characteristics of folk humor on the Internet, particularly as it manifests in the form of joke lists. Text-based, yet visually oriented in presentation, lists are a hallmark of the online medium, and they are regularly encountered via e-mail forward, discussion forums, and humor websites. Throughout the chapter, Oring explains the composition and various applications of list humor online—including the notable ways in which it differs from and is rather analogous to orally circulated forms of humor. However, Oring is hesitant to label such web-based humor as *folklore* outright, especially considering the term's historical and methodological application to the study of face-to-face communication. Nevertheless, he notes the presence of tradition in these online forms of expression and sees their proliferation as an indicator of vernacular culture's role in the transmission of humor across hybridized and digitally exclusive contexts.

In the late nineteenth and early twentieth century, Jewish jokes drew attention, both orally and in print, in connection with mass immigration from Eastern Europe to Western Europe and the Americas. But with assimilation and the passing of *Yiddishkeit* (cultural traits associated with Eastern European, Yiddish-speaking Jews), came the observation that the Jewish joke, of the analog culture of print and orality, was dead. The Internet, however, has signaled a new vitality or function for Jewish jokes, which have flourished online in a variety of websites. In chapter 6, "The Jewish Joke Online: Framing and Symbolizing Humor in Analog and Digital Culture," Simon J. Bronner discusses the dynamic qualities of Jewish ethnic humor online. Using a symbolist frame analysis (drawn from the ideas of Gregory Bateson, Patricia Wallace, and Sigmund Freud) of the most popular websites representing different uses of Jewish jokes within digital culture, Bronner argues that Jewish jokes provide a set of meanings communicated by the design and metacommunicative "frames" of the individual sites. And unlike analog culture, he notes, the Jewish joke online typically symbolizes Jewish humor as a way to construct "we-ness," or the sense of size of community, feeling for community, and the struggle of an individual against the big machine. By contrast, non-Jews use Jewish jokes as a symbol for anxieties related to the commercial, mass cultural implications of the Internet.

Elizabeth Tucker analyzes the transition of long orally circulated legends onto and in combination with the Internet medium in chapter 7, "From Oral Tradition to Cyberspace: Tapeworm Diet Rumors and Legends." In particular, Tucker chronicles and analyzes tapeworm diet rumors and legends from the 1960s to the present and explores the ways in which these narratives have permeated across oral, as well as increasingly electronic, modes of transmission. More explicitly, she observes that many digital manifestations of tapeworm-related folklore seem to coincide with times of anxiety about health and safety in a real-world context, as with the 2009 swine flu pandemic. Thus, in addition to facilitating and hosting the dissemination of oral traditions in new, digital contexts, present-day tapeworm diets and legends also demonstrate the hybridization of folkloric forms and the interchangeability of vernacular expression in response to social anxieties across corporeal and virtualized contexts.

In chapter 8, "Love and War and Anime Art: An Ethnographic Look at a Virtual Community of Collectors," Bill Ellis offers an extensive analysis of the Anime-Beta virtual community: a lively and complex locus of interaction for collectors of Japanese anime art to meet people and forge meaningful relationships. Drawing upon his years of participation within the Anime-Beta community, Ellis presents an expansive ethnographic inquiry that explores the anime genre (broadly), art collecting (as a specific locus for symbolic interaction and community-building through mutual exchanges over aligning interests), and the Anime-Beta virtual community (specifically). In doing so, he also provides new insights into how and why collecting authentic *cels*—transparent sheets used to display more traditional, hand-drawn, or painted animations—is so revered among anime art collectors as both a hobby and a form of therapy, especially the fetishistic, fantastical power that collectors derive from possessing such art, given its uniqueness and connection to a personally significant fantasy narrative from an anime series. But more than that, Ellis reveals the dynamics of a unique virtual community comprised of individuals who have to strike a balance between fostering relationships and fulfilling their own intrinsic desires relating to their hobby, which also requires gestures of restitution, symbolically "giving back," in order to keep the community peacefully together, despite the inherent competition therein. Along the way, he identifies key values and tensions within the Anime-Beta community, surveys serious public disagreements, and gives examples of how the group's sense of unity is restored in the wake of such conflicts.

In the final essay of this volume, "Face-to-Face with the Digital Folk: The Ethics of Fieldwork on Facebook," Montana Miller provides an indispensible analysis and methodological guide for conducting ethical and appropriate ethnographic fieldwork in online settings. She begins with a conceptual overview of ethnography, including the role and function of institutional review boards in human subject research and the traditional ethical applications and considerations for folkloristic fieldwork in years past. Juxtaposing examples from her own online fieldwork on sites like Facebook, Miller articulates the ways in which computer-mediated communication technology can blur the boundaries of an informant's actual and online lives, and thoroughly explains how this ambiguity should be addressed by folklorists in the course of ethnographic fieldwork online—by exploring such important considerations as how and when researchers need informed consent, identifying an individual informant's or a community's potential vulnerabilities, and protecting or masking the identities of informants and anonymizing data, among other conscientious matters of fieldwork ethics. In short, Miller touches upon important considerations for folklorists to incorporate into future ethnographic fieldwork online and closes this volume with a meaningful methodological treatise.

As these brief chapter descriptions suggest, the eclectic contents of this volume frequently juxtapose and analyze corporeal and virtualized forms of vernacular expression. In doing so, our aim is to not only identify the exclusive and contrasting dynamics that distinguish the respective expressive venues but to also draw attention to their increasingly *shared* qualities, which underscores the growing hybridization of folk culture in the twenty-first century. The boundaries and trajectories of folkloric expression and transmission are expanding and propelling forward, with profound implications on how the folk (and folklorists) will adapt. Folklorists must continue to reconcile the old with new and hybrid forms of vernacular expression and find common ground. By acknowledging the scholastic possibilities available to folklorists working in the Digital Age, it may be possible to see how we are, in the words of Tok Thompson, "in a very privileged position to be observing a whole new epoch of humanity and human culture unfolding before our very eyes, and during our careers."[30]

Finally, as this volume's title (and these chapters) suggest, we contend that folk culture can and *does* exist in the Digital Age. Even so, it merits repeating that folklore on and from the Internet and new media does not represent the antithesis of folklore resulting from face-to-face interactions. In practice, folklore and expression—whether from face-to-face or online contexts—can coexist in harmony (even if some scholars are not ready to give equal credence to digital forms of expression). To use an analogy, the differences between many forms of vernacular expression in face-to-face and online contexts are akin to those of name brand or generic versions of the same prescription drug:

they may not look or cost the same, but they nevertheless *work* the same and serve the exact same purposes with the same risks and results, despite being chemically composed through different means. Although some may favor a name-brand over a generic product, both serve the same end purpose; there is no genuine dichotomy despite their miniscule compositional differences.

Similarly, folklorists should not have to choose whether they support modernity or antimodernism. Embracing one form need not negate another. Instead, we should strive to highlight the diversity of our interdisciplinary field and acknowledge that there are numerous forms of folklore out there, waiting to be explored. On behalf of the contributors, it is my hope that this volume will provide readers with new insights and perspectives on the myriad ways in which folk culture manifests in the Digital Age and will contribute toward our greater understanding of vernacular expression in our ever-changing technological world.

NOTES

1. The title to this introduction is, of course, an homage to Henry Glassie's ground-breaking work, *Pattern in the Material Folk Culture of the Eastern United States* (1968). With respect, however, I should also convey that I am intentionally invoking Glassie's title in order to highlight this volume, specifically my introduction's departure from the traditional purview of folklore studies that his work so greatly influenced.

2. By making this blanket statement about American (U.S.) culture, as well as in some of my subsequent statements, I do not mean to in any way diminish or wholly ignore the applicability of these claims as they relate to other countries. The simple truth is that my geographical area of expertise lies deeply within the study of North America—namely, the United States. I do not wish to propagate an illusion of nation-centrism; however, I must acknowledge that my analytical lens and personal frame of reference *is* greatly influenced and informed by my own scholarly interest, research, and training in the study of American folk and popular culture. Thus, in this introduction, I comment upon (and direct my observations toward) predominantly American culture (regarding the usage, adoption, and/or behavioral nuances of interaction that I have observed) and toward American folklore studies because—given my training and expertise—this is where I am most qualified to make observations and/or generalizations.

3. See Humphreys (2005) for an elongated analysis of how these new mobile communication technologies influence social interaction. Also, see Hampton, Livio, and Goulet (2010).

4. And remember: this data (Pew 2011; A. Smith 2011; Zickuhr 2011) does *not* examine teenagers' use of cell phones and/or smartphones, which, following educational theorist Marc Prensky's (2001a, b) concept of "digital nativity," would likely reveal notably higher adoption and usage rates by virtue of the fact that youths have been immersed into using these technologies from birth (and thus socialized into and by their customs more naturally than those adopting the technologies later in life).

5.   Some scholars of vernacular expression and other computer-mediated communications online tend to forget that many people multitask while using the Internet—they watch TV or a movie, carry out conversations, or play a video game—and that their expressive content may reflect the influence of these mitigating factors; these external factors should at least be considered in future research. See Gray (2010) and Jenkins (2008) for examples of media studies approaches to managing these multiple planes of reality in the context of fandom across different expressive modes.

6.   Still, I do not wish to gloss over the fact that some remote, rural, and/or poorer areas of the United States have limited access to the Internet, which yields significantly lower rates of penetration in comparison to other parts of the country. For instance, the 2010 U.S. Census revealed that only 59.3 percent of residents in the state of Mississippi used the Internet—the lowest percentage in the United States—whereas 90.1 percent of New Hampshire's residents used the Internet, which amounted to the highest usage percentage (Internet World Stats 2010). Unsurprisingly, the census also revealed America's poorest and richest states to be Mississippi and New Hampshire, respectively (Christie 2010). More work is needed, but substantial and frequent progress is being made, especially as the U.S. Federal Communications Commission (FCC) continues to improve and implement its Universal Service Fund, designed to install complete nationwide access to advanced telecommunication services. For additional background and a critique of the initiative, see Jordan (2009).

7.   For example, see Bauman (1983); Bronner (2009, 32); Crystal (2006); Kirshenblatt-Gimblett (1995, 70; 1998, 310); and Levine (1988, 8). In some ways, it almost seems as though some folklorists perceive Internet and other computer-mediated communication technologies as slayers of tradition or inevitable displacers of folk culture, ready to atrophy oral traditions or distract new generations from inheriting or absorbing the folk processes and transmissions that folklorists have observed for decades. Others erroneously contend that the Internet's demographic composition has remained relatively unchanged since the early 1990s, suggesting that white, well-educated, and economically stable *American* users still predominately use the venue (see Frank 2011, 10). For well-reasoned counterarguments and compelling evidence against these kinds of false or incomplete perceptions, see Baym (2010) and Shirky (2008, 2010).

8.   See Hilmes and Loviglio (2001) for an interdisciplinary historical discussion regarding the cultural impact of American radio. For a discussion of radio broadcasting's correlation to perceptions of national tradition, see Camporesi (2002). Let us also not forget that the government's decision to begin regulating radio broadcasting in 1912 spurred the creation of underground radio stations that illegally broadcast their own pirate signals as well (see Walker 2004).

9.   However, as Bill Ellis observes later in this volume, Dégh (2001) strongly departed from the earlier, more inclusive viewpoints on folklore and mass media I cite here.

10.   To be fair, this is partly attributable to the ever-expanding reach and affordability of Internet and new media technologies; this growth and cultural penetration can quickly render some specific case studies obsolete as new cultural patterns and issues arise over a short period of time. For a few examples of antiquated research (i.e., publications where the findings no longer reflect contemporary Internet culture) that explore the barriers to Internet access for minorities and/or lower income families in America, see Compaine (2001); Eamon (2004); Ebo (1998); Martin and Robinson (2007); and Norris (2001). Of course, it bears noting that even these examples of

somewhat dated research nevertheless retain value as documentations of significant, albeit fleeting moments in a time of rapid technological innovation.

11. My thanks to Simon J. Bronner for this information; he has been researching the use of computer technology among the Amish of central Pennsylvania since 2010.

12. The Pew Research Center's Internet and American Life Project, April 29–May 30, 2010, http://www.pewinternet.org/Trend-Data/Whos-Online.aspx, accessed 28 October 2010.

13. Adults use the Internet for utilities, but it can also be an instrument of play for children and adults alike, although more youth use it for play and social networking (Bronner 2009; Danet 2001; see also Soffer 2010, 398). Even if the online medium appears to be dominated by a youthful culture, Americans from all walks of life still utilize it. For an interesting collection and analysis of how American middle school boys and girls conceptualize and use technology in their daily lives, see Hou et al. (2006).

14. A "learning environment" is a collaborative setting in which structured, semi-structured, or spontaneous interactions take place with the intention of facilitating an educational, social, or goal-oriented discourse on topics or objectives that pertain to the contextual needs and functions of the host or initiating parties. In a corporate business meeting, a college classroom, or at play with others, these interactions are ubiquitous and allow individuals to learn communal dynamics and develop knowledge hierarchies (see Gagné 1962, 1985; Gagné, Briggs, and Wager 1992). They imbue social knowledge and encourage the sharing and receiving of information while fostering cumulative learning throughout the life course, from the acquisition of basic cultural practices and norms to advanced philosophical understandings about a particular subject matter or cultural practice.

15. By documenting these patterns, folklorists can not only chronicle and analyze a single, individual moment or scene but can connect that scene to overarching contextual expressive patterns within the community network, and then connect those overarching expressive patterns to larger, broader observations as previously documented by folklorists.

16. Identifying, decoding, and explaining the meanings, functions, and characteristics of these patterns—this is where a folklorist is both needed and supremely qualified to comment! Folklorists' understanding of expressive patterns and human interaction—in all of its multifaceted forms—can greatly benefit the collective understanding of expressive discourse in contemporary society (while also serving to document the nuances of such discourse for future generations).

17. See also Bascom (1955, 1973); Bauman (1975, 1984); and Rudy (2002) for particularly salient examples of folkloristic scholarship on verbal art outside the context of computer-mediated communication.

18. Ironically, many individuals draw upon corporeal folk culture as an aesthetic guide for developing an online persona in terms of presenting their interactive identity or using an expressive screen name/handle to rhetorically reveal insight into the "real" person behind the textual dialogues that emerge.

19. For example, see UrbanDictionary.com for user-moderated definitions of folk speech, predominantly slang and subversive material, but also including explanations of terms and concepts popularized by users. Notably, it contains a feedback system that counts thumbs-up (positive) or thumbs-down (negative) votes on a user's submitted definition. Another site is NetLingo.com, which focuses more on Internet-derived vocabulary (though not exclusively). See also Danet (2001).

20.   Although I draw most of my supporting evidence from examples within the borders of the United States, this statement is also true of social movements and folk protests throughout the world, most notably in the civil uprisings of the Arab Spring, as discussed by Tok Thompson in chapter 2 of this volume.

21.   Although many supporters of the Occupy movement protest income inequality (between the top 1 percent of wage earners and the remaining 99 percent in America) while facing their own financial and economic hardships, it is interesting to see that technologically mediated communication has remained a central component of the movement.

22.   Interestingly, many individuals who conceptualize memes as cultural analogs to genetics/evolutionary processes describe the process of replication (or folkloristically, repetition and variation) along the same lines of argumentation and explanation presented by Dégh and Vázsonyi (1994 [1975]); for example, see Graham (2002, 196).

23.   "Image macros" essentially refer to examples of digital folklore that are distinguished by the practice of pairing a visual image (often humorous) with a catchy snippet of text (which may vary from a single word or phrase to whole sentences) that incorporate an emergent expressive pattern or delivery meter that has achieved popularity and recognition within a peer group; image macros usually follow a base template that is easily downloadable or transferable, which keeps things simple enough to invite many more Internet users to partake in creating their own variations. Indeed, the overarching meme inspiration installs an awareness of the macros' expressive patterns and the accompanying expectations that go into creating new images, but the image macro distinction becomes appropriate due to the general uniformity of presentation, in which creators insert either new text (and keep the popular image) or a new image (but keep the popular text associated with the macro's catchphrase), so as to tie new creation within the traditional frame of the original popular macro.

24.   Drawing again on a biological analogy (in this case, a spreading virus), *viral* is a vernacular term for the rapid dissemination process (which frequently includes repetition and variation) of computer-mediated folklore, be it a popular video, a Photoshopped image, e-mail hoaxes and urban legends, or a genuine news story, among other types. See Wasik (2009).

25.   In other words, folklorists may identify the patterns of folkloric expression circulating via computer-mediated communication and draw upon the existing documentation of correlating oral traditions (or other folklore deriving from face-to-face contexts) as a theoretical/conceptual model to help formulate their analysis and serve as a frame of reference.

26.   Note that many of these examples rely heavily on aesthetic components in their structure, thus giving a virtual tangibility to them as folk objects when consumed.

27.   In particular, see Blank (2009b) and Bronner (2009).

28.   There are exceptions to the general scholarly neglect by folklorists in studying the Internet and computer-mediated communication technology (pre-*Folklore and the Internet*). For example, see Baym (1993); Blank (2007); Dorst (1990); Ellis (2001, 2003); Fernback (2003); Foote (2007); Frank (2004); Howard (2005a, 2005b, 2008a, 2008b); Kibby (2005); Kirshenblatt-Gimblett (1995, 1996); McNeill (2007).

29.   I recognize that my description may come off as obnoxious or boastful (or both), but this is not my intention. I base these observations and contentions on my personal correspondence with numerous folklorists who have expressed their enjoyment of and appreciation for *Folklore and the Internet* and its efforts to disambiguate the

folkloristic study of the Internet. In some cases, these individuals, and others, have even adopted the book into some of the courses they teach (McNeill et al. 2010). To that point, a free downloadable teaching guide for the book has been compiled by contributor Lynne S. McNeill; it is available online at http://tinyurl.com/FolkloreInternetTeachingGuide or accessed by scanning the QR code embedded in the adjacent margin. Folklore and the Internet was also selected as a "Significant University Press Title for Undergraduates, 2009–2010" by Choice 47, no. 9 (May 2010).

30.   Personal communication, 20 May 2011.

1

How Counterculture Helped Put the "Vernacular" in Vernacular Webs

Robert Glenn Howard

In 1964 STUDENTS CONVERGED ON THE UNIVERSITY OF California's Sproul Hall. Protesting new policies that radically limited political speech on campus, some of these students wore punch cards, used to input data into the era's computers, around their necks. One protestor had a sign suggesting computers were a mechanism of oppressive institutional power: "I am a UC Berkeley student. Please do not fold, bend, spindle, or mutilate me" (Turner 2006, 2). In 1964 the computer could be invoked as a symbol of oppression. Some twenty years later, however, it had been transformed into a symbol of freedom. In January of 1984, Apple Computer announced its new Macintosh computer system. In a now iconic commercial, the Macintosh was presented as the liberating force that would keep George Orwell's dystopian vision of an autocratic future in his book *1984* from becoming a reality.

The commercial depicts what seem to be automatons watching a huge projection of a man orating, "We have created, for the first time in all history, a garden of pure ideology—where each worker may bloom, secure from the pests purveying contradictory truths . . . Our enemies shall talk themselves to death, and we will bury them with their own confusion!" As the man speaks, a woman with short, blond hair bursts into the auditorium, with helmeted guards in close pursuit. She wears bright red running shorts and a tank top bearing the new Macintosh logo. With a powerful swing, she hurls a sledgehammer through the screen and shatters it. A blinding flash of white light washes over the startled automatons. The commercial concludes, "On January 24, Apple Computer will introduce

DOI: 10.7330/9780874218909.c01   25

Macintosh. And you will see why 1984 won't be like '1984'" ("Apple's 1984 Commercial" 2011).

What happened? How had computer technologies been transformed from the oppressive mechanism of institutional control to a liberating force of empowered individualism? The simple answer to that question has far-reaching implications.

Only institutions with significant financial resources (like governments, large corporations, and major research universities and institutes) could afford to operate the expensive, large, and operationally complex computers of the 1960s. A decade later, individuals influenced by the counterculture movement of the 1960s developed personal computer (PC) and Internet technologies, infusing them with a sense of anti-institutionalism. Because the development of these two key technologies shifted the computer industry's focus away from institutions toward everyday people, the forms of online communication we see today bear traces of an ideology that values the "folk," or vernacular, over the institutional. The iconic Apple Computer commercial explicitly conveyed this ethos some ten years after the creation of the first personal computers. Today's computer users have been empowered by this ethos to create and consume their own complex media content alongside, but apart from, the content created by powerful institutions. The dynamic and interlocking networks of everyday personal connection that we create online now constitute powerful new webs of vernacular communication.

This chapter traces how a valuation of the vernacular came to be embedded in network communication. I first locate a rhetoric of vernacular authority that emerges in an amateur publication highly influential among hobbyist computer users of the 1970s: the underground introduction to computer programming and manifesto *Computer Lib* (Nelson 1974). This publication first popularized the idea of hypertext as a technology that could wrest the power of computers from institutions and bring it to the people. Ultimately, hypertext would become the basic technology that made vernacular webs possible. I next examine the *Homebrew Computer Club* newsletter. Here, another group of computer enthusiasts expressed the same valuation of the vernacular as they sought to create a personal computer that anyone could own and use. Prominent newsletter readers included Microsoft founder Bill Gates as well as the founders of Apple, Steve Jobs and Steve Wozniak. From the Homebrew newsletter, the second key technology of vernacular webs took shape: the personal computer itself.

Next, I describe how these communities' vernacular ethos emerged in the institutionally funded development of the basic computer code behind all Internet communication. But it was not until institutionally funded websites emerged that vernacular webs became observable online. Only afterward did it become possible to see the difference between everyday Internet use and more formal institutional Internet use. Finally, I demonstrate how the hybridization between institutional and vernacular influence is now inextricably woven into the vernacular webs of today. Although commercialism and institutional authorities certainly have a role in shaping the expressive behaviors that comprise vernacular webs, that fact should not keep researchers of everyday expressive behavior from looking online. The very technologies that make online vernacular communication possible also render that communication hybrid, and folklore scholars' expertise with everyday expression places them in a unique position to document and analyze the complexity arising in network environments.

Vernacular webs are, in many ways, nothing new. We humans have always devised clever ways to express ourselves to each other, and we have always done so by drawing from both institutional and vernacular sources of influence. However, as these new technologies press older analog media into the background, vernacular webs are creating a renaissance of everyday expressive communication rife with dynamic new forms of digital folk culture; this vibrant new arena presents powerful new research opportunities for scholars of everyday expression.

COMPUTER LIB

Theodor "Ted" Nelson self-published *Computer Lib: You Can and Must Understand Computers Now/Dream Machines: New Freedoms Through Computer Screens—A Minority Report* (or *Computer Lib* for short) in 1974. Half computer textbook and half fanzine, it was widely read by the small community of computer hobbyists of the mid-1970s (Abbate 1999, 214). Nelson's book gave voice to anti-establishment hippie-hackers who saw themselves standing in opposition to the powerful institutions of corporations and governments. Nelson argued that everyday individuals must learn to use computers because only computers could liberate them from institutional oppression.

In trying to make computers easier to use, Nelson imagined new kinds of computer interfaces he called "presentational systems" based on "branching" instead of hierarchical organization. In such systems, individuals could more easily access the information collected onto institutional computers. A branching system would shift the authority for the organization (the order and number of ideas accessed) to each individual user, privileging vernacular authority over institutional authority in the accessing of information. If authority is the power to determine what content is consumed and in what order, Nelson's systems would seek to frustrate the author-function of a traditional book or other media object where the order and parts of the content consumed are more subject to determination by the author or other content producers. The author of a book, after all, usually indicates which page is the first page a reader should read by numbering that page "1."

Exemplifying how such systems could work, Nelson's book, in contrast, seeks to frustrate this convention by having two first pages. Combined with other presentational system qualities, the book is an exercise in patience to read. After spending many hours with it, the reader is still not sure if she or he has read the entire thing because its structure has quite effectively made it impossible to read in any linear sequence. Figures 1 and 2 show the most obvious way Nelson tried to create a branching informational system: he gave it two front covers. From one side, *Dream Machines: New Freedoms through Computer Screens—A Minority Report* is, literally, a computer programming tutorial containing introductions to APL, BASIC, and other computer languages of the day.

Read from this cover, the book begins by offering Nelson's "credentials": a bachelor's degree in philosophy and a master's in sociology from Harvard University. If read from the other side (the *Computer Lib* side), Nelson's "counterculture credentials" include "a year at Dr. Lilly's dolphin lab" and "attendee of the great Woodstock Festival"(*CL* 127 [*DM* 1]).[1]

Throughout, the book offers manifestos, cartoons, mathematical equations, programming diagrams, quotes from computer textbooks, and descriptions of new technologies, both real and imagined. Nelson presents all this in a mix of often tiny typewritten and handwritten text blocks, graphics, and cartoons that seem to compete with each other for space on the pages as well as the reader's attention.

On one page, Nelson overtly references his choice of this confusing layout as an attempt to encourage readers to "jump around" and "try different pathways." He describes his choice in layout writing this way: "The astute reader, and anybody who's [*sic*] gotten to this point must be, will have

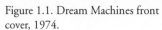

Figure 1.1. Dream Machines front
cover, 1974.

Figure 1.2. *Computer Lib*'s other front
cover, 1974.

noticed that this book is in 'magazine' layout, organized visually by ideas
and meanings . . . I will be interested to hear whether that has worked" (*CL*
85 [*DM* 44]).

For many readers, this format is more a challenge to overcome than an
effective informational system. However, for the computer hobbyists of the
mid- to late 1970s, the book was a printed representation of what they imagined a future medium would be able to do: overcome the limitations of print.
For them, this vision of a branching presentational system could empower
individuals to "build-from-the-bottom" by giving them more control over
their access to information. By forcing the reader to choose from which cover
to start reading, the two front covers at least symbolically shift some of the
authority from the author to each individual reader. In this sense, reading
the book forces the reader to enact her or his own vernacular authority to
determine the specific ideas and order of the information one accesses from
the book. In 1974, however, the actual technologies of the Internet would
not make these kinds of systems more practical for a long time:

> Deep and widespread computer systems would be tempting to two dan-
> gerous parties, "organized crime" and the Executive Branch of the Federal
> Government (assuming there is still a difference between the two). If we are

to have the freedoms of information we deserve as a free people, the safe-
guards have to be built at the bottom, now. (Nelson 1974, CL 70 [DM 59];
his underlining)

In the early 1970s, before the wide availability of personal computers like the Apple II, computers were so large and expensive, they were
almost exclusively owned by large institutions (Ceruzzi 2003, 109–141;
Freiberger and Swaine, 1984, 204–205). As a result, people generally seem
to have imagined them as distant institutional mechanisms. On the rare
occasions when the general public could access computer terminals, most
people found them too difficult to use. Before the graphical user interfaces,
or "GUIs," and the emphasis on ease-of-use common today, individuals
were required to have significant technical skills to actually use computers
of any kind. At the time of *Computer Lib*, the technical challenges presented to users compelled Nelson to argue that everyone should have some
knowledge of computer languages. This was the motive behind his book's
instructional component.

For Nelson, computer skills needed to be more widely distributed so
that vernacular voices could be better heard. He described a "computer
priesthood" that withheld knowledge by refusing to construct computer
systems in the vernacular of everyday people. He asserted, "Knowledge is
power and so it tends to be hoarded." For everyday individuals to stand a
chance against technologically empowered institutional forces, he argued,
"It is imperative . . . that the appalling gap between public and computer
insider be closed . . . Guardianship of the computer can no longer be left
to the priesthood" (*CL* 52 [*DM* 76]). Nelson figured himself as a computer
nerd Robin Hood. A noninstitutional agent, he and his computer-hobbyist
colleagues hoped to bring computers from the mountaintop to the masses
by distributing computer skills more widely among the population. At the
same time, they imagined developing branching informational systems that
would be much easier for these newly computer-empowered folk to use.
The difficult layout of *Computer Lib* invoked the folk-friendly systems he
and his colleagues imagined for the future.

While the difficulty of *Computer Lib* seems to have kept it from directly
reaching a popular audience, the central idea it attempted to exemplify
would eventually come to affect us all. While advocating ways to build at
the bottom with branching informational systems, Nelson described and
advocated for what he termed "hypermedia."

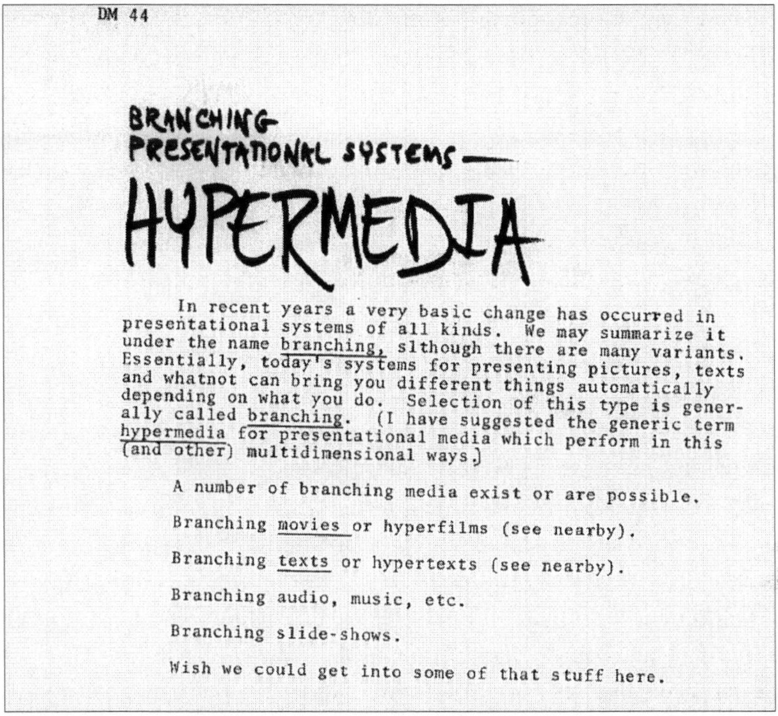

DM 44

BRANCHING
PRESENTATIONAL SYSTEMS —

HYPERMEDIA

In recent years a very basic change has occurred in presentational systems of all kinds. We may summarize it under the name branching, although there are many variants. Essentially, today's systems for presenting pictures, texts and whatnot can bring you different things automatically depending on what you do. Selection of this type is generally called branching. (I have suggested the generic term hypermedia for presentational media which perform in this (and other) multidimensional ways.)

A number of branching media exist or are possible.

Branching movies or hyperfilms (see nearby).

Branching texts or hypertexts (see nearby).

Branching audio, music, etc.

Branching slide-shows.

Wish we could get into some of that stuff here.

Figure 1.3. "Hypermedia" in *Computer Lib*, 1974.

For Nelson, using hypermedia instead of hierarchical organization would link information in more intuitive ways and thus encourage egalitarian access that gives the power of what and how knowledge is constructed to everyday people instead of institutions. Making this argument, Nelson became a countercultural hero championing the folk through his advocacy of hypertext as a form of branching or nonsequential writing. These technologies would counteract the power of institutions as held by the computer priesthood (*CL* 85 [*DM* 44]). Of course, the desire for a real-world application of Nelson's hypertext idea would later drive another hippie-hacker to develop the basic technology of the early World Wide Web in the form of the HTML computer language.

But even before individuals could use any sort of hypermedia, they needed a networked computer that could link the branching media. At the time, everyday people didn't have access to so-called minicomputers that were large and expensive and available only to institutions. The public needed something smaller and cheaper to plug into these imagined networks of branching media. In the next section, I look at the newsletter produced by the Homebrew Computer Club. Founded only months after Nelson released *Computer Lib*, active members of this club included some of the most important figures in the development of personal computer technologies. Much like Nelson had imagined vernacular empowerment through computer programming, many Homebrew club members were imagining new avenues for empowerment made possible by the creation of small, cheap, and widely available personal computers.

THE HOMEBREW COMPUTER CLUB NEWSLETTER

By 1974, a number of San Francisco Bay Area individuals had formed informal mechanisms for exchanging information about computers, computer programming, and electronics. At the time, a local activist named Fred Moore had started something he called the Whole Earth Truck Store in Menlo Park, California, as a way to create connections between people who wanted to share information outside of what he felt were oppressive institutions. Thinking that maybe a computer could help him, but not knowing much about them, Moore contacted a computer club called the People's Computer Company. Soon he was learning about, and loudly advocating for, computers as a source of noninstitutional empowerment (Freiberger and Swaine 1984, 104).

Meanwhile, the January 1975 cover of the hobbyist magazine *Popular Mechanics* featured the Altair 8800 Computer. An Arizona company sold the Altair as a minicomputer by mail order for only $400. The computer itself was little more than a metal box with LED lights on the front. However, the chip inside the box was an Intel 8080 (Ceruzzi 2003, 228). Intel had designed this chip at a time when that level of computing power was only available in the far more expensive and larger computers purchased by businesses, government agencies, and universities. As a result of new production technologies that dramatically reduced costs, however, the $400 Altair could house a chip with similar processing power to that of the 1974 IBM System/370 Model 115, which had a base price of $265,165. The LED-equipped Altair, however, did not come with screens, keyboards, or even software (IBM 1974).

Learning of the availability of the bare chip, H. Edward Roberts, of a small company called MITS, cut a deal to buy them in quantity from Intel for only $75 apiece. This was made possible because the cost of producing a chip was in the design and setup of its manufacturing. Once a single chip was built, it was very cheap to make many more chips. Because the Altair was not competing for the IBM System/370 Model 115 market (having no out-of-the-box functionality other than blinking lights), Intel could sell bare chips very cheaply (Ceruzzi 2003, 395n). But who would want a computer chip in a box? It had no keyboard, monitor, disk drive, or game controller. Roberts's genius was to realize that he could sell basically just the chip to computer hobbyists as a "kit" for $400 and turn a decent profit. Hobbyists wanted the chip because it was a "computer"—something usually only institutions could afford. While most people would find the Altair useless, hobbyists immediately recognized that they could build components to add whatever functionality they could imagine to the computer.

When Fred Moore heard of the Altair, he contacted everybody he knew who was associated with the People's Computer Company and interested in "building their own computer" to join him in a friend's garage on March 5, 1975. This informal gathering constituted the inaugural meeting of the Homebrew Computer Club. Thirty-two computer-hobbyist hippies came from all over the Bay Area (Freiberger and Swaine 1984, 104). While several of the new club's members began producing the now-famous newsletter, other members went right to building basic components to expand the Altair's functions. Not long after, Bill Gates famously rewrote the BASIC computer language so that it could be saved on a cassette tape and loaded into the expanded memory banks that users added to their Altairs. Later, Gates would print his "Open Letter to Hobbyists" in the Homebrew newsletter—a document often thought to mark the emergence of the software industry itself because it was the first in a popular publication to imagine a profitable industry producing computer programs to be sold as individual copies, much like books or recorded music.

Meanwhile, other Homebrewers formed businesses that built more computers small enough and cheap enough to be purchased and used by individuals in their homes. These personal computers were rendered more useful than the Altair by a rapidly increasing availability of gadgets to attach to them and software that operated with those gadgets. These computers became the means through which the Digital Age began to arrive, not just for large institutions but also for the everyday person. In the second issue of the newsletter, soon-to-be cofounder of Apple Computers Steve Wozniak listed his phone number and address, offering his "own version of [the computer game] Pong" as well as various other "homebrewed" equipment he had for sale in his garage (DigiBarn 2005a). Less than ten years later, the famous Macintosh TV advertisement specifically embodied the individualism and anti-institutional spirit of these computer hobbyists.

With the commercially driven ubiquity of computer technologies we have today, it is hard to imagine a time when the PC was just an idea, and it is easy to forget how the desire to empower vernacular authority drove that idea. However, early computer hobbyists were mostly young and idealistic men heavily influenced by the counterculture movements of the 1960s. For them, government and corporate institutions did not exist to help everyday people. Instead, as becomes clear in the Homebrew newsletter, their passion for computers emerged with a sense that these new technologies could empower individuals and the social networks they formed outside of institutions. Among the Homebrew hobbyists, Nelson's *Computer Lib* was required reading (Freiberger and Swaine 1984, 101). In 1976 Nelson was an invited speaker at an MITS-sponsored event, the World Altair Computer Convention (Freiberger and Swaine 1984, 180). Meanwhile, Fred Moore and the other driving figures behind Homebrew had become well-known countercultural activists. Seeking new ways to build networks of people outside of institutions, these influential hobbyists participated in Homebrew because they wanted to extend the vernacular possibilities of computer technologies. One of the most significant of these activists-turned-computer-geeks was Lee Felsenstein.

Felsenstein was an engineering school dropout who wrote for the liberal *Berkeley Barb* in 1969. The *Barb* was one of the nationally known publications expressing anti-institutional sentiments that resulted in rallies that followed the spirit of the 1964 gathering mentioned at the beginning of this chapter. After returning to the University of California, Berkeley, to finish his engineering degree in 1971, Felsenstein moved into an urban commune in San Francisco. The commune lived in an old factory building and pooled its resources to purchase a large minicomputer. Calling itself Resource One, it sought to use the computer to unify different "switchboard" groups around San Francisco that were trying to create noninstitutional activist networks of communication. Inspired by Nelson's *Computer Lib*, Felsenstein leapt at the chance to join Fred Moore at the first meeting of the Homebrew Computer Club (Freiberger and Swaine 1984, 100–101).

The club began meeting every month, and the number of participants swelled. When the group moved from Moore's garage to an auditorium on the Stanford University campus, Felsenstein emerged as its charismatic leader. Calling him Homebrew's "song and dance man" in the newsletter, Moore made it clear that Felsenstein was a central actor in the club as early as July 1975 (DigiBarn 2005d). A powerful public speaker, Felsenstein led the meetings like a talk show host. First came a "mapping session" where individuals spoke up about what interests they had or what projects or problems they were working on while he commented and moderated. A formal, pre-arranged presentation followed. Then came a "random access" session where individuals scrambled around the auditorium to make connections with others who had expressed shared interests. Soon projects based on the Altair and other computer technologies exploded among the Homebrewers (Freiberger and Swaine 1984, 106).

Homebrew's activities connected key players in the nascent personal computer and software industries central to the rise of Silicon Valley as the hub of the early Digital Age. But Homebrew was only part of a larger movement. In the mid-1970s, amateur computer clubs were popping up all around the country in response to the Altair: from Denver's Digital Group Clearing House to the Cleveland Digital Group in Ohio, from the Long Island Computer Association in Jamaica, New York, to the El Paso Computer Group in Texas. Many of these clubs produced newsletters and other amateur publications—from *Byte* magazine and *The Computer Hobbyist* to Felsenstein's alternate project, *The Journal of Community Communications*.

Still, the central importance of the Homebrew Computer Club to the development of Silicon Valley's computer and software industries makes a closer look at its newsletter a reasonable place to find evidence of the ethos driving these soon-to-be influential hobbyist-hackers. The newsletter captures the feelings of the time, and researchers have documented its embodiment of the early 1970s anti-institutional ethos (Freiberger and Swaine 1984, 108; Turner 2006, 114–116).

Writing in its second issue, Moore described how he was "intending to have it [the newsletter] out once a month," and he described its intended function as "mostly *a pointer* to sources, items, news etc." [italics in original]. The newsletter functioned much like the switchboard movement and publications like the *Whole Earth Catalog*. It was primarily a place for everyday computer hobbyists to find each other and share information about building computers and components outside of the institutional setting of that time. Describing its members as "learners and doers," Moore stated that the goal of both the club and its newsletter was to "facilitate our access to each other and the micro-[computer] world out there" (DigiBarn 2005e).

A look at the first three volumes of the newsletter clearly shows that this was precisely what they were doing.

The newsletter's first issues are filled with summaries of the club's meetings. They describe how members worked on various computer problems. They also contain notes submitted by members about their current projects, updates on the doings of computer equipment manufacturers, and provide addresses and points of contact for goods, books, magazines, clubs, and other resources. The newsletter functioned to disseminate this pragmatic information by helping members make connections in their efforts to generate homemade computer technologies.

While this information dominates the newsletter (making it less visionary than pragmatic), its overall ethos is clearly in line with Nelson's *Computer Lib*. For example, a cartoonish hand-drawn sketch representing the faces of a number of important early members dominates the front page of the third issue. Invoking an amateurish doodle, and poking fun at its own most popular figures, the sketch depicts eight men. Many of them sport long hair and beards, marking them as members of 1970s counterculture.

This counterculture ethos can more often be found seeping out in short bits of text sandwiched between sketches of design schematics for computer components and code. On the front page of the fourth issue, for example, one contributor discusses the positive impact of the popularity of the Altair. This individual writes that the Altair is encouraging the formation of computer clubs across the country. The writer goes on to argue that these clubs are important because they will function to "demystify computers." As the writer puts it: "Computers are not magic. And it is important for the general public to begin to understand the limits of these machines and the humans that are responsible for the programming" (DigiBarn 2005c). In another issue, Bob Lash, a well-known figure in the club also associated with the People's Computer Company, is quoted as saying during a meeting:

> You have so many people in society exercising an editorial function. In essence I see an electronic community bulletin board as uniquely different in that you are your own librarian. You select what it is that you are going to read of what is in the data bank. (DigiBarn 2005b)

Here Lash imagines the future of the linking systems that already existed in 1975. In activist networks of the time, individuals—sometimes through public computer terminals, other times on real-world bulletin boards—could find each other and share information of their choosing. The

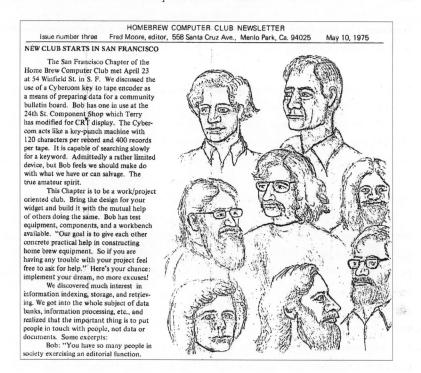

HOMEBREW COMPUTER CLUB NEWSLETTER
Issue number three   Fred Moore, editor, 558 Santa Cruz Ave., Menlo Park, Ca. 94025   May 10, 1975

NEW CLUB STARTS IN SAN FRANCISCO

The San Francisco Chapter of the Home Brew Computer Club met April 23 at 54 Winfield St. in S. F. We discussed the use of a Cybercom key to tape encoder as a means of preparing data for a community bulletin board. Bob has one in use at the 24th St. Component Shop which Terry has modified for CRT display. The Cybercom acts like a key-punch machine with 120 characters per record and 400 records per tape. It is capable of searching slowly for a keyword. Admittedly a rather limited device, but Bob feels we should make do with what we have or can salvage. The true amateur spirit.

This Chapter is to be a work/project oriented club. Bring the design for your widget and build it with the mutual help of others doing the same. Bob has test equipment, components, and a workbench available. "Our goal is to give each other concrete practical help in constructing home brew equipment. So if you are having any trouble with your project feel free to ask for help." Here's your chance: implement your dream, no more excuses!

We discovered much interest in information indexing, storage, and retrieving. We got into the whole subject of data banks, information processing, etc., and realized that the important thing is to put people in touch with people, not data or documents. Some excerpts:

Bob: "You have so many people in society exercising an editorial function.

Figure 1.4. Front page of the Homebrew Computer Club newsletter, issue 3, 1975.

editorial function Lash references concerned the institutional media acting as an intermediary between the public and the information they both shared and consumed. Computers, for Lash, could help remove that function from institutions, move it to everyday people, and thus give more power to the folk. For Lash and his peers, this shift to vernacular authority in both sharing and consuming information could replace the institutional authority for information access and dissemination associated with mass media. Today, of course, network communication technologies like file sharing and social networking sites have increased massively the power of individual actors for better or worse (see Howard 2011, 174).

For the idealistic young computer hobbyists of the 1970s, however, giving more people more access to more information was imagined as a clear route to a better world. If more people could learn about using computers in more personal and individually accessible ways, more power could be brought to those people. That would increase vernacular authority in information access and dissemination. For Homebrewers, this is exactly the role the club and its newsletter should play. Moore made this point succinctly in the newsletter's fifth issue when he noted the sudden explosion of similar clubs around the country. He echoed the general sentiments of his colleagues by writing, "I think this is great. We need more decentralized clubs to help the little guy" (DigiBarn 2005d).

The fifth issue of the newsletter's second volume marked a significant change. The newsletter (like the club members themselves) was professionalizing. Many of its members were forming companies. Some were doomed to fail, but others would be among the leaders in the upcoming technology boom that created both the software and the personal computer industries. Sporting a much more professional looking format, the newsletter, under new editor Robert Reiling, convinced a small company called Laurel Publishing to donate typesetting, graphics, and editorial assistance (DigiBarn 2005e). The club would expand and adapt over the years, and it still holds meetings—at least as of this writing.

With the rapid commercial rise of the PC and the now nearly ubiquitous commercialism on the Internet, the early idealism that invented these technologies seems hard to fully appreciate. But it is important to remember the sense of vernacular authority central to that idealism in order to understand how that ethos still infuses network communication technologies.

FROM HOBBYISTS TO CONSUMERS

Despite the anti-institutional ethos of both the Homebrew Computer Club newsletter and Theodor Nelson, it would take institutional resources to actually create the networks of personal computers and other computing devices surrounding us today. Even as powerful institutions brought their resources to bear in the development of these technologies, however, key designers continued to work out of a countercultural and anti-institutional sensibility. As a result, the basic technologies of the Internet emerged as hybrids between institutional power and individuals seeking to empower the vernacular.

Back in 1966, an earlier group of progressive computer engineers developed the concept of "Internetting." Internetting provided the foundational idea behind computer networks and consisted of layered structures of computer code in which bottom layers could act independently from the more rigid layers at the top of the hierarchy. While the top layers of code executed very specific functions that required relatively complex and specifically applied code, the bottom layers executed simpler code that would function across a wide range of applications. And although only a few computers might use the network's top-level code, the bottom layer of code had to be shared by all computers in the network because it governed the actual transmission of data. The base-layer code would form the common ground on which communication within the network could be established. This sort of idea underpinned (or maybe was underpinned by) the more philosophical statements of Nelson and the Homebrewers as they celebrated bottom-up technologies.

The base code that would come to underlie all Internet communication was developed with U.S. government funding through the powerful National Science Foundation (NSF). Formed in 1950, the NSF helped the country compete with the Soviet Union during the technology races of the Cold War. Although the most memorable moment in the history of those competitions might be the 1969 moon landing, the most consequential now seems to be the development of TCP/IP (Transfer Control Protocol/Internet Protocol) in 1973.

TCP/IP is a tiny piece of computer code that became the base layer of computer networks. This program is still the basis of all Internet communication today. As long as users deployed this basic gateway software, they could construct their own applications without the authority of the institutional powers controlling the network. The U.S. government seems to have been interested in creating a communication system that could better withstand massive attack. A distributed communication system in which each member of a network contained the base-layer code was more difficult to damage because each of its components could connect with each of its other components and thus could rout communications around damaged parts of the network. However, the builders of early Internet applications wanted to construct systems where individuals could create and apply specific applications without needing central approval or authority to implement new applications. As it turned out, the first really popular Internet application—e-mail—was in fact built in just this way: informally constructed and disseminated without any central authorization (Abbate 1999, 106).

The basic computer code for sending and receiving e-mail emerged when a few researchers using the early NSF computer network called ARPANET (Advanced Research Projects Agency Network) deployed a "mailbox" file that they kept on their networked computers. This allowed them to send messages to each other more easily. Never a commercial piece of software, the code was a useful add-on to TCP/IP that more and more network users added to their local machines. Later, of course, it was standardized and is still probably the most ubiquitous use of the Internet (Abbate 1999, 106–111).

A second transformative software application that emerged when individual network users began to place it on their individual machines came infused with a sense of vernacular authority: a functional implementation Nelson's concept of hypermedia (Abbate 1999, 214ff; Ceruzzi 2003, 320ff). In 1990 the multinational European nuclear agency CERN hired a counterculturally minded computer engineer named Tim Berners-Lee. CERN wanted Berners-Lee to develop a way for their scientists (who were spread around the world) to more easily share and retrieve scientific papers. Berners-Lee addressed the problem by developing a hypertext system that would operate over the CERN network and function on many different kinds of computers. He called his invention Hypertext Markup Language or HTML. By using this simple computer language, individuals could share formatted text, graphics, and other media in a linking web of information.

Like Nelson, Berners-Lee wanted to keep HTML very simple, so it could be easily learned and deployed by anyone. CERN, for its part, did not attempt to limit the use of HTML. Instead, in 1991 they gave away the first HTML browser to the public, and individual network users began to create HTML-based "sites" for other users to visit—the World Wide Web was born (CERN 2000; World Wide Web Consortium 2000). Although CERN was a powerful government institution, Berners-Lee was influenced by the anti-institutional ethos common among computer engineers of that day. When HTML sites began to pop up across the early Internet, it was not the result of any institutional directive. Instead, everyday users put the institutionally designed system to work out of their own volition and, at first at least, for their own vernacular purposes.

At this early stage, web users were mostly computer engineers who built webpages in their spare time. As a result, a distinctly institutional presence did not exist on the web. It was only when such a presence emerged that vernacular webs of webpages and websites could be recognized as distinct from the more institutional network media (Howard 2005b). Two main components inhibited the initial expansion of this presentational system to the broader public. First, HTML was relatively easy to use but not easy for individuals with little computer experience. As a result, many people just did not take the time to figure it out. Second, at the time, it was illegal to use the Internet for commercial purposes. As a result, no money was available to train and hire people to build the more professional network sites we are familiar with today.

That all changed in June of 1992, when the U.S. Congress's Boucher Bill offered an amendment to the National Science Foundation Act. This amendment changed the meaning of "fair use" for NSF projects so that the NSF-funded software TCP/IP could be put to commercial use (Segaller 1998, 298ff). With the sudden influx of commerce online, the popularity of the web medium exploded. Commercial interests put pressure on the simple but functional capabilities of HTML and a new kind of website began to emerge (Lessig 2002; Rheingold 1992, 2000, 2001). Commercial sites started to exhibit far more complex HTML coding. Meanwhile, the number of commercial sites dwarfed the simpler noncommercial websites. The web went from fewer than one hundred websites in 1992 to over ten thousand by January 1995. But the new population of web users had significantly less computer skills than did the early web community. In 1994 only 11 percent of web users reported being involved in computer programming for three years or less (GVU 2001a). One year later, the number jumped to 35.5 percent. The biggest increase occurred in those with no high-level computer experience at all, which leaped up from nearly zero to 16.78 percent (GVU 2001b, 2001c).

Instead of a network of hobbyists both creating and consuming web content, the web that emerged had few producers with many consumers for their products. This dichotomy between content producers and consumers set the stage for the emergence of observably different groups of networked websites. Because the vernacular only emerges dialectically—that is to say, it only emerges when something presents itself as distinct from that which is institutional—it *relies* on the existence of institutions from which to distinguish itself to exhibit its noninstitutional nature (Howard 2008b, 2011, 4–7). In the mid-1990s, corporations, governments, universities, and other powerful institutions hired teams of computer engineers to create just such an institutional presence online.

Because these institutional websites were the product of teams of professional builders, they exhibited more complicated features. While hobbyists and amateurs still put up sites, their sites appeared as vernacular because they exhibited features that rendered them clearly distinct. As the web of links these hobbyist HTML programmers made became distinct from institutional websites and networks, vernacular webs of amateur network content emerged in the electronic connections made between the software and

personal computer technologies springing up from the anti-institutional
ethos of computer hobbyists in the 1960s and 1970s (Howard 2005b).

THE VERNACULAR IN VERNACULAR WEBS

The combination of personal computers and software developed by
the Homebrewers and Theodor Nelson's vision of hypermedia combined to
create a network of connected computers that the public could access and
afford. This network developed further over the course of the 1990s and early
2000s to generate a mass of users who wanted to create, share, and consume
their own digital media content. In doing so, this network has in many ways
realized the anti-institutional ethos expressed by Fred Moore when he saw
computers as sidestepping the editorial function associated with institutional
mass media. In this sense, the Internet has become a powerful new venue
where vernacular authority can dominate because people act as individuals to pick and choose what information they share and consume. This has
become perhaps most starkly clear on the global stage where popular uprisings and movements in the Middle East and Asia challenge the authority of
dictators by employing vernacular webs for specific political ends. While not
necessarily countercultural, webs of like-minded content can connect the
public in ways and at a scale not previously possible. This fact should be of
particular interest to researchers of everyday expression of all kinds.

Mass-mediated institutional content has largely been understood as
having a limited ability to interact with the dynamic processes of lived
experience. Because its production is distanced from the individuals who
consume it, it is not typically available to local communities as a means to
express their own interests. In this sense, pre-network media like books,
newspapers, or Hollywood movies are primarily institutional because they
have a powerful institutional editorial function and are produced from the
top down. Older forms of mass media require institutional power to produce and disseminate them because they use highly centralized systems of
production. Participatory websites like Facebook or YouTube, on the other
hand, have the potential to be more empowering for everyday people by
offering network locations where individuals can express themselves without the editorial function of the media or other institutions. These technologies use distributed systems of production and cost very little to use.

At the same time, however, today's participatory media venues are not
totally noninstitutional, as Moore and Nelson seemed to have hoped. In

fact, the complexity of computer code at many levels has exploded since the 1970s, and very few nonprofessionals have the time to learn computer programming. Instead, complex but easy-to-use systems have emerged that allow people to deploy computers without the deep knowledge of their workings that Nelson hoped *Computer Lib* would encourage them to seek. As a result, powerful corporate institutions (the computer priesthood) built software that is easy for the public to use. Accessing the network locations of this software, individuals can then enact their own vernacular expressive behaviors based on the forms, modes, and norms established by institutionally produced technologies.

The technologies that create online locations for vernacular expression are typically produced, maintained, and funded by institutions. As a result, they generate content that is a hybrid between that of individuals and institutions. These communication processes give rise to what postcolonial critics Arjun Appadurai and Carol A. Breckenridge have termed "zones of contestation" where "national, mass, and folk culture provide both mill and grist for one another" (1995, 5). These zones are the domains of the vernacular, and the discourse that they host can be imagined as participating in a vast web of vernacular expression.

Generally, vernacular expression is characterized by what folklorist Henry Glassie (2000) has termed, "values alien to the academy" (20). These values emerge into meaning dialectically when individuals assert that something is noninstitutional. So the vernacular is imagined as diffused across a local community: learned informally, often face-to-face, and typically in small groups. Thus, vernacularity is often associated with the folk or grassroots not because it distinguishes itself by appealing to alternate institutions but because it invokes an alterity to all institutions. Since the inception of folklore studies in the nineteenth century, the field has attempted to preserve, understand, and even champion this extra-institutional power.

During the counterculture movements of the 1960s and 1970s, we see this interest at one of its peaks, and it helped drive the formation of some of the new media that are now transforming expressive human behavior. One of the most well-known and influential expressions of this technologically savvy vernacular ethos was in *Computer Lib* and another was clearly a powerful force in the emergence of personal computers among members of the Homebrew Computer Club.

From the invention of affordable personal computers to a layered network structure to which those computers can connect, to e-mail through hypertext to the World Wide Web to the myriad of mobile devices accessing the participatory media of today, the vernacular power Theodor Nelson called "building from the bottom" continues to exert influence through TCP/IP as the basic technology that allows individuals to create the vernacular webs of their own digital communication. As it does, it creates opportunities for the vernacular to enact its alterity from the institutional. Today, this opportunity is available to more people more of the time than ever before because of the emergence of online participatory media. Famously termed "Web 2.0" by computer media CEO Tim O'Reilly in 2005, these current forms of Internet media are characterized by network locations where users can connect with others based on the self-generated content they place online.

Running powerful new kinds of software, these sites are very easy to use. However, the ease of use comes at a cost. Vernacular voices can emerge in participatory media only in the ways that institutional interests have enabled. Institutional forces structure the content as the software adapts it to fit onto the institutional site. In particular, these sites require that advertising be placed on some personal webpages. As a result, individuals provide the content that corporations then use to forward their own interests. In many ways, this relationship seems to be at odds with the countercultural ethos that so powerfully influenced the development of these technologies.

On one hand, the alliance between institutional commerce and vernacular expressive behaviors makes it possible for people to connect "at the bottom" by sharing their personal photos, videos, and words without the editorial function of institutions. On the other hand, individuals act as proxies of corporations by forwarding agendas embedded in the media even as they rack up usage charges that further empower the institutions that have developed and sold them their mobile communication devices. This situation reminds us that everyday content emerging in the web of vernacular discourse made possible by these media are always and already hybrid. It seems that Nelson's vision of complete freedom from institutional power is not possible for two reasons. At a practical level, vernacular users of these technologies are being empowered by institutions that build technologies in order to be institutionally profitable. At a more philosophical level, expressing the vernacular relies on the institutional for its dialectical definition.

From wikis to social networking to photo sharing to file sharing, these new participatory forms of web use occur across network locations where vernacular and institutional agents hybridize expression in complex new communication processes. Taken together, this vast interconnected zone of informal discourse creates vernacular webs of interconnected digital content. In these zones of everyday digital life, a new renaissance of personal expression has emerged. Today, individuals increasingly watch excerpts from television and movies on their laptops and mobile devices instead of sitting down in theaters or in front of televisions. Here they can follow their friends to choose institutional content, edit it, and share it. Even more, they can combine mass media content with their own digital video and audio to create whole new hybrid media creations and share them with others in their vernacular web. Harvard law professor Yochai Benkler rightly describes how these vernacular webs foster a "new folk culture" that encourages "a wider practice of active personal engagement in the telling and retelling of basic cultural themes" (2008, 299). We owe the very existence of these webs, in no small part, to the countercultural vision of grassroots, folk, or build-at-the-bottom empowerment.

If it is true that a valorization of the informal, the everyday, and the communally held deeply influences these now ubiquitous forms of human communication, shouldn't the perspective of folklore studies offer a unique ability to speak to these expressive processes? It is not just that the Internet has bred new genres for folklorists to catalog (although that can, should, and is being done). Nor is it that there is some vestigial or resurgent orality in these forms (although there may well be).

Instead, it is clearly the case that the vernacular authority embedded in these forms enables researchers of everyday expression to speak about these new hybrid media expressions in profound ways. This can be done precisely because folklore studies has always concerned itself with how individuals act in small groups to locate themselves alongside but apart from institutions. Recognizing the dialectical relationship between the vernacular and the institutional in these webs of digital media, researchers of folkloric expression are in a unique position to be able to account for the complex dynamics of power made possible by new network communication technologies.

NOTE

1.   In citing Nelson's publication, each page includes both *Computer Lib* (*CL*) page numbers as well *Dream Machine* (*DM*) page numbers. In keeping with the document's format, I have placed both page numbers in the citations.

2

Netizens, Revolutionaries, and the Inalienable Right to the Internet

Tok Thompson

REVOLUTION 2.0

ON JANUARY 25, 2011, PROTESTORS TOOK TO THE streets of Egypt, demanding democracy and a change in regime. An election held in November 2010 was largely denounced as a sham. The 82-year-old leader and thirty-year autocrat, Hosni Mubarak, quickly moved to shut down the Internet in an effort to counter user-generated social networking sites such as Twitter and Facebook (see Ali 2011). Egyptians exploded in anger: who was he to control who they—the people—could speak with? There were appeals to the Internet as a human right, and debates on those appeals.[1] After a week of massive protests, the government restored the Internet in the hope of mollifying the community; some saw the move as a doomed ploy to regain some semblance of authority. But the Egyptian people harbored no illusions about their national government; they were well aware of the wider world and of issues such as freedom of the press, freedom of organization, freedom of religion, and true (rather than nominal) democracies. They were well informed of global discourse. And more importantly, they were *participants* in this global discourse.

The events in Egypt were not an isolated national story but rather part of a wider movement, quickly dubbed the "Arab Spring." Occurring first in Tunisia in December 2010, but spreading quickly to other countries throughout the Arab world, populations erupted in the first world political uprising in which the role of social media figured as a prominent constitutive factor in the revolution as well as in the public recognition of the discourse involved before, during, and after the Tahrir Square protest (among others in various countries within the region).[2] The world witnessed a global first: Revolution 2.0. While previous organizations such as the Zapatistas (see, for example, the account in Lindholm and Zúquete 2010) have made good use of global media in revolutions and social uprisings, the events that unfolded of a citizens' revolt against despotic national regimes nonetheless marked the first direct, successful political impact of Web 2.0 social networks. The implications of this are momentous: the inclusion of global networks in participatory culture and participatory social networks, the creation of a truly global discourse, and the birth of the postnational citizen.[3]

Before digital media, and especially the Internet, communications were much more controlled in Egypt. Under Mubarak, "emergency rules" suspended the due process of law for over three decades; the brutal secret police force easily silenced most "troublemakers." Newspaper editors, television programmers, and the rest of the citizenry participated in this common game of hegemonic discourse—one that ultimately confined the knowledge of citizens by confining the media stories available to them, often with explicit and implicit exhortations to nationalism.

But now citizens used the Internet to communicate, and the regime lost control of the story. When the unlikely protests started, in reaction to those in nearby Tunisia, Egyptian authorities identified the immediate threat of the Internet: the ability for protestors to organize mass protests online. Unquestionably, it was this concern that motivated the Egyptian government to close all Internet access at the first signs of civil unrest. Such a view makes sense from the standpoint of a despotic government, but the larger story may lay elsewhere: that its citizens became netizens— participants in a global discourse—and were not beholden to nationally produced narratives. The move of the national government to deny access to the global realm was no longer an acceptable possibility. Egyptians from all walks of life used the Internet and engaged in discourse on a global scale. Who was Mubarak, or any national government, to deny them this? The emerging ideas of the online world were more important (and more impressive) than the petty regional claims of national dictators. The reign of national media, national stories, and national control of social discourse was annihilated—swept aside—in a simple shift of public discourse and a refusal to submit to an overbearing version of the national.

A ham radio operator in the Egyptian desert circumvented the Internet clampdown and notified other hobbyists via Morse code: "Internet not working. Police cars burning." Another sent out the message "Today marks a great day for Egypt." The messages were relayed to the Internet, and global Internet-based groups such as Telecomix, Anonymous, and many others helped ensure that these dispatches circulated worldwide, bypassing the Egyptian national authorities.[4] When the protestors' demands were met and Mubarak stepped down from power, the people acknowledged and celebrated the influence of such discourses. Gamal Ibrahim, a jubilant young father, named his child "Facebook Jamal Ibrahim," honoring the power of global social networks to provide a new life, and a new political way of living, for his daughter (Olivarez-Giles 2011).

A new global right—the right to free speech in a global discourse of the net, the right of the netizen—may be the new ethical, civic, and political demand of our time. These ideas of global rights created by the Internet highlight the important role of new identity relations between individuals and global discourse, mediated through the Internet. They also suggest that new means of identity may be superseding national identities; with this comes profound implications for nation-states as loci for continuing political power in the world today. This is particularly relevant because many of the ways in which collective identity is being forged online are highly derived from individual interests (including occupational, hobbyist, political, ethno-national, local, religious, etc.).

THE MECHANICAL NATIONAL MEETS THE DIGITAL GLOBAL

Censorship used to be so easy. A nation only had so many printing presses churning out national books, newspapers, and magazines, so it was easy to know who had printed what. Shipments coming in from other countries could be stopped at the border by ominous-looking guards who could inspect deliveries and prevent "dangerous foreign" texts from entering the country.

Increasingly, "keeping a lid on things" became difficult. Printing became cheaper, and more widespread. International trade and treaties, tourism, satellite television, and various other developments all allowed people to gain more knowledge, and have more connections, to people in other nations. As mechanical technology improved, travel—of goods, people, and information—became much easier and much more common. Along with these new international connections came increased global discourse on such issues as universal rights, democracy, and freedom of the press and religion. Diasporas became more common. Refugees, immigrants, and visitors traversed the world creating complex overlaps of place and culture, from San Francisco's Chinatown to Indian communities in Kenya. The pace of communication technology, linking far-flung parts of the world, continued its astonishing developments: the telegraph transformed the world of its time, as did the radio, and then television. The ideal of the nation-state was already creaking at the seams by the time of the Internet's arrival, which pushed globalizing, democratizing communications into hyper-speed.

To be sure, globalization and postmodernity are also economic transformations, bringing people from widely separate geographies into business and economic relationships. The scope of industrial production is global in both production and consumption. Supra-national organizations of all kinds are also common. Tourism, currently the largest industry in the world, continues to swirl together people and places and thoughts thereof at an increasing rate.[5] Yet even with all these forces, it is the Internet, and digitally based communication in general, which has become the most pronounced site of global participatory culture. This is precisely what makes the idea of the netizen inherently postnational and, as such, a threat to despotic governments. National governments used to be able to control much of the discourse of their citizens and, therefore, what they thought about their national governments. A recursive system was set between political control and control of discourse *about* politics—in a word, hegemony.

Through the promulgation of national languages, textbooks, national holidays and celebrations, official religions, national museums, and controls over print, radio, and television networks, national governments have long enjoyed a near-totalizing formation of geographically based discourses and "imagined communities" (in the famous phrase of Benedict Anderson [1991]). The development of digital communications and the Internet have outmoded these discourses, allowing anyone in the world to share in the same discourse.

Subsequently, many nation-states have attempted to tighten controls on the Internet, perhaps nowhere more famously than in China, where the "great firewall of China" illustrates the enormous effort to exert state control over their citizens' digital discourses. It is easy to understand the motivations behind the actions. The Chinese government is not democratically elected by the will of the people; allowing citizens rights to free speech and free exchange of information threatens their continued existence. But to erect and sustain such a monumental project to monitor and control peoples' discourse requires an enormous amount of—for lack of a better word— spies (that is, people who are paid to monitor and control information). China's firewall is designed explicitly with the goal of nationally controlling discourse, yet such a construction runs the danger of a becoming a house of cards: a system built to protect itself, run by people who may no longer believe in it. In China, a brand-new creature has already challenged the great firewall: the grass-mud horse.

The Grass-Mud Horse

Perhaps the most famous reaction against censorship in China (although far from the only one), the grass-mud horse (*cao ni ma*) gained popularity via the Internet in a series of videos. On the surface, its story proposes new mythic beasts, the grass-mud horses, that live peacefully in an idyllic territory that is invaded by the evil "river crabs."

The pointed joke is that the Chinese word used to define grass-mud horse closely matches a rude obscenity (the only difference being tonal variations) meaning, essentially, "fuck your mother" while river crabs refer to censors. The message, coming from a nation chafing under despotic national control, is clear: the netizens, however profane they may be, are the heroes, and the censors, the vile river crabs, are the villains.

The idea of the grass-mud horse became enormously popular among China's netizens, with videos of an accompanying "folk song" sung by children alongside music videos and "documentaries." Rap songs echo the same song. Videos, and references, proliferate. Toys depicting the grass-mud horse (based on the alpaca) are hot sellers. The Chinese government now attempts to censor any mention of the grass-mud horse (making itself look somewhat ridiculous, petty, and fearful in the process), a move denounced by the country's netizens as "another invasion of river crabs"; but oblique references are now common and widely understood. This may have been another instance of locking the gate after the horses have bolted. Henceforth, China's censors, active as they are, are represented in popular discourse as crabs destroying the idyllic life of the peaceful grass-mud horse. The story, too, predicts an ending: the crabs will be destroyed and the grass-mud horses will emerge victorious.

Gaddafi sings Zenga Zenga

Another compelling Internet sensation resulted from the 2011 uprising in Libya (also following the mass protests in Tunisia and Egypt). Head-of-state Muammar Gaddafi delivered a series of fiery threats to the protestors on state television, vowing to hunt them down "inch by inch, house by house, home by home, alleyway by alleyway." An Israeli DJ, Noy Alooshe, created a mashup of this excerpt of his speech with the music of "Hey Baby (Drop It to the Floor)" by rapper Pitbull (featuring T-Pain).[6] The Libyan opposition adopted the song and requests flooded in from around the Arab world and abroad. Early on, some fans of the mashup asked Alooshe to create a second version, minus the scantily clad dancing girls of the first video (in order to be more acceptable to elder, more conservative people), and he did so. Multiple versions have since appeared on YouTube, many from the Arabic world. Gaddafi could not control the Internet and could not stop the parodies. The video was easy to copy and easy to spread around. Political control had to devolve to an almost medieval level of overt, brutal display of military force to try to maintain control.

"Zenga Zenga" was an enormous hit, enjoyed by an astonishing world-wide community of people, with nearly 3 million viewers in its first week alone. The video's aesthetic characteristics highlight the idea of representational control—away from despotic national regimes and national media into the digital global realm of the Internet—from person to person, who occasionally change it in the process. Its importance is not so much in what the video says against Gaddafi—after all, it uses his own words, even if they are indicative of his well-known and often mocked violent ramblings—but rather that it wrest control away from him and caricatures him in a way of the artist's choosing. The postnational aesthetic can also be seen in the worldwide spread of the video; although particularly popular in Libya and throughout the Arabic world, the viewership has been truly international.[7] Like the grass-mud horse, the video's grassroots artistry reveals a celebration of postnational identity, overlapping local and global—the *glocal*—something new in human history.[8]

Representation and the Future of Authority

Who controls the story? *Qui parle?* as the French say. If we admit the tremendous power of narratives in shaping social reality, then we must investigate how its larger, unifying stories are formed and influenced in order

to fully understand a society. In ancient Egypt, the rulers would periodically enforce a retroactive censorship, removing all evidence of a particular
ruler, or even of whole historical periods. Records inscribed in hieroglyphs
in the temple areas were chiseled away, literally stricken from the record.
At various times, purges of past material commonly took place, as different
ancients came in and out of favor—and where few copies of written text
existed, destruction was often more complete. Many times, as folklorists are
well aware, such repressed lore would live on in oral traditions, even (and
perhaps especially) when forbidden or purged from the literary realm, at
times to reenter the literary realm later on.

During the medieval era, prefiguring the modern, literacy was a tool of
the political establishment, and even more so of the church. Yet the reality
of Europe's Medieval and largely nonliterate society was that church and
political leaders constantly struggled to control the "grand narratives" (as
per Lyotard 1984 [1979]) of society, *vis à vis* the robust role that oral lore
played among the populace. The explosion of literacy after the development
of the printing press propelled the role of literature in transforming society
and organizing large-scale national identities in previously unimaginable
ways. National governments quickly became major factors in setting grand
narratives as the identities of the whole citizenry were established through
national education systems, museums, the press, and the like.

As in the example of the grass-mud horse, what emerges from netizen
artistic discourse is a strong aesthetic of claiming representation, claiming
the stage, and claiming the role of storyteller away from the primacy of
the national. This is especially powerful in the face of despotic, unelected
governments.

THE NETIZEN

Netizen, I would argue, is a particularly apt term for describing the
move into global discourse mediated by digital technology. The term itself
is a global one, particularly popular in Argentina and several Asian countries, including South Korea, Singapore, and China, reflecting the far-flung
Pacific nations. But people around the world increasingly use the word, and
it is rapidly appearing more frequently in newspapers and other media.[9]

Netizen is a conscious reworking of the term *citizen*, and as such contains claims of political and social identity. If the citizen descended from
ideas of civic social realities (participations, obligations, and the like), then

what has been shifted is not so much these fundamental ideas and ideals but rather their scope and locale. This is not entirely new either: long before current ideas of citizenship, the ancient Greeks held that the concept of citizens applied only to city-states and community-led governments of elite aristocratic men, representing the noble lineages. The Romans made great use of the Greek ideals of community and civilization, and the notion of the citizen grew along with the Roman Empire, creating differing levels of belonging at different times over its history. In the medieval period, people in many towns and cities often regarded themselves as citizens—with rights and privileges, as well as obligations, to the local town or city. This is the direct predecessor of the idea of the "national citizen," and the concept was expanded alongside the idea of the "national community." Efforts to formulate an idea of *international* citizenry still rely on the nation-state as the primary locus of political belonging (see Archibugi 2008).

Contrary to this formation, a netizen sees social and political discourse as via the Internet rather than via national media and the place of social interaction as global rather than national or even international. As historian Mark Poster asserts, "nation-states are losing their cultural coherence by dint of planetary communications systems" (2002, 98). Poster also sees that "the political formation of the netizen is already well under way, bringing forth . . . a humanity adhering not to nature but to machines, not to geographically local identity, but to the digitized packets of its own electronic communication" (103). Netizens are in touch with each other, however physically separated they may or may not be. In this way, these online forums help folk groups form new identities, ideologies, and political sensibilities.

The idea of citizenship as the participation in public life has moved from the local to the national, and now to the global. But how is such new participatory culture constructed? If the division is not territorially based, what constitutes the various levels of membership and participation? This is where a folkloristic approach may be useful, especially in examining the relationship between groups of participants and group identity, or in analyzing a social group in terms of its performances.[10] I have previously argued that aesthetics can be a mediating step between performances and identity concerns (Thompson 2003).[11] As many of the essays in this volume and its predecessor demonstrate (Blank 2009a), folklore is enjoying a tremendous renaissance online. Without question, online folk groups have become important in establishing new forms and thoughts of identity. This presents folklorists with a vital task: the opportunity to document the tremendous growth of new social and cultural networks. But what are the contents and contours of such expressive culture? Who takes part, and to what degree, and in what groups? All of these, and more, are useful questions to gain insight into the ways that the new netizen identity is being constituted.

THE TALE OF THE LONG TAIL

One concept to help approach the multitudes of new social and cultural groups online is the Long Tail. The Long Tail is a long-standing marketing concept that came to prominence with the rise of international media, industry, and, hence, the global consumer. Marketers, astute students of social behavior, noted that with the Internet, one did not have to aim for mainstream tastes (the "big bell" part of the statistical bell curve) to be profitable; instead, through the global reach of the Internet, one could profitably do business with non-mainstream tastes (the "long tail" of the bell curve). The Long Tail became a philosophy that guided growing diversity of the World Wide Web, invigorating many local-brand crafts and sidelining others.

Master guitar makers in Mexico from a region renowned for its prowess in folk music and guitar production now work in their small village shop for an upscale global clientele. Eskimo women weave delicate garments from musk ox wool in Alaska for a similar market. Niche markets of all varieties are suddenly possible since the *market* has become synonymous with the *world* (especially noticeable in digital products). If you have an obscure interest, all you need to do is reach out far enough across the globe to all the other people with the same obscure interest.

The development of the Long Tail of the market reflects broader social changes as well: people are free to spend their time and energy in a multitude of worldwide social networks. Identity in such a setting has the potential to be much more complex, as one can belong to widely diverse groups with multiple members. But, at the same time, the Internet can also support traditional identities such as families, loved ones, religious, ethnic groups and/or nationalities, and local communities. Identities—always multiple and overlapping—become even more heterogeneous when filtered through the globalizing medium of the Internet or other digital networks.

Groups' identities can easily include shared personal interests as well, ranging throughout the human spectrum of vocations and avocations: those who build boats by hand, or forge metal, or are interested in astronomy or particular celebrities, foods, technologies, or fashions. The range of shared interest groups on the Internet spans the range of human potential. Since most of these groups are based on interests and information, they have no need for a geographical base. They are open to interested people anywhere, and indeed often reflect this explicitly: a Google search of the phrase "international association of" resulted in 94 million websites.[12] The current ubiquity of such international links provides nearly everyone with extra-national contacts. The self-contained discursive realm of the nation-state has been supplanted in a most innocuous way by the plethora of international interest groups comprising the Long Tail.

Examples of Long Tail groups reveal many such networks clustered around personal interests, groups that are easily international as often as local. Scholars from folklore and media studies have published on topics ranging from games such as World of Warcraft (Lau 2010) to vernacular religion (Howard 2011) to global fan culture (Jenkins 2008). People may belong to many or few groups. All of these now have global potentials for social engagements and linkages. Such new possibilities for participatory groups allow for new ways to conceive of identity, both group identity and that of the self.

CHANGES AND IMPLICATIONS

Increasingly, the notion of place as a solid foundation for culture and political representation has become contested. The same technological advances that brought the printing press and modern nation-states also enabled large-scale population movements, both by choice and not, a trend that has only intensified over time. As anthropologists Akhil Gupta and James Ferguson (1992, 12) explain: "Both the ethnological and national naturalisms present associations of people and place as solid, commonsensical, and agreed-upon, when they are in fact contested, uncertain, and in flux."

One of the main ways in which the concept of the netizen is challenging the formerly supreme nation-state is by altering the fundamental ways in which people interact with place and the long-standing tendency to equate culture, and hence identity, with geography. If modernity was based on the individual and the national, then postmodernity has given new questions to these formerly accepted bases of personal, civic, and political identity. There is still, to be sure, the local—the actual space that one inhabits and in which one participates. You can always talk about the weather to a neighbor, no matter where you are in the world. The local remains powerful yet coexists at the same time with the new discourse of the Internet. The local and the global overlap—and easily so—just as local groups link to international societies, often leapfrogging over national concerns. But the local is no longer the only realm of folklore groups; both place and other earlier forms of identity exist as various *imaginaires* online, within which one can evoke identity discourses, or not.

It is true that one can still speak of a "digital divide" between the haves and the have-nots inhabiting this online agora, yet the massive expansion of digital communications has been a major democratizing influence on global discourse, swiftly empowering many previously excluded peoples and groups to voice their concerns and opinions. Digital communications have spread into many places that never witnessed electricity and are surely one of the most dramatic makeovers the planet has witnessed in terms of human communication and, hence, human society. Places that were never modern can now be postmodern, and tribal groups and others who have remained outside modernity and nationalism are now often eager participants in this new global discourse. Elders can be photographed telling oral stories in languages never written down; the stories then can be shared with the world at large. In many uneducated slums, street youths teach one another to be literate through their self-learned media proficiency.[13] And throughout much of the third world, cell phones have become ubiquitous.[14] These "phones" are in reality small personal computers, linking the user to the larger global media networks of the Internet. World affairs can now easily become everyone's affairs.

We may be witnessing for the first time the development of a truly new sense of citizenry, pointing the way for future global (or glocal) governance. Yet this would suggest a vastly different structure than the United Nations, a group built on the predominance of the nation-state in world affairs. Grassmud horses and rapping dictators may reveal a sense of frustration at the vast world netizenry against what is perhaps perceived as the dangerous, often violent, quarrels of nationalism.

CONCLUSIONS

The *vox populi* is now being heard loud and clear, as never before.

The emergence of folk groups online, sharing folklore and participatory culture, brings with it a renewed importance for the field of folklore studies.

After all, for over two hundred years, folklore studies has cultivated an expertise in the study of communally created, shared culture and the relationship between such participatory culture and identity. Identities are forged, confirmed, and celebrated in large part through shared expressive culture, and the social contexts of such performances are important. The digital realm allows an individual to have a corporeal, local experience as well as a virtual social life. It is important to note that the corporeal still implies face-to-face interactions and the importance of locale while the digital does neither. And the two may often overlap; the local world frequently plays a vigorous role in the online world. Importantly, what is eclipsed in this emergent discourse is a need for the nation-state as a locus of representation, and by extension, citizenry. National territory, the imagined community, fades in relevance in this newly emerging discourse.

With postmodernity in full bloom, postnational aesthetics are on the rise, signaling, in my interpretation, an emergent sense of global identities and global citizenry, with consequences for understanding an ongoing revolution in the philosophy of global civics, political identity, and representation. This is not to say that the nation-state will likely disappear overnight. Nation-states still control resources and armies, print money and the like. Yet, as discourse globalizes, nation-states seem to be moving together as well, joined through international law organizations, such as the United Nations, and non-governmental organizations, like Doctors Without Borders. The European Union promulgates law for its "sovereign" nation-state members, and various such supra-national groups connect nations in an overlapping web of regions and interests.

Further, the nation-state will most certainly continue to be a strongly held source of identity, even in its imaginaire state online; already one can witness online "nations" of dispossessed peoples. In the transnational world of vast diasporas and the worldwide flow of peoples, the idea of the nation-state may still remain an important imagined community for many people, blending with the ideas of homelands and other geographical imaginaires.

Yet alongside the development of the global arena, there are many more available sources of identity besides the national, and people are increasingly likely to identify themselves in strikingly postnational terms. The tensions between national interests and emergent folk groups online is already one of the most dramatic of the postmodern world. The questions concern nothing less than the future of identity: who will our children/grandchildren consider themselves to be? We might like to assume that identities are fixed, but history shows us this is an error. In times of great societal flux, particularly in great shifts of communicative technologies, identity itself has become open for questioning and change.

In order to improve our understanding of this emerging situation for human culture, we must examine this new folklore and its aesthetics: who is sharing, who is performing, what do they perform, and what does it mean to them? It is the same old field of folklore studies, albeit in new contexts, and with critically heightened importance. In this way, the study of online folklore—Folklore 2.0—may help us to understand these new identities, which in turn may be grounds for new political representations and philosophies.

Communication builds groups. Forms of communication create forms of political groups. The age of the nation-state relied on print technology and mechanical culture to push the nation-state as the dominant locus of political power and representation in the world (as the current supreme global organization, the United Nations, makes explicit).

Now we have entered a new age of humanity, one relying on digital communications that are notable for fostering global discourses and therefore global political thinking. Along with the tremendous social and political changes brought by these new technologies (including the toppling of several dictatorships), the world recently witnessed the introduction of a brand-new global human right: the right of Internet access (as recommendations of the Special Rapporteur to the United Nations Human Rights Council have already indicated). Every person's voice, it seems, should be heard in the forum. Take heed: the rights of the netizen, the first truly global citizenry, are being formulated and proclaimed. Multitudes of new groups, new social formations, and new identities are being formed. More important than any economy or leader or army are the views of the people; and the folk, these days, are netizens. The postnational glocal models of citizenship and politics will have to grapple with this fact in reorganizing our societies and philosophies and in building a new future for humanity.

NOTES

1.	During the preparation and writing of this chapter, first Finland, and then Estonia, guaranteed citizens an inalienable right to broadband Internet access. The United Nations later declared Internet access a fundamental human right. See United Nations report A/HRC/17/27, http://tinyurl.com/AHRC1727, accessed 11 November 2011

2. Another point to consider is that the execution of coordinated mass protests relied heavily on social media, which served to further cement its influence and importance in the contexts of these uprisings.

3. There is a voluminous record of discussions on postnationalism. See, perhaps especially, Habermaus (2001) as well as Appadurai (1990, 1993, 1996), and Bhabha (1990). These scholars see, as I do, that global flows, particularly of communication, continue to erode the idea of the nation-state as the locus for political representation and power. However, there have also been critics of this term, (see, e.g., Bloemraad 2004), who emphasize the ongoing power of the nation-state. In this chapter, I focus more on aspects of postnationalism that are cultural and identitarian in nature rather than social, political, economic, or military, and it is these aspects, I would argue, which have witnessed the most globalization.

4. For an in-depth account, see Ryan (2011).

5. As per the reckoning of the World Travel and Tourism Council, http://www.wttc. org/eng/Tourism_Research/Economic_Research, accessed 21 March 2011.

6. For an argument of mashups as a form of folk music, see Thompson (2011).

7. Also note the easy acceptance of "foreign" authorship that seems to transcend national, ethnic, and even religious identities, that being the acceptance of the work of an Israeli Jewish DJ.

8. Since writing this chapter, events further confirmed the power of international social networks to influence world affairs: Gaddafi's regime fell spectacularly and others have come under pressure. Even Russia has witnessed remarkable demonstrations against the government, again enabled by social media.

9. Google Analytics; s.v. "netizen," accessed 24 May 2011.

10. This follows Richard Bauman's (1971, 33) call for folklore to be an empirical discipline focused on the actual objective cultural performances, along with the subsequent scholarly attention given to performance studies. For an introduction, see Kirshenblatt-Gimblett (2004).

11. For example, when you ask people why they like a joke, they might reply, "because it's funny." But answering the question as to *why* a particular joke is funny can provide deeper insights about the culture performing and enjoying the joke. The same logic applies to all such cultural performances.

12. Google, accessed 29 January 2012.

13. See Hannson and Wihlborg (2011).

14. See, for example, "Not Just Talk" (2011).

3

Performance 2.0
Observations toward a Theory of the Digital Performance of Folklore[1]

Anthony Bak Buccitelli

INTRODUCTION: WHERE IS THE "FACE" IN FACEBOOK?

A FEW YEARS AGO, I VISITED "SEAN," AN OLD college friend, in San Francisco.[2] As we sat in his apartment catching up, our conversation turned toward a mutual acquaintance, "Jake," whom neither of us had seen in some time. When I relayed what information I had about recent happenings in Jake's life, Sean conjectured, "So I guess you keep in pretty good touch with him, huh?" I clarified that I had not talked to Jake in over a year but that I had been informed about his life by following his Facebook status updates. "Then it makes sense that I didn't know about what he was up to," Sean explained. "I deleted my [Facebook] account." I inquired as to why he did so, expecting the usual litany of valid concerns about Internet privacy and professional etiquette. Instead, Sean revealed that using social networking services, such as Facebook, eventually began to make him feel narcissistic. As he recalled, "I kept posting things in my status and then just sat around waiting for people to comment on or 'like' them. When I started feeling hurt that no one responded to a post, I decided that I needed to stop."

I begin with this anecdote because it personally opened my eyes to some interesting questions about performance in digital environments. Since joining Facebook almost a decade ago, I have often thought of it as merely a way to occasionally catch up with friends and colleagues with whom I do not interact on a regular basis. But, as Sean's comments suggest, social media has increasingly taken on a performative function, allowing participants to

DOI: 10.7330/9780874218909.c03

engage in numerous forms of communicative interaction. Just as one might feel disappointed or self-conscious if an audience poorly receives a personal performance, Sean's self-consciousness about the reception of his posts on Facebook make sense when framed as a kind of performance. To put his comments in familiar folkloristic terms, Sean felt that he had assumed the role of a performer in front of a group of people he knew and, hence, he had become responsible for a display of communicative competence. The assumption of this type of performative role places the performer in a dialogic, socially governed relationship with his or her audience (Bauman 1984; Briggs 1988; Georges 1969). Thus, when his audience fails to respond to his posts, Sean reads this as a direct comment on what he has created.

This familiar performative feel expressed by Sean is not a coincidence. A closer inspection of the poetic features of a number of forms of digital expression reveals distinct points of overlap with social and aesthetic features that folklorists commonly recognize and study in face-to-face contexts. Accordingly, the dynamics of performance familiar to folklorists remains most relevant to creative expression that takes place on social networking sites like Facebook. The increasing recognition of the sociocultural complexity of digital environments offers a new way to study digital culture as continuous with the actual world in some ways. Of course, this continuity can be a false friend. Points of overlap often belie important distinctions between online and offline contexts of performance.[3] In the emerging media environments of digital folklore, familiar forms occur in markedly unfamiliar ways.

Although I argue in this chapter that folklorists can and should apply their unique insights into the dynamics of traditional performance to the digital world more extensively than they have in the past, there are valid reasons why this has largely not yet taken place. As folklorist Trevor J. Blank aptly notes in the introduction to this volume, the extent to which the criterion of "face-to-face" contact[4] has permeated the study of folklore performance has contributed greatly to the reluctance of folklorists to study digital folklore as performance.[5] Since the earliest work on media and folklore, scholars have worried about the implications of mediated communication in general—let alone communication that potentially spans vast global networks—for a set of practices famously defined as "artistic communication in small groups" (Ben-Amos 1971). For instance, in one of the earliest treatments of digital folklore—penned well before the explosion in popularity of the Internet in the 1990s—sociologist William S. Fox (2007 [1983]) articulates some of the basic features of digital folklore that seem problematic for the consideration of folklore as situated performance:

> [C]omputerized folklore tends to be highly anonymous and individualistic—perhaps even more so than paperlore. It resembles graffiti in this respect. The creators and disseminators of material cannot determine recipients with any precision and they cannot be identified. Materials are mediated by the computer and appear as anonymous contributions. Consequently, disseminators of a joke for example, can only anticipate or indirectly experience reactions to it. With grafffiti [*sic*], creators of computerized folklore cannot easily control access to materials. The best they can do is to place general restrictions on who may gain access, but in doing so they unnecessarily and undesirably restrict availability. This defeats the purpose of creating the folkloric materials in the first place. (2007, 10)

Like Fox, many folklorists and other cultural scholars have accepted the notion that digital spaces are inherently spaces that efface familiar components of social identity, allowing users to remain anonymous or assume fictitious identities.[6] Given that performance has been importantly understood as a communicative interplay between performer and audience, and thus necessarily concerned with esoteric and exoteric understandings of social identity (see Bauman 1992, 48; Dundes 1980, 28),[7] it seems counterintuitive to apply theories of performance to a milieu in which social identities have often been described as irrelevant, attenuated, or nonexistent.[8]

In keeping with the difficulties of locating performer and audience identities in the same way that might be done in offline performative settings, the study of digital folklore has often forsaken performance-oriented approaches for textual studies that can be more easily conducted without direct knowledge of performer identities. Hence, work on digital folklore has often taken two related foci: text and transmission rather than performance and digital technology as a medium for communication rather than a site for performance (cf. Runnel 2001, 170–171).

Interestingly, both emphases have direct parallels in some of the most influential earlier work on the relationship between folklore and technology, particularly in the study of photocopier lore (or "Xerox lore") famously examined by Alan Dundes and Carl R. Pagter in their groundbreaking volume, *Work Hard and You Shall Be Rewarded: Urban Folklore from the Paperwork Empire* (1978 [1975]). In this treatment, Dundes and Pagter set forth a convincing case for the idea that photocopied pictures, poems, or jokes that had never been in oral circulation could be considered folklore, despite the widespread reliance on orality as a defining feature of folklore at the time. In doing so, they formed what has become one of the signature conceptual and argumentative frameworks in the study of folklore and media in general:

> The materials contained in this study are traditional: they manifest multiple existence in space and time, and they exist in variant forms . . . Except for the oral criterion, these materials would doubtless pass muster as folklore for most American folklorists. Had we lied and claimed that we had elicited all of the texts orally from informants, these materials would surely be considered authentic folklore by folklorists. Since the materials are *not* in oral tradition, there are two possibilities; one can either throw out the data or throw out the theory! (1978 [1975], xvii; italics in original)

Mathematician Alan Turing (1950) once suggested that the true test of artificial intelligence (AI) would be whether it could fool a real person into believing that the AI was another real person. In *Work Hard and You Shall Be Rewarded*, Dundes and Pagter similarly structure their understanding of technologically mediated expression as a kind of Turing Test: they suggest that photocopier lore is folklore if it can fool folklorists! The evidence for their case consists of a survey of the versions and variants of photocopier lore, which clearly showed its textual similarities to oral forms of folklore in terms of transmission and traditional variation.

Of course, Dundes and Pagter would go on to publish several popular follow-up compilations (1987, 1991, 1996, 2000) that further built upon the theoretical foundations presented in their original effort, especially as increasingly sophisticated communication technologies emerged and further complicated—or, in some cases, reinforced—their argument that technologically mediated expression contained genuine folkloric elements, regardless of orality. These texts, and other works on Xerox or photocopier lore,[9] are often cited in studies of digital folklore as examples of analogous instances of folkloric production through technology (see Blank 2009a; Bronner 2009; Dorst 1990; Fox 2007 [1983]; Frank 2009).

Dundes and Pagter's work was seminal inasmuch as it opened up the possibility of examining technological devices as tools in the creation and transmission of folklore. But while the circumstances of production and reception may have analogs in some areas of digital folklore, they are quite different from those of photocopier lore. To begin with, the question of identity in digital environments is far more complex than in earlier technological instances. There is no doubt that in many contexts, it remains difficult to pin down a correspondence between online and offline identities. While some folklorists have rightly observed that it may be possible to reconstruct information about online participants after the fact (Ellis 2003; Langlois 2005), this arduous task may not be possible in all situations. More importantly for this discussion, however, the systematic reconstruction of identifiable information is not likely to be a realistic practice for the average user and therefore is not likely to play a significant role in the performance process.

Despite these difficulties, a number of studies challenge the basic assumption that digital environments are necessarily situations either of anonymity or where individuals have complete freedom to fabricate identities. For instance, Barbara Kirshenblatt-Gimblett observes that while some digital environments intrinsically rely on anonymity, others actually either promote or result from personal offline relationships (1996, 29, 39–41; see also Varnelis 2008). Ethnographer danah boyd[10] (2006) argues that digital environments, given their function as key venues for expressions of approval or disapproval by peers, have become indispensable arenas for interaction between youth friend groups; furthermore, she argues that the ability to construct an online version of personal identity on sites like MySpace or Facebook has become an important way that teens construct their offline identities. Finally, in the context of video games or immersive digital environments, folklorists Kimberly Lau (2010) and Kiri Miller (2008) both observe that users importantly perform identity in accordance with the often overdetermined identity constructs of digital environments and the understood parameters of the anticipated audience.[11] Even if the identities do not correspond to their offline selves, Lau argues that this lack of correspondence does not undermine the performative possibilities and weight of online discourse (2010, 387).

It is clear, then, that the linkages and politics of identity in digital environments are significantly more robust than they had initially appeared.[12] Thus, as scholars have come to understand the dynamics of identity in digital environments in a more sophisticated way, it is now possible to critically examine digital interactions in terms similar to actual world interactions. At the same time, acknowledging the difficulties with the application of standard theories of performance to the new social spaces and poetic possibilities offered by digital technologies, folklorists must adjust their performance lens to account for both the marked similarities and vast differences between digital and actual performances.

Proceeding along similar lines to Dundes and Pagter, some Turing Test examples, which display various aspects of performance as they are understood by folklorists, may point to a few of the ways that expressions in digital environments bear striking resemblances to offline performances of similar materials. Ultimately, however, this strategy will only take scholars so far; therefore, following a discussion of parallels between digital and actual performance, the following section considers the unique aspects of digital performances and offers some initial observations about the circumstances of production and reception in digital environments that can contribute to the development of a more robust, performance-centered study of digital folklore.

DIGITAL FOLKLORE THROUGH THE PERFORMANCE LENS

Five Minutes in the Comments Forum: Humorous Bids on the Internet

The emotional reaction of my friend Sean to the process of posting on Facebook certainly suggests that the social dynamics of Internet posting evoke many familiar issues about performative competency and the assumption of performance roles. Even so, without knowing the actual content of his posts, it is an open question as to whether Sean's creations were "traditional," or, in Richard Bauman's terms, whether they involve "the situated production of generically informed discourse [that] indexes prior situational contexts in which the same generic conventions have guided discursive production" (2004, 3). But other examples of digital expression more clearly display attributes of traditional performance. Take, for example, the following series of responses to an unusual news story posted on an obscure right-wing forum site, FreeRepublic.com:

'HYPNOTIST' THIEF HUNTED IN ITALY

BBC | 22 Mar 2008 | BBC

Posted on 03/22/2008 1:28:04 PM PDT by BGHater. Police in Italy have issued footage of a man who is suspected of hypnotising supermarket check-out staff to hand over money from their cash registers.

In every case, the last thing staff reportedly remember is the thief leaning over and saying: "Look into my eyes," before finding the till empty.

In the latest incident captured on CCTV, he targeted a bank at Ancona in northern Italy, then calmly walked out.

A female bank clerk reportedly handed over nearly 800 euros (£630).

The cashier who was shown the video footage has no memory of the incident, according to Italian media, and only realized what had happened when she saw the money missing.

CCTV from the bank showed her apparently being hypnotized by the man, according to the reports.

Italian police believe the suspect could be of Indian or North African extraction.

 Filed under the topic of "Crime/Corruption" and associated with the keywords "hypnotism," "hypnotist," "italy" [*sic*], and "thief," the comments section below the news story elicited several colorful responses (including replies to the original poster, "BGHater"):[13]

Awesome, Drudge needs this one.
   1 posted on 03/22/2008 1:28:05 PM PDT by BGHater

To: BGHater
Hey, our govt been doing this to us for YEARS now!!
   2 posted on 03/22/2008 1:29:52 PM PDT by prophetic (I'm not afraid of calling his full name: Obama's full name is BARAK HUSSIEN OBAMA!!)

To: BGHater
Don't gaze me Bro!
   3 posted on 03/22/2008 1:30:48 PM PDT by Into the Vortex

To: BGHater
Was it this guy? [with a hyperlink to another site]
   4 posted on 03/22/2008 1:34:54 PM PDT by TruthShallSetYouFree (Abortion is to family planning what bankruptcy is to financial planning.)[14]

Here, commenting on the unusual and perhaps already somewhat comical news story, the second poster makes an attempt at a humorous con-
 nection between the hypnotist and contemporary political leaders. The third poster moves away from the political commentary but stays within the general topic by constructing a humorous wordplay on the phrase "don't taze me, bro," used by a student protester during a speech given

by 2004 Democratic presidential candidate John Kerry. The video of this event, in which the student was tasered and removed by the University of Florida's campus police, was widely distributed on the Internet.[15]

Finally, the fourth poster simply asks, "Was it this guy?" placing a hyperlink in the text. The user follows the link to this text at Jokesy.com:

AMAZING CLAUDE THE HYPNOTIST

It was entertainment night at the senior center, and the Amazing Claude was topping the bill. People came from miles around to see the famed hypnotist do his stuff. As Claude went to the front of the meeting room, he announced, "Unlike most hypnotists who invite two or three people up here to be put into a trance, I intend to hypnotize each and every member of the audience."

The excitement was almost electric as Claude withdrew a beautiful antique pocket watch from his coat. "I want you each to keep your eye on this antique watch. It's a very special watch. It's been in my family for six generations."

He began to swing the watch gently back and forth while quietly chanting, "Watch the watch, watch the watch, watch the watch . . ."

The crowd was mesmerized as the watch swayed back and forth, light gleaming off its polished surface. Hundreds of pairs of eyes followed the swaying watch until suddenly, it slipped from the hypnotist's fingers and fell to the floor, breaking into a hundred pieces . . .

"SHIT!" said the hypnotist . . .

It took three days to clean up the senior center.[16]

Elliott Oring (2003, 139) rightly observes that posting on Internet joke sites is less like building a performative repertoire and more like building a text archive. Yet this user did not merely post a joke text for anyone to read later but linked to the text as part of a fast-paced dialogue of direct responses to the original article posting. All four posts were made within minutes of each other, a fact recorded in the time stamps at the bottom of each message. Furthermore, the general aim of each message is contextualized by the visible Reply stamp, which is placed at the top of each message. In this case, each message is shown as a response to BGHater, who posted both the original article and the first response to it. These types of stamps help the audience understand who is speaking to whom in the forum environment. Although not present in these posts, many forum-type posting sites place conversations such as these in dedicated "threads," which allow users to visually mark off their response posts as related to a certain previous set of posts. Some sites also automatically reproduce some or all of the previous message in their reply posts, which further contextualizes each post in terms of the earlier utterances in the thread (Kirshenblatt-Gimblett 1996, 56).

On top of visual or technological features intended to help the audience contextualize discourse on the forum, the posters' communicative strategies display a marked similarity to those observed by folklorists in face-to-face situations. Treating the article as the beginning of the discussion, the second responder, "prophetic," attempts both political commentary and very general political humor by comparing the hypnotist-criminal to government leaders. Although the textual component of this expression is quite brief, the contextual information enhances the meaning available to the audience. The venue for the post (a conservative political site) and prophetic's signature line (a short text that users can automatically attach to any message they send) both provide contextual cues for the interpretation of the text as an expression of radical right-wing discontent with the government.

Building on the second post, "Into the Vortex" shifts the context to a specific well-known incident involving a liberal politician and a right-wing protester. But this commenter's expressive move involves more than just the introduction of a specific event for discussion. Instead of moving the conversation in a serious direction, Into the Vortex attempts to amplify the playful frame of the communicative setting by both engaging in wordplay and incorporating a reference to a noted bit of Internet humor.

Charles Briggs argues that while some forms of performance represent definitive breaks with normal discourse, others such as scriptural allusions are much harder to distinguish. These forms, which sit on the "fuzzy boundaries of performance," may be linked more by content than by form to traditional performance (1988, 17; see also Bauman 1992, 44–45). These fuzzy boundaries begin to emerge in the post by Into the Vortex. While this post does not clearly "breakthrough" into a performance (Hymes 1975), the amplification of the humorous frame combined with the use of an intertextual reference to the arguably traditional "don't taze me, bro" video, which spawned video remixes, T-shirts, slogans, and other forms of Internet humor, certainly seems to edge the conversation toward a performative mode (Stirland 2007).

The fourth poster, "TruthShallSetYouFree," whose signature line also marks him/her as a political conservative, takes advantage of a communicative dynamic hovering on the border between serious and playful frames.

Posting a question with an opaque tone leaves open the issue of which direction the poster will take the discussion. But this opacity turns out to be part of a larger humorous strategy. By incorporating a link to a joke text on a humor website, TruthShallSetYouFree does not just allude to a piece of traditional humor, as Into the Vortex does, but requires the audience to follow a link to a version of the actual joke in order to understand the full meaning of the post. Furthermore, rather than reproducing the text of the joke in the post itself, TruthShallSetYouFree skillfully plays with the opacity of hyperlinking to amplify the audience's surprise and, hence, the humorous effect of the joke. Finally, TruthShallSetYouFree's humorous play also engages intertextuality on a couple of different levels. First, the introductory question "Was it this guy?" invites the audience to consider the humorous possibility that the hypnotist in the news article matched the character described in the traditional joke, linking these two texts with a brief performative move. Perhaps more tellingly, however, TruthShallSetYouFree quite literally links the text of the post to a previous joke text; this creative use of hyperlinking both demonstrates the poster's expressive skill and "reproduces" a traditional text within a specific performance situation.

In addition to considering the communicative strategies in relation to the specific content of each post, it is also useful to take a step back and look at the posts as a single communicative event. Much of this interaction would seem quite performative if imagined as a transcript of a spoken conversation. The participants here are engaged in a series of increasingly amplifying expressive moves that eventually culminate in the performance of a traditional joke. As part of this process of amplification, the complexity of each similarly evolves—from a few aimless phrases at the beginning of the conversation to the more in-depth and sophisticated humorous plays in posts 3 and 4. In this sense, TruthShallSetYouFree's use of a hyperlink is a kind of breakthrough into performance that keys the subsequent text "so that communication within that frame will be understood" (Bauman 1992, 45; see also Goffman 1974).

To properly key the joke, however, it is crucial to note that TruthShallSetYouFree uses expressive techniques that are not possible in face-to-face situations. The humorous amplification achieved is made possible only because of the opacity of a hyperlink. By incorporating this kind of device, the performer indicates an intertextual connection without showing the actual text at that moment. Furthermore, the use of hyperlinks shifts the performative framework away from the poster. Just as an oral performer might signal to the audience a shift away from personal voice to traditional voice with phrases like "What I myself have heard" or "As they say,"[17] TruthShallSetYouFree moves the joke into a different communicative frame through the act of linking.

Although some users in earlier stages of the Internet experimented with the use of links as tools for movement within a single text,[18] the expressive use of hyperlinks in the later phase—commonly dubbed "Web 2.0"—tends to incorporate links as ways to direct the attention of the reader/audience to different texts rather than different pieces of the same text. For instance, weblogs (or blogs), the Web 2.0 version of the personal homepage, were originally conceived of as a way for users to more easily embed links to external websites, videos, pictures, or other multimedia products as well as to other blogs (see "It's the Links" 2006). As a result, the use of hyperlinks now often moves a user outside of a text produced by one user and into one produced by another. Thus, by hyperlinking, rather than pasting the joke text into the post, TruthShallSetYouFree necessarily forces the audience to leave their personal communication and enter into a joke-posting site, a place where all texts are necessarily keyed to the generic conventions of jokes.[19]

Are Digital Performances Face-to-Face?

Despite the expressive similarities I have just discussed, there are many distinct differences between digital and actual performances. For instance, in an analysis of e-mail forward, folklorist Russell Frank observes that

> The other half of the folklore-as-performance equation, of course, is the audience. We can . . . ask receivers and forwarders what they thought of this or that joke, but we cannot reconstruct their facial expressions, body language, and verbal responses, if any, at the moment they opened the e-mail. (2009, 100)

Frank suggests that merely asking an audience member to describe his/her reaction later is not the same as observing that reaction in the context of the performative event. However, I submit that the reactions of audience members are themselves a kind of performance. Since there are many contextual and often socially governed factors that influence the communicative display of the audience, it is overly naturalistic to suggest that people's in situ reactions precisely match their inner states. But if the reactions in a face-to-face setting are communicative fronts constructed by audience members in accordance with their accepted social and performative roles (Bauman

1984, 29–31), then response postings on the Internet, themselves a kind of communicative display, must also be examined as socially governed forms of expression that can be profitably thought of in similar terms to audience reactions in face-to-face settings. It is certainly true that audience reactions in digital environments often do not occur in real time, or in simultaneous temporal frames, in the same way that they do offline. And yet the audience does react to communicative displays in a wide variety of ways that range from subsequent performance to mere indication of approval or disapproval, from elaborate video-recorded responses to simply clicking the "like" button above a Facebook post.

So while understanding audience reactions online as similar to offline performance may require a reconsideration of what defines the boundaries of a digital performance context, the interactivity allowed in digital environments suggests that folklorists should not let what is unfamiliar blind them to important similarities. Frank (2009) himself notes that text-based performers and audiences have developed a set of metalinguistic expressions intended to approximate the missing proxemics of a face-to-face performance:

> These kinds of interchanges can be approximated by newsgroup or forum members who participate in threaded discussions, or by instant message partners who may, in addition to commenting verbally, deploy such Internet slang as LOL (laugh out loud) or even ROTFL (rolling on the floor laughing), or emoticons like the ubiquitous :-) or ☺ .[20] (101)

However, in addition to these emerging expressive conventions, we should also consider certain situations of digital performance that actually allow for the expression of many of the nonverbal cues one might find in a face-to-face setting. The following game of rock-paper-scissors, created as an exchange between several video bloggers (vloggers21) on YouTube (Figure 3.1), is an example of this kind of situation:

In this series of videos, the initial poster, "spectrem," asks the audience to engage in a game of rock-paper-scissors.[22] spectrem explains the rules and then makes the initial motions to begin the game. In some of the follow-up posts, vloggers posted short videos of the shape they chose (Figure 3.2). Later, spectrem posts a series of video clips showing various players making one of the three symbols, revealing his original choice of paper and explaining the outcome of the game to each group accordingly.

Here the use of video as a particular performative medium allows both the performer and the audience to directly experience some of the nonverbal

Figure 3.1.

Figure 3.2.

cuing that is missing from text-based performances. Each participant's facial expressions, body motions, posture, and hand gestures are available to the audience and other performers. There is a clearly established central performer who, while his real name may be unknown, is visible to the audience and susceptible to their understandings about the social identities of gender, race, and age.[23] Similarly, we can see the reactions of the most active audience members in the form of their response videos, which provide the same type of social information prima facie about each audience member and his or her reactions to the original post.

We still lack a great deal of information about the social dynamics in play. For instance, it is not clear what preexisting relationship, if any, exists between the posters. But it bears noting that this type of information is not always available or evident in actual world settings. In practice, face-to-face performances may occur between family members who have known each other for many years (Dundes 1980, 7) or between vendors and customers in a marketplace who have no preexisting history (Kapchan 1993, 314). But the fact that some observers may not be aware of certain kinds of contextual information, say, a preexisting relationship between vendors in the marketplace, does not render actual world expressions as nonperformances anymore than it does online.

While certainly not identical, the events I have highlighted share enough of what folklorists know about performances as they occur in face-to-face settings that they deserve a fuller consideration as traditional performances.

In digital settings, the potential exists for both verbal and nonverbal communicative interaction between performer and audience members who often utilize familiar communicative strategies. Digital environments also provide at least certain kinds of social contextual information such that the "emergent quality of performance" should be considered (Bauman 1984, 37–45). Given both the interactive and expressive potential of many forms of digital media and the striking parallels between online and offline performative situations, it is clear that folklorists must stop thinking of digital technologies as simply media that record or transmit offline folklore. Instead, we must think of them as *places of performance*.

Digital Places, Digital Performances

Still, while online and offline contexts may have some similarities, there are vast and important differences between their performative possibilities. For instance, as Frank (2009) notes:

> Though forwarding lacks most of the elements of a real-time performance, it may be a more naturalistic medium than humor websites—to the extent that receiving a joke via e-mail is more like hearing a good one from a colleague who pops his head in your office door, whereas going to a website is more like going to a comedy club or watching a comedy show on television . . . [also] it lends itself to a genre of humor—the visual joke—that is barely possible in face-to-face joke telling. (116)

Frank's observation should give pause to any attempt to directly transfer theories of performance to digital environments. As he shows, while some digital contexts appear similar to offline ones, the hidden parameters of digital environments often restrict or enhance the use of certain kinds of expressive strategies or structure performative events in ways that are distinct from offline contexts. The example of the YouTube game of rock-paper-scissors is a case-in-point.

First and foremost, while popular technologies such as Skype, iChat, FaceTime, and Chatroulette allow users to video chat in real time, YouTube is inherently a non-real-time format.[24] While posters can react to each other via text or response video, they will never have the same kind of contact that a face-to-face or real-time video setting would provide. Also, because of the public nature of YouTube as a forum,[25] the number of visible reactions to a video is frequently far less than the number of people who see it. The final video in the game posted by spectrem, for instance, has more than 13,000 views but less than 500 text comments and only a handful of video responses at the time of this writing. Thus, while it may be true that the visible responses by audience members have commonalities to offline performance, it is also important to observe that performers likely understand that their audience may be vaster than those who directly engage with their performance (Dobler 2009, 181). Therefore, any consideration of this exchange as performance would have to consider the implied as well as the participatory audience.

The foregoing points are primarily concerned with the dynamics of digital performances in general, but there are several other important specific generic differences between the performance of rock-paper-scissors in the context of these videos and the game's performance in the actual world.[26] For instance, while this performance is outwardly similar to an offline game, closer inspection reveals a very different set of practices and expectations in play, largely as a result of the technological constraints of the performative setting. So while a game of rock-paper-scissors in an offline context might be performed as either entertainment (Roberts 1949, 19) or an informal decision-making tool (Leventhal and Cray 1963, 243), the lack of real-time context prevents decision making as a reasonable use in a digital environment.

The user spectrum announces quite a different intention at the start of the initial video. Inserting a text frame early in the video with the words "I'm bored," spectrum follows up with a second text frame saying, "I have an idea! Let's play a game!" Going on to explain the rules of the game in the same way that they are played in offline contexts, spectrum concludes by asking viewers to produce response videos that will be posted in a later follow-up. Thus, although the rules, as spectrum announces them, bear similarity to the offline rules, it is clear that neither the method of play nor the possible functions of the game are understood as exactly the same as offline versions. Instead, what could have been a counting-out game that stresses strategy within a group (Goldstein 1999 [1971]) in an offline context, is restricted to an online diversion, a form of entertainment and social connection among vloggers that emphasizes the production of engaging video posts. So although it may be generically informed expression that "indexes prior situational contexts" involving many of the same generically informed features of production, we are actually witnessing a subtle shift in the mode of play, the understanding of the generic possibilities of production, and the explicit function of the game.

TOWARD A THEORY OF THE DIGITAL PERFORMANCE OF FOLKLORE: ASPECTS OF DIGITAL PERFORMANCE

Despite the differences between digital and actual performances, folklorists currently have much of the needed theory to adequately understand digital performance. The combination of similar social and expressive dynamics with changes to context resulting from production in new performative situations points to the idea that what is required is not a new theory but a new orientation toward the object, a shift from a view of digital context as recording media to performative setting. But this shift requires a critical understanding of digital expression as being (in some ways) analogous to face-to-face performance *and* as something quite different. A few further observations may illustrate the unique features of digital performances but also indicate some areas where these features overlap with existing theories of performance.

Temporal Extension

Going back to some of the earliest work on performance, folklorists have quite frequently described instances of performance as "events" (Georges 1969). When conceptualizing events, as Barre Toelken (1996) astutely points out, there is a certain ambiguity between thinking about the production of discrete traditional expressions and thinking about the sum total of those productions that takes place in any one particular contextual setting. In order to clarify this concept, Toelken argues that events should be viewed as coterminous with the process of production. So while the recitation of a proverb may take only seconds, and thus many proverbs may take place in a single contextual setting, the building of a barn may take days and encompass numerous changes to its context (1996, 178–179). Thus, it is also clear that, as a general rule, verbal or bodily performance events tend toward shorter durations while the performance events for material objects often have much lengthier timelines of production and reception.

But Toelken's observations break down in digital contexts. The vlogger game of rock-paper-scissors took almost a month from start to finish and, in theory, could have taken months or years. By contrast, the posts on the news forum, which may have constituted discrete discursive events in Toelken's terms, actually took place within minutes of each other. But similarly, the process of discourse that eventually resulted in the performance of a joke could have been temporally extended much further. Because the extension of the time of a performative event or contextual setting is possible, these verbal/bodily performances appear to have more in common with many material genres than with verbal or bodily genres.

While the possibility of temporally extended digital performances that use verbal or bodily modes does not necessarily undermine our current concept of a verbal/bodily performance event, it does complicate it in a variety of ways. For example, while the communicative medium, the understood performers, the understood audience,[27] and the communicative context remain consistent over the course of both instances, quite a few elements external to the event but accessible to the performers could have occurred between the initial and final postings. These elements could bear on the process of production. While folklorists are accustomed to considering these aspects of performance in the most elongated instances of material creation, verbal- or bodily-mode performances have generally not been examined in this way.

So then, should a theory of digital performance look more like, say, the theory of "material behavior" as developed by folklorist Michael Owen Jones? Indeed, in terms of the circumstances of production, there are many similarities. For instance, in his 1997 study, Jones recounts a quilt making event in which the patchwork for a quilt was created by a single individual several years earlier and the quilt itself was assembled by ten individuals working in various combinations over the course of three days (206–207). This sort of temporal extension of the event and sporadic group collaboration, while not the same as the rock-paper-scissors game, certainly suggests some relevant conceptual similarities. In this sense, any folkloristic models of the process of online performance should begin by considering the similarities of production between offline material behavior and digital folklore, even that which is ostensibly produced in verbal or gestural modes.[28]

Durability and Audience-Mixing

There is yet another aspect in which digital performance seems similar to material behavior: they both result in a product that endures in an external form past the production event. Just as the result of a barn-building event is a barn, the result of a textual or video posting is a text or video that can be accessed by an audience well after the original process of production. In this sense, just as the subsequent evaluations of other skilled performers, community members, art gallery viewers, or purchasers of folk art or material products have often been the backbone of the performance theory of material behavior, similar possibilities should be considered in digital performance, not just in performances that are more discernibly working in visually oriented modes such as ASCII art or traditional images, such as userpics or LolCats.[29]

Intimately tied to this durability is the potential for what I term "mixed audiences," a feature common to many digital performance settings. Digital discourse is often characterized not by the non-presence of social identity but by a difficulty in controlling the identities of those to whom the performance is directed. Take, for example, this posting from my own Facebook page:

Figure 3.3.

In this posting, I personally placed a link and short comment about a humorous site I had discovered. Several people responded to this posting, giving their takes on the link. These people were not unknown individuals; quite the opposite: each had a distinct relationship with me. But, brought together by my post, I suddenly found myself in conversation with three individuals who existed in otherwise separate social spheres. This aspect, like the durability of digital performances, may be one of the most important ways that digital performance differs from real-world performance and is potentially among the most influential contextual features.

Richard Bauman (1986) observes a similar effect of technology on the context of performance in his landmark study of the narrator Ed Bell. Bauman argues that the process of fieldwork recording fundamentally shifts the context of narration, not because it necessarily occurs in a non-natural setting but because it both creates a durable product and affects the narrator's ability to control who hears the recorded speech (1986, 105–106). However, in the age of digital interactivity, Bauman's observation can be extended to include the possibility that a recording may not just be heard by a faceless group of strangers at some later time, but rather that various people the performer knows from many different contexts will hear and respond to it in a relatively short time frame. While a performer could more readily control earlier technological forms such as tape recording, which could, at times, be recontextualized and reconstituted as performance by the original performer (Dégh 1994, 110–152), the loss of performative control in digital media happens at a much greater pace. So in a highly identity-oriented venue like Facebook, a performer must expect that a performance will be received not just by one social group or an anonymous mass but by a number of different social spheres within the performers' acquaintance as well as by the general public. Thus, the tension in digital performances between social frames is not just between private and public but between many different private spheres and many different publics.

Serialization

Digital performances also display a tendency toward serialization. In contrast to a face-to-face context, where there is often room for overlapping or intersecting forms of speech, action, or expression by different participants, the structure of the technological environment in which many digital performances occur requires that such expressions take place sequentially rather than in direct juxtaposition. Text, audio, or video posts, however close together they are published, are inherently serialized on the web in the order that they were submitted to the server. Even in some real-time media such as instant messaging (IM) chat programs, where participants in a discourse event must be present online at the same time, the discourse remains serialized.[30] While the potential exists that party B can make an intervening statement in the time that party A is typing, these statements will necessarily appear as discrete elements on the page. Take, for example, the following IM exchange between myself and another individual:

Line 1   (*4:13 a.m.*) Me: so you will send me the spreadsheet to show him and then we send it back with changes?

Line 2   (*4:14 a.m.*) "Darcy": haha no i'm coming over today remember

Line 3   nothing is happening before i get there

Line 4   Me: but we are in ohio

Line 5   Darcy: im just opening it on your computer

Line 6   wait what?
Line 7   Me: we are in youngstown ohio
Line 8   Darcy: i thought u werent leaving til today?
Line 9   after mass
Line 10   (*4:15 a.m.*) u left yesterday?
Line 11   Me: plans changed, i thought you knew...
Line 12   Darcy: no
Line 13   oh ok
Line 14   (*4:16 a.m.*) Me: that explains it

In this discourse of about three minutes, the IM interface (in this case, Google Talk) parses out the conversation in a very specific way. Each participant's discourse is represented discretely in a serialized back-and-forth. The communicative effects of this structural framework are most readily apparent in lines 5 through 10. In this sequence, "Darcy," not knowing that I was traveling, suggests that she will come to my house later that day. Although I type quickly that I am traveling (line 4), she is most likely engaged in typing her next line (line 5) and unaware of what I said until slightly later (line 6). In an offline context, overlapping speech might occur in this situation. But in the setting of an IM chat, this is simply not possible; instead, the speech of both participants is metered out on the screen.

In addition to the constraints on expressive simultaneity in the context of IM, it is important to note the way that the program automatically parses the linguistic expressions of each individual. Line breaks, especially those between shorter linguistic elements, indicate where the IM participant has pressed the Enter key or hit the Send button, and so suggest a certain sense of rhythm in both the typing and thinking of each participant.[31]

The Poetics of Mediation

Because digital folklore encompasses a broad range of genre, expressive strategies, and performative settings, it is fruitless to attempt to create any totalizing theory about it. Part of folklorists' difficulty in understanding digital folklore stems from our tendency to paint all of these variations with the same brush. While it is true that there are spaces on the web where anonymity rules (like many news forums), hyper-identification and hyper-location are the norm in others, as with Facebook and foursquare.[32] And while some digital technologies inherently structure interaction through temporal extension and serialization, technologies like video chat allow interaction to take place in real time. The net result of this wide range of technological environments, as well as how they are used, is that folklorists must consider each performative setting separately, as we do in face-to-face settings, and try to understand all of the contextual and poetic features in play at any given moment.

While folklorists should consider digital environments as places of performance rather than as media that represent performance or transmit text, digital technology *is* still an important form of mediation between performers and audiences. Indeed, many of the differences between online and offline performance noted above demonstrate both new poetic possibilities and new limitations imposed by the mediating effects of technological venues. The media itself structures communicative events in digital spaces.

Looking at digital contexts as places of performance structured by the mediating effects of technological environments may reveal theoretical parallels with actual contexts in unexpected ways. For instance, revisiting Richard Bauman's (2004) observations on "mediational routines," actual-world performances that rely on "speech routines organized around the relay by a mediator of at least one utterance from a source to an ultimate targeted receiver" (129), could embolden folklore scholars to further consider how the dynamics of these routines provide a structure for thinking about digital contexts. Bauman writes:

> Mediational routines are organized by their very design to spite the power of time, to transcend the ephemerality of the spoken word. The phase structure of such routines confers upon the source utterance a projected lifespan that extends beyond the source dialogue, at least as far as the target dialogue and in some cases beyond it. By the conventionalization of the mediational structure of the routines, the source utterance anticipates reception—detachment from the source dialogue, the source speaker, the context and circumstances of production, and recontextualization in the target dialogue. Moreover, the shaping of the source utterance prepares it for this decontextualization and recontextualization. (2004, 147)

While Bauman principally studied traditional performances in a face-to-face context, his remarks begin to suggest a new focus for the study of all forms of mediated cultural performance. In one sense, this opens up the question of the expectations of users who produce expressive forms online. Do Internet users expect their creations to be received as productions situated in their own identities? Or do their techniques of production rely on the assumption that their performances will be disassociated from them personally? Or alternately, do those who consume these performances share the same expectations?

In another sense, Bauman's observation also calls attention to an important gap in much of the current work on digital culture. Folklorists often take for granted that despite the mediating effects of technological environments, "[a]gency resides with the author; the mediator is denied an active role in the formation and entextualization of the message" (2004, 152). But in mediated environments, these conventional assumptions break down or merge in novel ways.[33] An adequate theory of digital performance must account for not just how users express themselves online but how the forces that mediate these expressions, whether human or technological, are themselves fundamentally part of this mediational routine. Folklorists must understand how this synergy between producers, strategic consumers, and technological infrastructure contributes to the emerging poetics of digital life.[34]

CONCLUSION: BEHAVING DIGITALLY

Folklore's long engagement with performance theory is one reason for the unique position of folklorists to contribute to the understanding of digital culture. In many ways, emerging forms of digital expression can usefully be contextualized within existing theories of performing folklore. At the same time, while adequate resources exist to theorize digital performance, these theories are not directly transferable. While some digital performances show marked similarities to offline performances, they also include performative features either unique to digital environments or that generally occur offline in different generic modes. Thus, digital folklore performances must be studied on their own terms, with a full consideration of the unique contexts in which they are created. To borrow a phrase that Michael Owen Jones used in his own recasting of material culture, folklorists must recognize that the "subject matter consists not of isolated entities, but cognitive, sensory, communicative, and interactional processes occurring within unique circumstances have their own dynamic all of which determine the nature of the thing produced." Digital folklore objects are not "things in themselves,"[35] but manifestations of digital behavior.

NOTES

1. My thanks go to Trevor J. Blank for his helpful and constructive editorial commentary on this chapter.
2. My use of quotation marks around the first reference to names in this essay indicates that I am using pseudonyms.

Anthony Bak Buccitelli

3.   I use the term "digital performance" to indicate the process of aesthetic production, reception, and response in digital environments. Here I am primarily concerned with performances on the Internet, but the same conceptual distinction could also apply to performance that takes place in digital environments created by other forms of digital communication technology. I prefer the term *digital* to the broader but often conflated term *virtual* because, following Shields (2003), I see the virtual as something that extends well beyond the bounds of digital media. For instance, virtual experiences can also occur offline in the form of dreams or intense memories. Thus, the possible contexts of virtual performance are much more diverse than the contexts of digital performance than this paper is concerned with. At times I may also substitute the oppositional pair *online* and *offline* to stand in for the digital/actual relationship. It should be understood, however, that I intend the term *online* to encompass both the Internet *and* other digital technologies.

4.   Indeed, this criterion was a significant aspect of the "performative turn" in folklore most famously articulated in Américo Paredes and Richard Bauman's edited volume, *Toward New Perspectives in Folklore* (1972).

5.   Furthermore, the rapid pace of technological development has made thorough study of emerging technologically based cultures, which develop with equal rapidity, difficult to pin down. As Barbara Kirshenblatt-Gimblett deftly observes, one of the key tensions in writing about digital culture is to resist the temptation to try to account for the new developments that have taken place even in the relatively short time between research and writing (1996, 23).

6.   For some specific examples, see Blank (2007, 19; 2009b, 9; 2009c, 73); Dégh (2001, 114–116); (Dorst 1990, 183); Fine and Turner (2001, 77, 210–229); Mason (1998, 323); Titon (1995, 441).

7.   Although not concerned with performance per se, the esoteric/exoteric dimension of folklore is brilliantly explored in William Hugh Jansen's (1959) article "The Esoteric-Exoteric Factor in Folklore."

8.   Scholars of rhetoric have developed a large body of work dedicated to conceptualizing different types of audiences, including those where a determination of definite social identity is either not possible or not desirable. Perelman and Olbrechts-Tyteca (1969, 13–33), for instance, have long ago pointed out that performers must often consider the possibility of "multiple audiences," composites that can include both known and unknown individuals, as well as "universal audiences," an abstraction that helps performers avoid the appearance of pandering to a particular group. As concern with media has increased in the work of folklorists, this aspect of rhetorical scholarship has begun to make its way into folkloristic work (for example, Howard 2005a). Also, drawing on the insights of media studies scholarship, some recent work in folklore has begun to articulate a more nuanced understanding of the role of social identity in performance. Sawin (2002, 42–48), for example, argues that the ways that viewers react to the gender identities of performers shifts when the venue of performance moves from face-to-face to various forms of mass media.

9.   See, especially, Preston (1974, 1994). For additional examples, see also Hatch and Jones (1997); Pimple (1996); and Roemer (1994).

10. danah boyd spells her name with lowercase letters.

11. Specifically, see Lau (2010, 374, 382, 388) and K. Miller (2008, 257, 264, 267).

12. This also reflects both changes to the existing technology and the ways that users interact in digital spaces. For instance, the expansion of technological

environments that connect online and offline identities has popularly been dubbed "Identity 2.0" (Nowak 2005).

13. All message board verbiage is quoted exactly as it appeared.

14. "'Hypnotist' Thief" (2008).

15. "University of Florida Student Tasered" (2007).

16. "Amazing Claude" (2006).

17. See Bauman (1984 [1977], 21).

18. An example of this might be artistic creations such as the hypertext novel, a text with embedded hyperlinks leading to different story elements (Titon 1995, 441–443).

19. To be clear, I am not arguing that posting on the joke site itself necessarily constitutes the performance of a joke, but rather that, within a conversational frame, the expressive and strategic use of hyperlinks to joke sites can be seen as a form of performance that has many analogs in our understanding of offline performance.

20. For a discussion of the political implications of this creative use of typed text, see Mason (1998, 323–324).

21. Vloggers are users that compile series of self-created videos on video sharing sites like YouTube or Google Video. Like blogs, the contents and orientations of these videos vary greatly.

22. "Rock Paper Scissors" (2008).

23. For a detailed discussion of the politics of social categorization in virtual worlds, see Lau (2010, 374–375).

24. Skype and iChat are video conferencing programs that are essentially video telephones. They allow users to place calls directly to specific people. Users can both see and hear each other in real time. Chatroulette is an anonymous video chat technology. It allows users to be randomly connected to other users in a video chat setting. Thus, while users on Chatroulette can also see and hear each other in real time, they likely have no previous social connection.

25. It is possible to set up more restrictive privacy settings on YouTube; these videos were publicly available.

26. I thank my fellow panelists, Tok Thompson and Merrill Kaplan, in the "Online Folkloristics" panel at the 2011 Western States Folklore Society meeting for a lively discussion. I also benefited a great deal from the audience questions and discussion, especially comments by Elliott Oring and Robert Glenn Howard that pushed me to elaborate on this point.

27. Although, as I have already discussed, much of the audience may be unknown, it is likely that the performers are aware of this feature of their performance and hence understand exactly who they are performing for.

28. Dealing with the production of a "digital quilt," Kirshenblatt-Gimblett also notes that the "pieced and collaborative nature" of the quilt was amplified in online environments "even as the quilt itself dematerialized" (1996, 30). See also the special issue of *New Directions in Folklore* 9, no. 1 (2011), which explores "Quiltmakers in the Digital Age" (http://scholarworks.iu.edu/journals/index.php/ndif), or McNeill (2007), on serial collaboration.

29. "Lolcats" are a tradition of user-created digital images of cats labeled with humorous non-sequiturs (Ramos 2009). Although each image is unique, certain patterns and conventions of variation have developed that govern the production of new images (Dash 2007). For a nice discussion of similar dynamics in the case of userpics or

avatars, see Foote (2007). ASCII art is a much older tradition of digital art. In this form, users create unique images using only the ninety-five printable characters of the ASCII standard character set. For a number of examples of ASCII art, see Danet (2001) and Kirshenblatt-Gimblett (1996).

30. Kirshenblatt-Gimblett has previously described Internet Relay Chat (IRC)—a chat format similar in technological structure to instant messaging interfaces—as a form of synchronous communication (1996, 45–46). However, the inherently serialized nature of chat conversations both makes them slightly asynchronous and distinguishes them from offline conversations. In this regard, I view IM chat environments as similar to e-mail in that they produce "microconversational turntaking . . . but in a way that is very different . . . from face-to-face conversation" (56). But unlike e-mail, this turn-taking is not produced retroactively.

31. Compare this emically produced representation to the etically produced representations of natural speech as employed by folklorists including Henry Glassie (1982, 2006) and Ray Cashman (2008) in their works on storytelling.

32. Users check in on foursquare using a computer or mobile device from anywhere in the world. The exact geospatial location of a user's last check in is made available to other users who are his/her "friends" on the site, or to "friends" on other sites such as Facebook. Also, users that check in to a particular location frequently can become the "mayor" of that location. Their image and profile will appear to anyone that checks in to that location subsequently until a new mayor is named. Finally, users can also leave "tips" for each other about the features or points of interest in any particular location. These tips are available to anyone who checks in to that location in the future.

33. See, for example, Howard (2005b) and (2008a).

34. For engaging discussions of the interconnections between technological infrastructure and poetic expression, see Coleman and Golub (2008); Howard (2005b, 2008a); Kirshenblatt-Gimblett (1996, 57).

35. See Jones (1997, 208–209).

4

Real Virtuality
Enhancing Locality by Enacting the Small World Theory

Lynne S. McNeill

THE TEXT MESSAGE ARRIVES ON MONDAY: "PILLOW FIGHT mob, Saturday, 11:45 a.m., Union Square." The message is forwarded to friends, posted to Facebook, picked up by a popular blog, and forwarded again. By the time Saturday morning rolls around, close to 5,000 people are casually converging on Union Square in New York City, pillows hidden under jackets or in tote bags. At 11:45 exactly, a whistle blows, and thousands of people seemingly spontaneously begin to whack each other with pillows—much to the shock and bewilderment of those present who were not in on the plan. Feathers fly, fabric tears, bystanders pull out their smartphones and film the chaos. By Sunday morning, twenty new videos of the pillow fight are posted to YouTube. People across the country and across the world watch the videos, laugh (or scoff) at the fun and the vicarious sense of surprise, and set off to organize their own pillow fight mobs.

The above scenario, strange or silly as it might sound, is an increasingly common one, and it is an excellent example of the kind of web-based local events that this chapter addresses. The idea that technologically mediated communication affects cultural expression is not a revolutionary one—social scientists have been considering the cultural impact of distanced communication since the telegraph and landline telephone became common—but in recent years, with the rapid growth in Internet and wireless communications technologies, we are seeing the changes in cultural expression develop more and more rapidly. We are also being called to account for an increase in interplay between mediated and unmediated communication; folklorists

DOI: 10.7330/9780874218909.c04   85

can no longer treat the virtual world as one wholly separate from the physical world. Everyday people are developing traditions that reflect the reality of their lived experience, which increasingly encompasses both digital and analog modes simultaneously. The type of cultural expression exemplified by a pillow fight mob, which would be impossible on any sizable scale without the use of communications technologies, is an excellent example of a vernacular practice that defies the strict separation of the real from the virtual. A pillow fight mob is planned via digital networks, enacted in a physical place, and before the event is even over it is recorded, promoted, observed, and then revived in virtual space. Through the use of communications technologies, standard expectations of place and locality are thrown into disarray.

Communications scholar Nancy Baym (2010, 24) notes that there are four general perspectives on the ways that technology and society interact and influence each other: technological determinism (the belief that technology controls us), the social construction of technology (the belief that we control technology), social shaping (the belief that control goes in both directions), and domestication (the eventual assimilation of technology into everyday life so that it is no longer seen as an agent of change). This chapter examines three different examples of web-based collaborative events that support the social shaping perspective: flash mobs, alternate reality games, and small world activities. While technology may affect how, when, and where we communicate, I argue that we in fact adapt technology to our unique social and cultural expressive needs. A close consideration of these case studies reveals that everyday people are using the new social realities of multilocality and translocality to enact a small world model and enhance their experience and perception of place.

WEB-BASED COLLABORATIVE EVENTS

Flash Mobs

As Howard Rheingold (2002) notes, one result of digitally enhanced networking ability is the development of smart mobs: large groups of people who can work together and unite their efforts without ever having to meet each other in person. Flash mobs are a subset of smart mobs; according to Wikipedia—a good source for emic definitions of informal digital culture—flash mobs are a form of performance art in which a group of people arrange to meet at a central location and put on some kind of unified performance, usually to the bewilderment of other bystanders.[1] Invariably, these events are coordinated via some online communication medium, usually through a blog, website, Twitter, or mass text message. Flash mobs can be highly planned and coordinated, such as the Swedish dance group Bounce's tribute to Michael Jackson that took place in Stockholm ("Michael Jackson Dance Tribute" 2009). The event seemingly begins spontaneously with just a single dancer but soon grows with the addition of dancers in groups of two or three, all performing the same choreography. By the time the spectators have realized that something prearranged is happening, they get another surprise when an enormous number of their fellow audience members—who had initially been playing the part of similarly confused and surprised bystanders—suddenly join in as well, almost doubling the size of the dance.

Flash mobs can also be much more informal and involve much less official preparation, such as the popular pillow fight mob described at the beginning of this chapter (see "San Francisco Pillow Fight Flash Mob" 2006). Another common and easily enacted flash mob is the freeze mob, which asks participants to suddenly cease all movement at a predetermined time and hold their poses for a few minutes.[2] As can be seen from the videos, flash mobs can run the gamut from formal to informal; however, in cases where they are orchestrated by a major company for promotional purposes and subsequently posted (as a video) to the Internet, those who comment are often quick to point out and criticize the "inauthentic" origins of such flash mobs.

One of the most interesting qualities about flash mobs—and the focus of their consideration here—is that while they utilize the enhanced networking that virtual communities provide, they are physically enacted in the real world.[3] This blend of *real* and *virtual* in flash mobs is not unique within the culture of digital media, which regularly flows into and out of real life, but it does uniquely represent the normally invisible concept of a "social network" in starkly physical terms. The blending of physical and virtual reality in flash mobs creates some confusion when it comes to the classification of flash mobs as an expressive form of Internet culture. As noted in this book's introduction, the term *meme* has been adopted by the Internet community to refer to viral image macros, texts, and videos that circulate and evolve on the web.[4] The website KnowYourMeme.com, which documents and explains Internet memes, notes that while most Internet memes originate within and are shared within the confines of virtual space, flash mobs are unusual given their enactment in physical space. The fact that the self-appointed arbiters of Internet memes acknowledge that flash mobs are uniquely non-virtual in some aspects argues for their placement in a unique genre of expression.

Alternate Reality Games

A related expressive form is the alternate reality game (ARG), or the web-based collaborative production game. ARGs are interactive group games—similar in basic structure and purpose to traditional scavenger hunts that take place in the real world—that involve the use of communication technologies for the planning, distribution, and organization of tasks, clues, and instructions. As with flash mobs, games like these can have both official and unofficial iterations.

Companies initially generated ARGs for commercial purposes as they became aware of the value of viral marketing and the possibility of using the multiple networks within which consumers, especially younger consumers, were already enmeshed. According to a March 2009 article in The Economist, the first commercial ARG—"The Beast," a promotion for the 2001 film, AI: Artificial Intelligence—brought activities like these into popular awareness (Technology Quarterly 2009). As is common with ARGs, The Beast never formally announced a start to the game; players instead found random clues inserted on posters or websites and had to piece together the narrative for themselves. This subtlety of execution is a common practice. For example, in 2006, the popular television show Lost used an ARG called the "LOST Experience" to promote itself, placing fake commercials for companies featured in the show among the real commercials aired during the show, which prompted viewers to either call phone numbers or visit websites, which in turn revealed further information. In employing such tactics, the boundaries between real and virtual blurred as participants determine for themselves whether the information they receive is part of gameplay.

While film and television production companies can afford large-scale publishing and fake commercials, this form has been enacted in vernacular ways as well. One of the most well-known examples is SFZero, a web-based community game in San Francisco that lets participants plan tasks online and enact them in the city. Ryan Blitstein of *SF Weekly* explains: "the basic structure of SFZero is simple: create a character on the *SFZero* site, complete tasks as that character, document them online, and score points" (Blitstein 2006). Documentation can be a piece of writing, a photograph, or a video clip and is posted online for others to acknowledge and appreciate. Blitstein goes on to explain that "the catch is that the 'character' you create is basically you, or, at least, a version of you, and that the alternate universe of *SFZero* occupies the same space as the real world." A player takes on his or her character's identity whenever necessary to complete a task. Tasks are incredibly diverse—"from the deceptive (tell your family you joined the CIA) to the charitable (pay the bridge toll for the car behind you) to the absurd (bring a fish to an accountant)" (Blitstein 2006).

One significant way in which SFZero differs from commercially sponsored games is that it is collaborative—players can design tasks for other players and have a hand in shaping the overall user experience.[5] David Terdiman of CNET.com feels that games like SFZero are "appealing to a small but growing number of people interested in the way real-world communities can take on the collaborative characteristics of Internet wikis" (Terdiman 2006). A *wiki*, as many Internet users are familiar with through Wikipedia, is a website—a virtual location—that is collaboratively created and edited (see Westerman 2009). Casting an alternate reality game like SFZero as a wiki brings the features of virtual reality to reality, creating what could be called real virtuality.

Similar to flash mobs, the documentation of completed tasks—or *praxis*,[6] in the game's terminology—brings us back again from reality into the virtual setting. One task, entitled "1000 Small (Heavy) Things," asks players to purchase or acquire 1,000 small and, if possible, heavy things. The website suggests objects such as bolts or nuts. Participants must then take their 1,000 small, heavy things to a public space and drop them on the ground. There is flexibility in how they can be dropped—all at once, one by one, in a trail—and the SFZero site suggests that if "anyone harasses you, apologize profusely and then leave." The results of a number of people completing this task in public can be found on various websites, including SFZero and YouTube ("1474 Small Things" 2006). As is the case with many flash mob videos, the reactions of bystanders are often part of the documentation; here again, we see a technologically mediated experience (in the planning) merging into an unmediated experience (in the enactment), before again moving back to a virtual setting for additional mediated performance and transmission.

Small World Games

Alternate reality games may often involve smaller numbers of people than flash mobs—at least in terms of the real world performative aspects— but my third case study includes even smaller activities that similarly mirror the pattern of real virtuality. Small world games or activities—serial collaborative events that test real-world networking possibilities and are tracked and documented online— also utilize communications technologies to bring the power of technologically mediated networks to bear on mundane reality (see McNeill 2007). Activities such as BookCrossing (bookcrossing.com) and Where's George (wheresgeorge.com) involve the passage of objects from person to person in the real world and utilize the Internet to track the journeys of those objects, thus providing proof of success or failure of the network in a way that could never before be determined with much certainty. For example, the long-standing practice of leaving a book in a public place for another reader to find,[7] perhaps after writing your name and hometown on the inside cover along with a note suggesting that the next reader do the same, is indeed a test of how far an object can travel in a network, but the outcome can only be surmised. The BookCrossing website, on the other hand, lets people give their books identification numbers that enable an accurate tracking of the book from person to person. Thousands of BookCrossing books have traveled the world, and there is no guesswork about the reach of the networks involved.

Where's George is similar; the website uses the serial numbers of paper currency (there are versions for most countries—Where's George is specific to U.S. currency) to track individual bills as they travel through normal monetary transactions. It used to be a popular tradition for people to paint coins or mark bills in order to discover whether they or someone they knew would ever get the same ones back, but with national banks and ATMs keeping cash out of purely local circulation, the chances of finding a released bill or coin are slim these days. With Where's George, however, bills can be tracked all the way across the country. The bill that the website lists as its most tracked has traveled 4,191 miles in the past three years, making stops in Ohio, Kentucky, Florida, Texas, Louisiana, Tennessee, Utah, and Michigan. The second most tracked bill has traveled over 7,000 miles in just over two years. Notes that participants leave about the bills range from reports about where they acquired them to comments on their condition. Just as with flash mobs and ARGs, we again see the use of communications technologies to enhance experiences in the unmediated world.

THE SMALL WORLD THEORY

In their structure, serial collaborative activities like BookCrossing and Where's George are near replicas of social psychologist Stanley Milgram's experiments in the mid-1960s to test the small world theory: the idea that any random members of the general public are closely interconnected, with an average of only five or six degrees of separation between any two people. As journalist Elizabeth Devita-Raeburn explains:

> [Milgram] gave 60 people in Wichita, Kansas, envelopes and the name of a target person—a stranger—along with a few details of that person's life. Their mission: to get that envelope to someone they knew on a first-name basis who then might be able to pass the envelope a step closer to the target person. (2008, 44)

Milgram stated that the initial idea for his study came from social scientist Ithiel de Sola Pool and mathematician Manfred Kochen, who attempted to uncover a mathematical formula that could explain the interconnectedness of large populations. They were unsuccessful at accurately representing the complex realities of society, and so Milgram drew up the package-sending experiment as a tool to solve the problem (Devita-Raeburn 2008, 45).

According to Milgram, the phrase "small world" implies that social networks are "full of unexpected strands linking individuals seemingly far removed from one another in physical or social space" (Travers and Milgram 1969, 426; see also Milgram 1967). Jeffrey Travers and Milgram summarize the phenomenon as follows:

> "[W]hat is the probability that any two people, selected arbitrarily from a large population, such as that of the United States, will know each other?" A more interesting formulation, however, takes account of the fact that, while persons a and z may not know each other directly, they may share one or more mutual acquaintances; that is, there may exist a set of individuals, b, (consisting of individuals b_1, b_2, ... b_n) who know both a and z and thus

link them to one another. More generally, *a* and *z* may be connected not by
any single common acquaintance, but by a series of such intermediaries, *a-b-
c-* . . . *-y-z*; i.e., *a* knows *b* (and no one else in the chain); *b* knows *a* and in
addition knows *c*, *c* in turn knows *d*, etc. (1969, 425)

The interconnectedness that Milgram describes is an incredibly absorbing idea for many people. While Milgram certainly brought the "six degrees
of separation" concept to the American public's attention and imagination,
he was not the first writer to conceive of the notion. In 1929, Hungarian
writer Frigyes Karinthy penned a short story entitled "Chains" (*Láncszemek*),
which posits that no more than five links exist between any two people. An
excerpt explains:

> To demonstrate that people on Earth today are much closer than ever, a
> member of the group suggested a test. He offered a bet that we could name
> any person among earth's one and a half billion inhabitants and through at
> most five acquaintances, one of which he knew personally, he could link to
> the chosen one. (Barabási 2003, 26; emphasis original)

Karinthy's characters first link one of themselves to a Nobel prizewin-
ner via the King of Sweden and two famous tennis players and are then
challenged to make the same type of connection without the assistance of
notoriety or celebrity. The connection between one character and a worker
in a factory pans out just as successfully:

> The worker knows the manager in the shop, who knows Ford; Ford is on
> friendly terms with the general director of Hearst Publications, who last year
> became good friends with Árpád Pásztor, someone I not only know, but is to
> the best of my knowledge a good friend of mine—so I could easily ask him to
> send a telegram via the general director telling Ford that he should talk to the
> manager and have the worker in the shop quickly hammer together a car for
> me, as I happen to need one. (Barabási 2003, 27)

The fascination with the invisible links between disparate people that is
so evident in Karinthy's work in the 1920s and Milgram's work the 1960s
has not changed in contemporary culture. Consider the popularity of the
vernacular theory of six degrees of separation, which manifests in games such
as Six Degrees of Kevin Bacon,[8] unofficial experiments such as the "snowball effect,"[9] or various six degrees of separation projects on Facebook[10] as
well as in the traditional sharing and enjoyment of small world stories,[11] as
documented by folklorist Amy Shuman (2005). I believe it is this desire for

a small, meaningfully interconnected world—a perception promoted not only by the object-passing games but also by the other activities addressed here, which similarly create a perception of surprisingly deep interconnectedness[12] in a previously random-seeming group—that is at the heart of the popularity of the activities described in this chapter.

DELOCALIZATION AND MULTILOCALIZATION: A NEW PERCEPTION OF PLACE

In response to the contemporary social shaping that takes place between people and their communication technologies, several new concepts have emerged to aid in the understanding, identification, and description of new modes of social interaction. In their study of the social implications of mobile telephone and Internet advancements, Andre H. Caron and Letizia Caronia (2007) discuss the related concepts of *delocalization* and *multilocalization* as results of technologically mediated interaction. They explain how current socioeconomic contexts that allow for regular travel and usage of mobile communications technologies enable more and more places to become settings for interaction (Caron and Caronia 2007, 15). In other words, we have redefined the idea of "where" our social relationships take place—they have been *delocalized*. Similarly, place no longer determines our social roles, even at the most basic levels: public interaction can happen in private locations and vice versa; work-related interaction can happen in family settings and vice versa. With regard to our identity in different locales, we have become *multilocalized*, embodying multiple localities—and our roles within those various localities—all at once.

A focus on place and location is common to studies of mobile technologies. The increasing separation of social space from physical space has been noted by social scientists for many years now, and the opportunity for a more functional *translocality* is still emerging. It is pertinent to observe how the stock greeting for phone calls has gone from "how are you?" to "*where are you?*" We no longer call a place—a home or an office—we call a person, regardless of where he or she is, making the delocalized individual an autonomous node in a social network outside of any place-based identity.

The impact of mobile communications on sense of place was evident even at the inception of mobile technology. At the 1984 Summer Olympics in Los Angeles, Sam Ginn—a pioneer in the wireless communications industry who worked at that time for Pacific Telesis Group—took a $3,500 Motorola cell phone[13] into the stands with him and began to make phone calls from his seat. As the crowd in the stands began to notice that Ginn appeared to be speaking on a wireless telephone, Ginn started offering the phone to them so that they themselves could call far-flung family and friends from inside the Olympic Stadium. Those who used the phone evidently couldn't wait to report on the new technology to their call recipients; they would "inevitably shout to some distant friend or relative—inaugurating what would become one of the rituals of mobile telephony—the statement of location" (Galambos and Abrahamson 2002, 3). "Guess where I'm calling from?!" had new meaning in the context of delocalized communication; calling *from the stands* at the Olympics had simply never been possible before. Ginn recognized that these phones "were more than an incremental improvement on existing technology. They created a whole new paradigm for communications" (4).

Current technology has far surpassed the simple mobile telephone; text- and image-based communication can now also take place from mobile devices, and the disruption of locality is at an all-time high. This disruption has both positive and negative effects. On one hand, our society is experiencing an unprecedented reduction in uncertainty; when plans go awry, people can contact each other with ease to change meeting places or times, update travel plans, or clarify directions. A lack of shared space is no longer a liability for social interaction, organization, or coordination; whether at opposite ends of a department store or at opposite ends of a continent, people can immediately connect and communicate with ease. On the other hand, this ease of communication has resulted in a distinct lack of effort *for* certainty these days. People no longer plan in advance as they used to. For example, while parents may be able to get in touch with their children at any moment, the children can rarely let parents know ahead of time where they will be on any given evening—plans are made at the last minute or change en route. When it comes to practical benefits, some people feel that communications technologies have not seriously improved situations of communication at all (see Baym 2010, 50–59).

Many people are also disturbed by the ways in which participation in private social interactions in public spaces is alienating people from even the most basic levels of acknowledgment of their fellow citizens. As Nancy Baym explains,

> One of the defining qualities of communication technologies is that they rupture the otherwise-mandatory connection between message delivery and shared space. The ability to communicate in the absence of shared space in

real time invokes fears of separation from physical reality . . . As we lose connection to space, do we also become detached from the family, friends, and
neighbors whose social support comprised communities of old and on whose
interconnections civil society depends? (2010, 92)

The concerns about delocalization that are rampant in society are not
unfounded; technology has developed so quickly that society has not yet
formed generally shared customs and conventions to address the awkward
or impolite situations that arise. It is still an unfamiliar[14] and potentially
distressing experience to be in a crowded public space, surrounded by people who are all multilocalized: people taking work calls, flirting with their
partners, planning their vacations, sharing their playlists, interacting with
unseen multitudes, and yet apparently oblivious to the people standing next
to them.

CONCLUSION

The popularity of flash mobs, alternate reality games, and small world
activities grows from the often stressful contemporary contexts of de- and
multilocalization. In the face of a delocalized, alienated public, the underlying deep interconnectivity of the small world model is a very reassuring
thought. While digital culture networks are certainly noteworthy in their
entirely virtual forms, the manifestation of such networks in real life and
physical space—especially on a massive scale—allows us to more tangibly
reconceptualize social reality in a new way, if only for a brief moment. The
physical manifestation of a virtual network allows us to believe that *any* random, disconnected crowd could in fact be full of people who are deeply and
meaningfully interconnected. The reaction of the crowd in the Stockholm
Michael Jackson tribute flash mob video is telling: it isn't until the actual
extent of the insider mob is revealed that the audience audibly gasps and
cheers. A small group seemingly coming out of nowhere is fun; an enormous, intimately connected group emerging from within a disparate crowd
of strangers speaks to a deeply meaningful achievement: an extreme level of
social dispersion was overcome and united into a singular identity for the
duration of the event.

The technology that creates situations of alienation among the general public is the same technology that enables moments of relief from that
alienation. Not only in the use of cell phones and the Internet to plan the
events, but in the use of these technologies to reach a broader audience with

the re-virtualized record of the events, we can see the reciprocal social shaping of technology and culture. Real virtuality is powerful; the far-reaching translocality of a virtual network creates the impression of an impossible level of hyperlocality when enacted in the real world, one that greatly overrepresents the interconnectedness of an apparently random group. Huge numbers of people who seem to coincidentally be in the same place at the same time suddenly know the same dance, the same timing, the same actions; they carry the same props, they say the same words, they play the same game, they handle the same money. Most importantly, they *know* that they share these things. The network is realized rather than assumed; it is made present in the physical world. Certainty reigns, in a time where prearranged certainty is being increasingly devalued. The empowerment of smart mobs through technologies that support the formation of a digital culture turns the impersonal randomness of public space into momentary physical evidence of a very small world.

NOTES

1. The designation of flash mobs as a form of "art" is not always accurate, and to call a mob "smart" does not always indicate positive motivations; flash mobs have been convened for both political and criminal purposes in addition to the more performative goals described here.
2. See "World's Biggest Flash Freeze Mob in Paris" (2008).
3. Not only in the coordination of times and locations via digital media but also in the posted videos of dance choreography or suggested activity that may appear on the web as well as in the resulting videos of the events themselves.
4. From its original proposed usage as the cultural analog to *gene* (Dawkins 1976).
5. It is important to note that even commercially sponsored ARGs are often collaboratively developed, but typically by teams of game developers rather than by participants.
6. The usage of praxis by SFZero game designers is similar to the usage of it by Simon Bronner in *Grasping Things* (2004 [1986]), in which he defines *praxis* as "activity resulting in the production, and I would add consumption, of an object, but one where the doing, the *processes involved* and the *conditions present*, rather than solely the end, is paramount" (20; italics added).
7. This is a common tradition for travelers, and the locations are often trains or hostels.
8. This game challenges participants to identify the links between a given celebrity and the actor Kevin Bacon; the popular belief is that any celebrity can be connected to Bacon through works shared with other celebrities in less than six steps (the number of steps that any given celebrity is away from Bacon is referred to as his or her "Bacon number"). An example would be the actor Dick Van Dyke, who has a Bacon number of 2: Dick Van Dyke was in the film *Dick Tracy* (1990) with Dustin Hoffman, who was in the film *Sleepers* (1996) with Bacon.

9. This is a common experiment played out within online social networks to test the breadth and speed of a potential network. One person begins the experiment by linking (via a group page or requests for friendship acceptances, etc.) to their friends with the request that those friends forward the request to others that they know. The goal is to see how fast and far the group can grow. The term *snowball effect* comes from the idea of rolling a small snowball down a hill, watching as it picks up more snow and gains momentum.

10. Similar to the snowball effect experiment, these are Facebook groups that aim to connect as many disparate people as possible through one Facebook page.

11. Small world stories, as defined by Shuman, are stories about "coincidental meetings in everyday life" (2005, 89), stories that are "extraordinary in [their] reliance on the completely unexpected connection between two seemingly unrelated events" (91).

12. It is important to note that it is the *perception*, and not the *reality*, of deep interconnectedness that is promoted here; none of these activities can be said to objectively prove the small world theory. However, it seems that the subjective perception of proof is all that is needed for these events to create the impression of a small, meaningfully interconnected world; people are rarely driven to test the limitations of the activities for themselves. The world *appearing* to be small is seemingly more important than it actually *being* small.

13. It was the infamous "brick" phone or, as it is known by younger generations, the "Zach Morris phone," in reference to a teenaged character on the popular 1990s after-school show *Saved by the Bell*, who carried one of these early mobile phones.

14. Unfamiliar for some; sadly common for others.

5

Jokes on the Internet
Listing toward Lists

Elliott Oring

WHEN CONFRONTING THE ISSUE OF HUMOROUS FOLKLORE ON the Internet, certain questions necessarily arise. What part of humor is folklore? What constitutes folklore on the Internet? When does humor on the Internet become the concern of the folklorist? After all, not all humor is considered folklore. Most folklorists would not regard a spontaneous witticism made in the course of a social encounter to be folklore. Innumerable witticisms are generated in conversation each and every day and no folklorist has ever set out to document them. Nor would many folklorists regard television situation comedies as falling within their province. Although some blurring of boundaries between folklore and popular culture has occurred in recent years, television sitcoms remain firmly in the popular culture camp. Old situation comedies, whether broadcast on television or streamed from an Internet site, would be unlikely to attract folklorists' scrutiny. The question of what constitutes folk humor in cyberspace is entertained in this essay and explored with reference to a humorous genre that in some ways seems emblematic of the Internet as a whole.

If humorous folklore is considered to consist of specific genres—jokes, riddles, bawdy songs, pranks, witty proverbs, comic tales, and the like—there will be an inclination to see these genres as folklore on the Internet as well. Once something has been labeled as *folklore*, there is a tendency for that label to stick. No one defines folklore as an invariable list of genres, however.[1] Expressions, behaviors, ideas, and objects are regarded as folklore because they are the result of some process. The key processes that have served to define folklore are "tradition" and "art" (Leach 1949, 403).

DOI: 10.7330/9780874218909.c05

Contemporary formulations of folklore as tradition see it as forms and practices from the past passed on by means of oral communication or customary example (Brunvand 1998, 11). Those who focus on the aesthetic character of folklore regard it as "verbal art" (Bascom 1955) or "artistic communication in small groups" (Ben-Amos 1971, 13). Some have also held folklore to be the culture of certain social groups and classes: peasants, farmers, the urban poor (Leach 1949, 401). Such groups and classes were singled out because they were held to preserve traditional knowledge and maintained traditional practices. The association of folklore with these groups divorced from, or at the margins of, mainstream society gave rise to the idea that folklore constitutes the unofficial or vernacular culture in modern society, as opposed to the culture of those at the centers of social, political, and economic power: the corporation, the government agency, the university, the museum (Dorson 1968; Howard 2005b).[2] Thus, there are three potential ways to conceptualize folklore on the Internet:

1. Folklore is the product of traditional or artistic communications that emerge in oral, face-to-face interactions in society that then move onto the Internet.
2. Folklore is created by processes not unique to face-to-face social interaction. It is created on the web through means *analogous* to those processes. This presumes that web-based traditions or artistic communications are wrought in web-situated groups.
3. Folklore is the unofficial or vernacular culture of the World Wide Web. It is a culture distinct from the corporate, bureaucratic, governmental, or other institutional cultures that inhabit cyberspace (Bronner 2009, 23; Howard 2005b, 324–325).[3]

To date, it would seem that references to traditions on the web have been mainly directed at materials that first circulated through oral channels before migrating to a digital environment. To some extent, all culture is traditional since everything depends on models from the past. Even corporate webpages, for example, depend on layouts and designs derived from other media or other sites. Nothing is ever completely new. Consequently, the concept of folk traditions born and bred on the web remains somewhat hazy, although it may not be difficult to identify certain specific web-based traditions.

Emoticons are one example. The term is a portmanteau word composed of *emotion* and *icon* and originally consisted of ASCII characters employed to serve paralinguistic functions in textual communication ("Emoticons";

Kirshenblatt-Gimblett 1995, 74–76). Thus, :-), when rotated 90 degrees clockwise, resembles a smiling face just as :-(resembles a frowning one, and each can be employed to indicate the emotional tone of a statement. Etymology notwithstanding, however, emoticons are less concerned with registering emotion than marking the intent of the statements in which they are embedded. Emoticons are largely concerned with pragmatics (Dresner and Herring 2010). But even emoticons, which seem unique to computer-mediated communication, have antecedents in telegraphy and Teletype, and the magazine *Puck* compiled a short list in 1881 ("Emoticons").

Transporting "artistic communication in small groups" into an Internet context raises the question of what constitutes a small group and how one assesses the nature of web-based interaction. Certainly, some videos displayed on YouTube have attracted thousands, even millions, of viewers. The audiences for them cannot in any sense be considered "small." And although there are mechanisms for submitting feedback to content providers, as well as responding to other viewers, these communications are asynchronous and differ from what goes on in the joke-telling or song-singing environments of small, face-to-face groupings. YouTube videos seem more akin to television broadcasts, although individuals rather than corporations produce them. The producers of the content—unless they are actually in the video—are likely to be anonymous.[4] Yet there are also chat groups, discussion lists, or even interactive games in which aesthetic expressions may be created or deployed much as they are in face-to-face groups. All in all, the question of what constitutes folklore or, more specifically, folk humor on the Internet would not seem to be entirely a straightforward one.

Because of the range of humorous materials that needs to be considered, and the variety of ways that humor can appear online, the discussion that follows will be limited to examining a certain type of verbal joke in a digital environment. A joke is a brief communication whose humor is abruptly apprehended only at its conclusion (Oring 1992, 81–93).[5] Furthermore, only canned jokes are considered—those that can be shown to exist as relatively fixed forms in space and through time. Jokes can be verbal and/or visual, although identifying the conclusion of a purely visual joke—a cartoon, for example—may prove a matter of some difficulty.[6] There are several potential environments for the appearance of verbal jokes on the Internet: e-mails, listservs, forums, chat, archives, and streaming video performances. Unfortunately, even these venues cannot be addressed in the space of a single essay.

Even if one does not go looking for jokes on the Internet, they can hardly be avoided. Jokes are regularly included in e-mails; in fact, the communication of jokes is the sole point of a good number of e-mail messages that people receive. Jokes received via e-mail can then be forwarded to other individuals. There is no need to retype the joke or transform the text of the e-mail in any way. The forward can remain completely faithful to the text which was received and passed on without any alteration whatsoever.[7] If the notion of tradition is rooted in the replication of past ideas, behaviors, and expressions, then the Internet allows for the faithful reproduction of the form and substance of a message. The modern era, in fact, has produced all the great replicative technologies: printing, machine manufacturing, photography, broadcasting, analog and digital audio and video recording. It is a wonder, then, that modernity has not been designated the Age of Tradition.

The theoretical stability of jokes in e-mail forwards distinguishes them from jokes communicated in oral, face-to-face channels. While e-mail jokes may be disseminated in a manner that parallels oral joke dissemination—to sets of friends and acquaintances known to appreciate jokes—there are some very noticeable differences. E-mailed humor lacks the texture of "actors, scene, and setting" (Frank 2009, 100). It does not demand a reaction, and a purveyor of e-mail humor usually cannot be sure that the humor is read, let alone appreciated. Consequently, purveyors often preface their e-mails with some affirmation of the humor's quality to persuade the receiver that the humor is worthy of scrutiny (101). While such attestations can occur in oral communication ("I heard this great joke"), the oral teller must take responsibility for the quality of the presented material at the moment of its performance. Testimonials in these situations are optional. "Have you heard this one?" or "That reminds me of a joke" or even breaking directly into performance with "A guy walks into a bar" can serve as sufficient attestation to the joke's quality since the performance is subject to immediate communal evaluation. In the face-to-face communication of humor, even a nonreaction is registered as a reaction (101). Given the great volume of e-mail communication, users must rapidly develop a small list of people whose joke forward they come to trust to be worth their while. When a joke forward is received, the viewer does not assess either the materials (they remain to be viewed) or the performance (there is none), but the source (102). Receiving jokes from an unknown or dubious source is likely to result in communicative failure. The e-mail may be deleted without being opened.[8]

It seems obvious, but worth noting nevertheless, that verbal jokes that regularly appear in e-mails (unlike some other humorous forms) have no analogies in the paperwork lore circulated in written, hand-drawn, or, more often, photocopied form. There are virtually no photocopied verbal jokes. When people want to communicate a joke in-person, they do not hand over a piece of paper with a text on it. Nor do they send someone to consult a book of jokes (e.g., "There's this great joke on page 25 of Isaac Asimov's *Treasury of Humor.*"). One communicates the joke orally or not at all. Only when such communication is not possible—usually because distance makes oral delivery difficult or secrecy is required—does a verbal joke get encoded as text.[9]

Visual humor does not operate under the same constraints. Face-to-face communications utilized photocopy lore (Dundes and Pagter 1978 [1975], 1987, 1991, 1996, 2000). Visual jokes (e.g., cartoons) are difficult or impossible to transmit verbally without undercutting their humorous qualities. A verbal description of a cartoon, for example, may sacrifice its economy of expression or reduce the interpretive challenge to the receiver. Consequently, a cartoon might be handed over to a recipient, although a written copy of a verbal joke will not. Obviously, visual jokes can also be mailed, faxed, or otherwise digitized for communication at a distance. There are types of verbal jokes, however, that can be transmitted in document form: jokes organized as *lists*. The best way to grasp the nature of the form is to look at an oral narrative joke that was reformulated as a list in the Internet environment. First, the oral narrative:

> There was a young priest who was just starting to preach and stuff. And one day, it was the first time for him to lead the Sunday Mass, and the head priest was giving him some little hints to follow and told him to come back to his office when Mass was over and he would tell him what he did wrong. So the young priest goes into the church and leads the Mass and makes announcements and everything, and when it was over he went back to the head priest's office, and the head priest told him what he did wrong. The head priest says, "You did three things wrong, but other than that you did fine. First of all, we do not refer to Our Lord and Savior Jesus Christ as the late J.C. Second, Daniel slew the lion; he did not stone the bastard to death. And worst of all, the Ladies' Circle is having a taffy pull at St. Peter's and not a peter pull at St. Taffy's." (Mitchell 1977, 327)

Oral narratives that become lists generally end with a brief set of (usually three) statements (Olrik 1965 [1909], 133–134). On the Internet, however, the number of statements may be greatly extended. A forwarded e-mail joke sent in 1996 had a setup similar to the above text but the list of the older priest's corrections grew substantially:

> A new priest at his first Mass was so nervous that he could hardly speak. After Mass, he asked the monsignor how he had done. The monsignor replied, "When I am worried about getting nervous on the pulpit, I put a glass of vodka next to the water glass.[10] If I start to get nervous, I take a sip." So the next Sunday he took the monsignor's advice. At the beginning of the sermon he got nervous and took a drink. He proceeded to talk up a storm. Upon return to his office after Mass, he found the following note on the door:[11]

1. Sip the vodka, don't gulp;
2. There are ten commandments, not twelve;
3. There are twelve disciples, not ten;
4. Jesus was consecrated, not constipated;
5. Jacob wagered his donkey, not bet his ass;
6. We do not refer to Jesus Christ as the late J.C.;
7. The Father, Son, and Holy Ghost are not referred to as Daddy, Junior, and the Spook;
8. David slew Goliath, he did not kick the shit out of him;
9. When David was hit by a rock and fell off his donkey, don't say he was stoned off his ass;
10. We do not refer to the cross as the Big T;
11. When Jesus broke the bread at the Last Supper he said, "Take this and eat it for it is my body." He did not say, "Eat me";
12. The Virgin Mary is not referred to as Mary with the cherry;
13. The recommended grace before a meal is not: "Rub-a-dub-dub, thanks for the grub, yeah God";
14. Next Sunday, there will be a taffy pulling contest at St. Peter's, not a peter pulling contest at St. Taffy's.

Two of the three lines in the oral joke are found in this e-mail version. Another e-mail received a year earlier contains the same list word-for-word in the same order except for a fifteenth entry: "And finally, the names of the four apostles are NOT Leonardo, Michelangelo, Donatello, and Raphael."[12]

Fifty websites that contain versions of this joke list between six and fifteen statements by the priest. Most contain between ten and fourteen. Unlike the oral version, all employ a setup in which a priest—it is invariably a priest—drinks during his sermon. It is clear that some of the versions of the joke on different websites are identical. One website provides a word-for-word version of the 1996 e-mail joke above, although the list is not numbered; dashes substitute for numbers ("HK Expats"). Another list is also a word-for-word duplicate of the 1996 e-mail joke but contains some typographical errors.[13] Perhaps in formatting a joke for a new environment some words are deleted and need to be retyped and are retyped incorrectly. So it is not entirely a matter of copy-and-paste. Something analogous to scribal error seems to be taking place online as well.

More than scribal error is involved, however. Often the list is reworked so that it exists in different versions on different websites. There is, for example, considerable variation in the specific items included and the order of their presentation. Yet this variation is not entirely random. It is, to some extent, rule governed. For example, if item 1 (about sipping rather than gulping the alcoholic beverage) is present, then it is always item 1, probably because it is directly related to the setup and grounds all the other mistakes. Items 2 and 3 ("There are ten commandments, not twelve; There are twelve disciples, not ten") always appear as items 2 and 3 unless item 1 is absent. In that case, they become items 1 and 2; they never appear in any other positions. This is probably because they are metrically balanced in a chiasmic structure and establish a rhythm for the unfolding of the list. Furthermore, they represent only minimal speech errors. In any other position, these entries might undercut a sense of the increasing outrageousness of the priest's blunders. It would seem that later entries must be just as or more outrageous than previous entries and that the list is meant to be perused in the order of its entries, and not haphazardly skimmed.

Most of the lines in the fifty other versions collected were contained in the e-mail joke as well, although there might be some variations in their formulation (e.g., "And you should refer to the mother of Christ as the blessed Virgin and not Mary with the cherry"). Occasionally there are lines in some versions that are not found in the 1996 e-mail text: "Jesus' parents were not Peter, Paul, and Mary"; "Moses parted the waters of the Red Sea, he did not pass water"; "The Pope is consecrated, not constipated (related to item 4) and we do not refer to him as 'The Godfather'"; "We do not refer to Judas as 'El Finko' [or 'El Bastardo']"; "Do not refer to Jesus and the Twelve Apostle as 'J.C. and the Boys'" (related to item 6); "When the multitude were fed with loaves and fishes, Jesus did not mention chips"; "Walk down from the pulpit; don't slide down the banister"; "'It's hallowed be your name'; his name's not Howard"; "Last but not least, in marriage we say, 'Till death do us part,' not 'dying because of fart'." These lines, however, are dispersed throughout the fifty lists. Only on one website do as many as three of these anomalous entries appear together in a single list ("Tristan Café").

In jokes, the final position is critical. In the above list, it also seems to be important. Theoretically, any item might conclude the list. However, as items 1 through 3 of the e-mail version invariably occupy the opening positions, they are necessarily eliminated as choices for the final slot. Even so, the remaining choices are not equal candidates. On the fifty websites that I visited, nine items were found in the final position, but there was a considerable discrepancy in their distribution: "Peter pull at St. Taffy's" (60 percent); "Mary with the cherry" (24 percent); "Rub-a dub-dub" (4 percent); "The Godfather" (4 percent); "Consecrated, not castrated" (2 percent); "Holy Spook" (2 percent); "Eat me" (2 percent); "Dying because of fart" (2 percent); "Don't slide down the banister" (2 percent). In other words, 84 percent of the lists used only two items in the final position.

To a great extent, the final position in a joke is governed by aesthetic criteria. Even though it is presented as a list, the text remains a joke. The final line is a punch line and must, to some extent, break the pattern set by the previous entries. Since only two items dominate the final position on the list, it suggests a considerable degree of agreement as to what constitutes the "best" line to fulfill this function.[14]

Not only can certain narrative jokes be elaborated as lists on the web, but lists can serve as the underlying structure of humor. A great deal of humor in e-mails, social networking sites, forums, and Internet archives appear in the form of lists. For example, the following list was received in an e-mail in 2006, and variants can be found on numerous websites:

We all know that:
    666 is the Number of the Beast

But did you know:
    668: The Neighbor of the Beast
    606: The Area Code of the Beast
    1-800-666-HELL: The Toll-Free Number of the Beast
    666-6667: The Wrong Number of the Beast
    666 . . . 999: The Quotation Mark of the Beast
    2 × 4 × 666: The Lumber of the Beast
    666A: The Tenant of the Beast
    555: The Number of the Wannabeast
    $665.95: Retail Price of the Beast
    $699.25: Price of the Beast plus 5% Sales Tax
    $769.95: Price of the Beast with All Accessories and Replacement Soul
    $656.66: Walmart Price of the Beast

00666: The Zip Code of the Beast
1-900-666-0666: Live Beasts! One-on-one Pacts! Call Now! Only $6.66/
    minute. Over 19 only please.
Route 666: Highway of the Beast
666°F: Oven Temperature for Roast Beast
666k: Retirement Plan of the Beast
6.66%: 5 year [*sic*] CD interest rate at First Beast National Bank, $666
    minimum deposit
i66686: CPU of the Beast
666i: BMW of the Beast
DSM666: Diagnostic and Statistical Manual of the Beast
333: The Beast's Better Half

The list plays off a single theme: the number of the Beast mentioned
in the Book of Revelation (13:18). Each item in the list (except for the
first) constitutes a joke. Most of the lines are relatively independent of one
another, and individual entries could be dropped or reordered without any
significant effect on the list as a whole. Certain lines, however, can generate
subthemes. An example is the series of items that deal with dollar amounts.
The first example—"$665.95 The Retail Price of the Beast"—can stand
alone, but some of the other prices would not work well in the absence of
that one. In other words, sub-lists with subthemes may be generated within
lists, although they still adhere to the theme of the list as a whole.

The list plays off a single theme: Although each item in the list is humorous, there is no narrative setup,
no necessary denouement, and consequently no entries with greater claim
to the final position. In fact, there is no concluding position, and websites
reveal considerable variability in the order and final entries of their lists. It
may be convenient to regard this type of humor as a *joke list*, as each item in
the list is humorous but does not add up to an integrated joke with a punch
line, and to regard the example of the misspoken priest as a *list joke*, since
the whole must still add up as a joke where the final position remains critical
(Oring 1992, 81–93). Joke lists can vary considerably:

Okay, we all know that 666 is the Number of the Beast. But did you
know that:
    660: Approximate Number of the Beast
    DCLXVI: Roman Numeral of the Beast
    666.0000: Number of the High Precision Beast
    0.666: Number of the Millibeast
    /666: Beast Common Denominator
    666^{-1}: Imaginary number of the Beast

1010011010: Binary of the Beast
0000001010011010: Bitmap of the Beast
6, uh . . . what?: Number of the Blonde Beast
1-666: Area Code of the Beast
00666: Zip Code of the Beast
1-900-666-0666: Live Beasts! One-on-one pacts! Call Now! Only $6.66/
    minute. Over 18 only please.
$665.95: Retail Price of the Beast
$699.25: Price of the Beast plus 5% state sales tax
$769.95: Price of the Beast with all Accessories and
    Replacement Soul
$656.66: Walmart Price of the Beast
$646.66: Next Week's Walmart Price of the Beast
Phillips 666: Gasoline of the Beast
Route 666: Way of the Beast
666°F: Oven Temperature for Roast Beast
666k: Retirement Plan of the Beast
666 mg: Recommended Minimum Daily Requirement of Beast
6.66%: 5-year CD interest rate at First Beast of Hell National Bank, $666
    minimum deposit.
Lotus 6-6-6: Spreadsheet of the Beast
Word 6.66: Word Processor of the Beast
i66686: CPU of the Beast
666i: BMW of the Beast
DSM-666 (revised): Diagnostic and Statistical Manual of the Beast
668: Next-door Neighbor of the Beast
667: Prime Beast
999: Australian Beast
Win666: Operating system of the Beast ("Laugh Break")

While numerous items from the previous Numbers of the Beast list can be found on this one, there are many items that are different (e.g., many of the mathematical and computer-inflected items). Items that appear in the previous list are absent in this one (e.g., "666A The Tenant of the Beast"; "666 . . . 999 The Quotation Mark of the Beast"), and some items are expressed differently ("Route 666: Way of the Beast" vs. "Route 666 Highway of the Beast"). The positions on the list also vary ("668 The Neighbor of the Beast" comes at the top of the previous list but is fourth from the end in this one). What seems clear is that there is great variation in joke lists, despite the ease of digitally copying and pasting materials into new online environments. Joke lists on the Internet manifest "multiple existence in space and time, and they exist in variant forms," as had previously been found to be true of photocopy lore (Dundes and Pagter 1978 [1975], xvii). Despite the theoretical possibility of the exact reproduction of humor in cyberspace, it is not what happens. Versions and variants are inevitably generated (Shifman and Thelwall 2009, 2571).

Oral narrative jokes seem to grow by slow transformation over time. Modifying a narrative joke requires constant attention to the whole text. A single word change can destroy the joke (Clements 1973). Such jokes develop by means of small and subtle changes. As jokes undergo these changes, the whole must remain a joke if it is to continue to exist. Consequently, the alteration of a narrative joke is never just a matter of addition. A narrative joke, for example, cannot be filled with irrelevant details that may distract from the elements necessary to grasp the punch line. Nor can material simply be appended after a punch line (Oring 1992, 81–93). Joke lists or list jokes, however, only require the generation of new entries that conform to their structural, metrical, and thematic patterns. Appropriate materials from other sources can be included, and new material can be invented. In other words, joke lists and list jokes are *compiled*, they do not *evolve*.[15]

Although all kinds of jokes and humor inhabit the World Wide Web, lists especially seem to have proliferated. They can appear as a series of test or application questions and answers, formulas, rules, proverbs, aphorisms, greetings, quotes and misquotes, bumper stickers, signs, instructions, laws, translations, glossaries, product names, menu items, letters, excuses, calendar entries, haiku, photographs, and answering machine messages. The question is: why has the web been so hospitable to humor in list form?

Of course, lists have been staples of American popular culture for some time: the top ten or one hundred most popular songs/albums/books/films; the richest, most influential, best- and worst-dressed people; the poorest, most robust, and most corrupt economies; the top news, science, and sports stories of the year. There are books of lists and lists of lists. Many of these invoke a spirit of play, but the list does not seem to have been a template for humorous production. There are exceptions. Looking back, there is Pooh-Bah's inventory of potential victims in Gilbert and Sullivan's *The Mikado* (Act 1); the remarks that Cyrano de Bergerac contends could be made about his nose (Act 1, Scenes 1, 4), chapters in François Rabelais's *Gargantua and Pantagruel*, and perhaps the proverb paintings of the Elder and Younger Brueghels.[16] But it is hard to retrieve a plethora of examples. As a humorous genre, the list seems new.

Oral, face-to-face communication does not seem conducive to the performance of humorous lists, although lists are performed on late-night television talk shows. Johnny Carson, Jay Leno, and David Letterman, among others, have all performed comic routines based on lists. Lists are not exclusive to the Internet; such lists appeared in photocopy lore before its invention (e.g., Dundes and Pagter 1978 [1975], 39, 50, 51–56, 59, 60–63, 73–75, 200).[17] The Internet, however, seems to have greatly accelerated the growth of the format.

To begin to grasp the significance of lists on the Internet necessitates noting their specific qualities. Lists are essentially visual. They are an outgrowth of writing. And while oral lists exist—genealogies, rosters of kings, ritual recitations of objects or names—they are relatively rare.[18] When writing was first developed in ancient Mesopotamia, inventory, not literature, constituted the bulk of the output from this new medium: administrative and economic lists documenting production, expenses, receipts, accounts receivable (Goody 1977, 78–79, 105). In any event, humorous lists are textual and not oral. Even the lists performed by television comedians are written and read rather than orally recreated. The Numbers of the Beast list is particularly visual since most people have difficulty processing numbers aurally. From the beginning, computers pushed users toward visual imagery. Emoticons and signatures often involved the creative use of ASCII characters (Bronner 2009, 27; Kirshenblatt-Gimblett 1995, 82–86), and cartoons and other elaborate images were created as well. Programs were even written in BASIC to animate those primitive computer images.

Lists, theoretically, are open-ended. They have no natural boundaries. They can be added to or subtracted from without any violation to the sense of a whole.[19] Such changes, however, depend on the medium in which the list has been textualized. In cuneiform, a list with additions and subtractions might require laborious recopying. A handwritten list also needs to be recopied. Additions and cross-outs are possible but evidence of the changes remains. Typewritten and printed lists also have to be retyped or reset and reprinted. Digitization, however, leaves no traces behind. Consequently, computers make lists into creative structures amenable to easy revision and elaboration.

Lists can speed one up or slow one down (Belknap 2004, xiii). Some lists can be skimmed and sampled as well as perused. This is also true for humorous lists. One can skip through the entries in the Numbers of the Beast list, grasp its overall sense, and appreciate those particular entries that one happens to light upon without dwelling on each and every item. Narrative jokes cannot be so easily skimmed and sampled, however. Every word is potentially important. Some lists can impose an order—an order that it may be perilous to ignore. Skipping over entries in an itinerary, a recipe, or a preflight checklist can prove disastrous. List jokes share something of this order. While it is possible to skip through the "Sip, don't gulp" list, it is still important to register the final entry. Thus, joke lists, unlike narrative jokes, do not have to be accessed serially; they can be randomly accessed.

Individuals make their own contributions to humorous lists. If someone thinks up a suitable entry, it can be inserted; the new edition may be posted or otherwise passed on. Since the Numbers of the Beast list centers on a particular number, it is not surprising that those with a penchant for mathematics or computing seem to have made more than a fair share of the contributions. Consequently, the list is a collaborative effort, although the collaboration—as in oral folklore—remains invisible.[20] In theory, lists can go on forever; in practice, they cannot. They have a "load limit" (Belknap 2004, 31).

Lists also tend to replace quality with quantity (Goody 1977, 88). Items of very different qualities can be added to a list, and this seems particularly true of humor lists. It may never be known how the oral joke about the misspoken priest came into being, but it is not difficult to imagine what happened to the joke once it began to circulate in its Internet form and establish itself on webpages.[21] Individuals felt they were capable of adding to the three-part mini-list of the oral joke with their own creations or by the addition of extant linguistic formulas that they felt suited the joke's structure and theme. For example, "Dying because of fart" seems to be an addition with limited circulation since it only appears in texts on a single website.[22] "Rub-a-dub-dub, thanks for the grub, yeah God," however, is a mock grace that exists independently of its inclusion in the joke ("Grace before Meals").[23] "Howard be thy name" is known independently as a line from the Lord's Prayer as understood by children ("Children's Answers"). Unlike the epic poet working with a set of memorized formulas that are stitched together in the act of oral composition, the Internet bard generates new formulas on the basis of previous models that are compiled in a register (Ong 1988 [1982], 22). Although it has been claimed that orally based thought is *additive* (37–38), it would seem to be true of these web-based forms as well. The list is predicated on the conjunction *and*, even if that word never appears in the surface of the text.

Lists can be reviewed and reordered (Goody 1977, 89). Thus, the Numbers of the Beast, as has been noted, can be found with different entries and in different orders. But a list can also be broken down and scavenged for its constituent elements. Hence, individual entries from the Numbers of the Beast list have been used to create T-shirts, bumper stickers, and coffee mugs ("Sick, Sick, Sick"). There is a rock album called "668 The Neighbor of the Beast" and an album track as well (Shredd 2000). There is also a beer of the same name ("New England Brewing"). One website offers a video made up of bits of *Star Wars* footage cobbled together. The video pretends to be the opening credits of a television show titled "Han Solo, P.I." and closely adheres to the format of many of the opening credits of detective and police dramas from the 1960s and 1970s ("666A The Tenant of the Beast"). The video, like the website's name, contains the cannibalized parts of greater wholes. In some sense, the list is the quintessential mode of aesthetic humor production on the web; it is bricolage: compilation, recombination, and cannibalization for parts.[24]

It is interesting in this light to reconsider the use of emoticons in computer-mediated discourse. Lists of emoticons were published early on, but only a few emoticons really had pragmatic functions. Most were simply the result of playing with the set of 128 ASCII characters to produce representational images. In other words, lists of emoticons often were joke lists rather than dictionaries. For example:

:-{ "Count Dracula" and

:_) "I used to be a boxer, but it really got my nose out of joint"

were of limited paralinguistic utility and were created as jokes to reflect the ingenuity of their creators (Kirshenblatt-Gimblett 1995, 75–76; Raymond 1996, 173). In this vein, //:^=) was fabricated as an Adolf Hitler emoticon, and there are webpages with variants of this type (see"Hitler Emoticons"). But again, these lists can be scavenged for parts, and artist Dan Piraro published a cartoon in which a German soldier presents a piece of paper with the Hitler emoticon on it to his senior officer and asks, "What is, 'backslash, backslash, colon, caret, equal sign, right parenthesis?' Is the Fuhrer [*sic*] using a new code?" ("Bizarro" 2011).[25]

A question naturally arises with respect to the relation of joke lists and list jokes to joke cycles that have been circulating for more than a half century beginning with "little moron" jokes, sick jokes (e.g., "Mommy Mommy" jokes), knock knock jokes, Polack jokes, Italian jokes, elephant jokes, light bulb jokes, dead-baby jokes, Jewish American Princess jokes, space shuttle jokes, dumb blonde jokes, Princess Diana jokes, lawyer jokes, and the like. These cycles of jokes were invariably constructed in a riddle (question-and-answer) format. Riddle-jokes were rarely performed singly. They were reeled off orally in a series, although there was no necessary order to the sequence except when a subset of jokes played off one of one another (Oring 1992, 16–28). Unlike lists, however, these joke sequences were *exchanged*, so that when tellers paused, other jokes in the cycle would be forthcoming from members of the audience. Nor did they come together as fixed lists since the jokes in the cycle and the sequence of their presentation substantially changed in subsequent performances. In other words, if the jokes in an orally performed cycle could be considered a list, it was a completely ephemeral one. It would never survive except perhaps in the documentary recording of an observing folklorist.

Online, cycle jokes appear as posts, as lists, and in archives where large numbers of jokes are sorted by category (see "Blonde Jokes"). Posting jokes in a forum seems closest to face-to-face exchange.[26] In a forum devoted to scale modeling, there was a posting of blonde jokes—some in narrative form. Responses acknowledging the success of jokes were forthcoming as they might be in a small, face-to-face group: "ha thats billiant kiwi!!! deffinatly [*sic*] got some chuckles out of me!!" and "lol, very good duncan!" ("Scale Models 1"). One individual offered a blonde joke indicating that it was their "first post ever," so the joke was used by way of introduction and to break the ice, as one might do when joining a face-to-face group in the midst of telling jokes. The forum moderator welcomed this new member, thanked them for the joke, asked about the member's scale modeling experiences, and extended an invitation to make the most of the website's resources ("Scale Models 2").

In another forum where people post questions for which they want answers, a blonde joke was posted with the request, "Can someone please explain to me what this means? I don't get it. I saw it on Facebook and I got confused." The joke was

> Okay, so a brunette was jumping over railroad tracks and chanting "22" over and over again. A blonde comes by and thinks it looks fun, so she copies the brunette. When a train comes by, the brunette jumps out of the way at the last second and the blond doesn't. The brunette starts jumping over the tracks again chanting "23."

A number of respondents helpfully explained, "It's the 23rd blond she killed"; that is, the brunette had lured a total of 23 blondes into the path of oncoming trains with her antics. Another person offered a non-blonde version of the joke. One respondent, however, was less charitable: "You're 24" ("Yahoo Answers"). These kinds of responses might occur in face-to-face interaction as well, as some people offer to explain a joke, allude to or perform other versions, or ridicule a friend's inability to understand.

Similar responses to blonde jokes were forthcoming in the forums of eBaum's World: "pur good. my favs would be . . ."; "Hahah, those were great. Another"; "haha i like that last one, but chekc [*sic*] this"; "Nice"; "Those are pretty good!" ("eBaum's World Forum" 2011). As laughter signals appreciation in oral joke-telling situations, users employ textual laughter or statements of approval to register approval in forums and chats. There is a difference, however, between the two. Laughter can be, and often is, an involuntary response to humor. Textual laughter or expressions of appreciation are always delayed and deliberate and may be offered even when a joke was not genuinely appreciated. While laughter in face-to-face situations can be feigned, it can also be real. In computer-mediated communication, appreciation is not an automatic response but the report of a response. Nevertheless, such responses may be necessary for cooperative expression and to insure, as much as possible, appreciation for one's own joke contributions. All those in this forum who reported laughter or commented favorably on a previous joke immediately contributed a joke of their own.

Even though jokes posted in a forum can resemble aspects of face-to-face communication, those joke exchanges do not evaporate. They remain on the forum webpage as a series of posts. In other words, the exchanges look a lot like lists as they accumulate, and they can be scanned, perused, and copied in whole or in part. Contributors to the blonde joke thread on the scale modeling website initially offered only one or two jokes until one poster offered twelve:

Blonde year in Review
January—Took new scarf back to store because it was too tight.
February—Fired from pharmacy job for failing to print labels....
   "duh.".. bottles won't fit in typewriter!!!
March—Got excited.....finished jigsaw puzzle in 6 months.....box said
   "2–4 years!"
April—Trapped on escalator for hours.....power went out!!!

May—Tried to make Kool-Aid.....8 cups of water won't fit into those little packets!!!

June—Tried to go water skiing... couldn't find a lake with a slope.

July—Lost breast stroke swimming competition... learned later, other swimmers cheated, they used their arms!!!

August—Got locked out of car in rain storm.....car swamped, because top was down.

September—The capital of California is "C."....isn't it???

October—Hate M&M's.....they are so hard to peel.

November—Baked turkey for 4 1/2 days.....instructions said 1 hour per pound and I weigh 108!!!

December—Couldn't call 911....."duh."....there's no "eleven" button on the phone!!!

What a year!! ("Scale Models 1")

This series of blonde jokes has been assembled into a list organized by calendar month. In addition, they have been stripped of their question-and-answer format and reduced to one-liners. This listing and reduction would be unlikely to ever happen in oral performance. It is unlikely that the poster composed this list as it can be found word-for-word on other websites. There seems to be a compulsion toward producing lists online even in the midst of the most amiable, single-joke exchanges.

It has been suggested that the serialized nature of folk creation—graffiti tags, joke cycles—can be understood as the dominant culture's "ultimate penetration of the vernacular" (Dorst 1990, 187–189). In the style and the speed of their spread, graffiti tagging and joke cycles have the quality of mechanically automatic—industrial—production (1990, 186; Eco 2009, 353). The case of graffiti tagging perhaps more easily illustrates why the folk would mimic the modes of production of the dominant order. Graffiti tags are a folk version of advertising. Taggers seek to compete with the dominant order on its own turf—public space (Sahlins and Service 1960, 88). Taggers can only achieve their goals by means of a rapid, if hand-wrought, reproduction of a message over a broad landscape. Joke cycles and Internet joke lists are different, however. While individuals broadcast graffiti tags to be recognized as nearly identical items, they purvey joke cycles and joke lists as a differentiated series of entries. Unlike industrial commodities, the jokes in a list are not meant to be facsimiles but distinct items. Furthermore, the joking is a cooperative venture and rarely the product of a single source. All in all, the analogy between serialization and capitalistic production seems strained.

The relationship between lists and the Internet would seem to lie in the strong analogies between them. The conspicuousness of the list on the Internet owes largely to the fact that the Internet is more a visual than a verbal medium. The list is also a visual creation that is visually processed. To be grasped, it needs to be *seen* as a whole and in its parts. The list is also an open structure. It invites modification—slight and significant—and therefore participation. A large part of what makes the Internet attractive is that it is not a passive medium. It is interactive, and that interaction can be immediate, unedited, and uncensored. The Internet is democratic and common, although sometimes at the lowest of denominators. The list, consequently, is a structure that captures the virtues and vices of the medium itself as it allows the easy incorporation of contributions from disparate sources.

Lists also seem to dwell comfortably on the Internet for another reason. Although the list must be grasped as a whole and in its parts, it is not necessary to grasp each and every part. Often it is sufficient to grasp a sense of the whole and a few representative parts. In other words, a list may be perused, but it can be and often is skimmed or—in the language of the Internet—*surfed*. Surfing connotes moving from place to place by gliding over the surface of things.[27] One does not need to read each and every entry of the Numbers of the Beast list in order to grasp its overall sense and how individual parts contribute to that sense. A list is open to surfing much like the pages of the World Wide Web itself.

A final relationship between lists and the Internet seems more than an analogy. Lists confront Internet users at every turn: lists of folders, files, e-mails, and bookmarks; lists of hits produced by search engines; menus that guide access to its numerous sites. Although not visible, the whole of the Internet is directed by programs that are nothing more than lists of serially executed instructions. The World Wide Web is itself a list as every entry leads to yet some other entry. In the words of Umberto Eco, it is "The Mother of All Lists" (2009, 360).[28]

What can one conclude about joke lists and list jokes as folklore in the Internet environment? While there are lists that underlie oral rhymes, songs, and even tales (e.g., Bronner 1988, 68; Hugill 1969, 171–173; Hunt 1884, 2, 208–209), the structure holds a relatively minor place in the inventory of oral creations. If joke lists and list jokes are folklore, it is not because it is a genre imported from the oral to the digital world. While they certainly could qualify as forms of unofficial or vernacular culture, these terms are so broad that they cannot easily serve to ground a term like *folklore*.[29] Joke lists and list jokes, however, are creations fashioned and purveyed *in a manner analogous to orally communicated artistic forms.* Although certain texts can, and sometimes do, replicate others exactly, they are not eternally fixed. Joke lists and list jokes are used, and in that usage they undergo the communal recreation characteristic of oral folklore in the real world. Like folktales and folk songs, the lists are collaborative productions that can be and are reshaped in the acts of their conveyance. They are transmitted person-to-person in e-mails much as friends convey jokes in one-to-one conversations. They are posted in special-interest forums as a joke might be performed for a small group of people assembled for some specific purpose. Like oral folklore, these lists escape the confines of local groups, find their way across social boundaries, and persist over stretches of time. These artistic forms become traditional, even if that tradition is situated only in a virtual world. Joke lists and list jokes are examples of humor that not only inhabit the Internet environment but are wrought by that environment. That is why they are central to any discussion of folklore on the Internet.

NOTES

1.   Alan Dundes would seem to have done so in *The Study of Folklore* (1965, 3), but as this was an introductory text, he was merely illustrating the kinds of material that constituted folklore. He never did offer a definition of the subject matter, however.
2.   In fact, folklore can appear in all of these sites, but it is apart from or grafted on to the official business of the organization.
3.   It might be argued that there could be processes that are unique to the web that generate folklore. However, while there may indeed be processes that are unique to the web, it is hard to imagine why they would generate anything that should be called *folklore*. Using that word can only occur because some analogy with older meanings of the term is recognized. If there are unique processes that generate unique products on the web, these would necessarily be identified with a unique name.
4.   This is not to say that something could not be found out (see Oring 2003, 129–140).
5.   Humor may be expected from the very beginning, but *how* the humor is achieved is surprising.
6.   Studies that track eye movements can examine the order in which visual jokes are processed to determine how humor is apprehended.
7.   The viewable list of recipients can change in the course of the forwarding.
8.   There are people who forward joke e-mails without having read them. Theoretically, it would be possible for a joke to be distributed to hundreds—even thousands—of people without the joke being read.
9.   Jokes are undoubtedly told on the telephone and web-based platforms that enable voice and visual transmission. The characteristics of joke telling in these situations

would more likely resemble oral telling in face-to-face environments, but the research remains to be done.

10. I presume it was, in some early version, "next to the water pitcher."

11. It seems significant that when the errors are extended beyond three examples, they are contained in a *written* list posted on the office door. The older priest does not enumerate the younger priest's errors orally in a face-to-face situation.

12. These are the names of Renaissance artists, but the allusion is to the Teenage Mutant Ninja Turtles popular in comic books, television, and movies in the 1980s and 1990s. This line does not seem to appear on any other website today.

13. "Fortune City," accessed 31 January 2011. http://www.fortunecity.com/bennyhills/proops/125/Jokes/Religion_Jokes/First_Mass.htm. As of July 2011, this site is no longer active.

14. One might think that these two choices predominate because they are sexual in nature, but that would not explain the fact that "Eat me," which is also sexual, served to end only 2 percent of the examples.

15. Narrative jokes sometimes seem to undergo radical structural change, but this process is neither well documented nor understood.

16. Certain legends circulate in list form (Fine and O'Neill 2010), but humorous lists would seem to far surpass them in both number and popularity.

17. Also see "sequential graffiti" (Longenecker 1977).

18. Also see "catalogue songs" (Renwick 2009 [2001], 59–91).

19. Goody feels that because lists have a precise beginning and end, they are bounded (1977, 81); but while lists have a precise beginning, they do not have a precise end. They can always be extended (Belknap 2004, 31; Eco 2009, 15).

20. It is not always completely invisible. In the Numbers of the Beast list in the 2006 e-mail, the forwarder suggested his own contribution to the list: "OSDCLXVI = the new Mac Operating system of the Beast." It was not placed at the end of the list but at the beginning of the forwarded message. It does not seem to have gained any currency, as it does not show up in any web searches. Both "DCLXVI = the Roman numeral of the Beast" and "Win666 = the operating system of the Beast" do, however.

21. There are many old tales about parsons' sermons (AT 1824–1839), and there is a possible precursor in Tale LV in *One Hundred Merry Tales* published in 1525 (Klaf and Hurwood 1964 [1887], 84–86).

22. In Tristan Cafe Pinoy Forums but on three different pages. See http://tristancafe.com/forum/113140,/99657 and http://tristancafe.com/forum/87331. It seems to be associated only with this Filipino website. One version is interspersed with little animated emoticons.

23. The grace is, in part, a parody of the nursery rhyme that begins "Rub-a-dub-dub, three men in a tub." A similar and well-known type of grace is "Good bread, good meat, good God, let's eat!" ("Grace Before Meals").

24. It is not just the market that captures folklore for commercial purposes; folklore captures elements of the market for use in jokes and other genres. One example is the enormous number of video clips on YouTube that attach humorous subtitles to Adolf Hitler's diatribes in the German film *Downfall (Der Untergang)*. There is even a clip where Hitler rants about the enormous number of parodies that have been posted on YouTube ("Downfall").

25. I presume the cartoonist hoped that his readers had never seen it before.

26. While all kinds of verbal humor abound in synchronous chat, it would seem that canned jokes are rarely exchanged (Baym 1995; Nilsen and Nilsen 2000, 167).

27. There is no etymological connection between *surf* and *surface*, the latter deriving from the French *sur* + *face*—that is, "on the face of."

28. "Mother" is used not in the sense of an ancestor but in how Saddam Hussein used the term when referring to the forthcoming 1991 Gulf War as "the mother of all battles"—that is, the greatest battle of all.

29. Should the exchanges on book discussion websites, for example, be considered folklore because they are unofficial or vernacular—not taking place in such institutional settings as university classrooms or the corporate offices of a publishing house? Why would a folklorist be interested in these exchanges? The term *vernacular*—dialectically defined—is likely to include almost everything under the sun (Howard 2005b, 328–331).

6

The Jewish Joke Online
Framing and Symbolizing Humor in Analog and Digital Culture

Simon J. Bronner

As THE PERSONAL COMPUTER BEGAN REPLACING THE TYPEWRITER on office desktops during the 1980s, folklorist Paul Smith (1991) reported that workers delighted in the new machine's capacity to enable unofficial, playful activity that he called folkloric. Although he sensed that many colleagues wedded to definitions of folklore around face-to-face oral transmission might be skeptical of his folkloric label, he pointed out the continuity of repeatable, variable material on the Internet with previous folk forms. The material in question was not games that had already been commercialized and packaged for computers. What he noticed beneath the surface of work life was definitely vernacular, often edgy humor in the form of jokes and cartoons that he recognized from earlier office communication technology such as the typewriter, photocopier, and facsimile machine (see Barrick 1972; Bell, Orr, and Preston 1976; Dundes and Pagter 1978 [1975], 1987; Preston 1974, 1994; Smith 1984, 1986).

Noticing that the behavior of "playing on the computer" (often perceived by office managers as "misusing" the computer) primarily involved sharing jokes, Smith dubbed the computer "The Joke Machine" and predicted the exponential growth of its humor-generating function. This label implied that the machine was more than a storehouse of information. If the Internet merely provided a cabinet in which to file one's favorite joke, it would not brandish the expressive, interactive features or cultural functions of folklore that frequently lodge as commentary on popular culture. More than being a reproductive medium, however, the computer, as it became

DOI: 10.7330/9780874218909.c06   119

more of a home appliance, fostered the creation of new material that, in Smith's words, could only exist "within the machine" (Smith 1991, 274; see also Foote 2007; Fox 2007 [1983]; Jennings 1990, 120–141). Users at home and work manipulated images and adapted texts, often commenting on the technology and inviting social feedback that distinguished the humor as "computer lore" (Bronner 2009; Preston 1996).

Why joke in and around the machine? Smith implied that it is a natural process for humans to appropriate new technology for folkloric transmission, and he drew an evolutionary pattern from user-controlled media of the typewriter to the photocopier, fax machine, and computer. Yet the high volume of traffic on the Internet and the creative, interactive forms therein suggest something more at work (and play) on the computer. In its personalized consumer version, the computer promised more self-reliance in a growing culture of modernistic individualism, but at the same time risked alienation and corporate, mass cultural control over individual users. As a result, I contend that joking became associated with digital transmission for several reasons: first, because it emotionally and psychologically serves to respond to anxieties of diminished human control and competency for users; second, it signals for them an intimate social connection that questions a dominant corporate order; third, it creates symbols that provide or project a satisfying transgressive or aggressive effect; and fourth, its brief and often visual form adapts well to the physical screen frame.

Twenty years after Smith made his observations, a Google search of "jokes" results in an astounding figure of 324 million hits that clearly indicates a development well beyond the adaptation of photocopier lore. Most of the sites are lists of texts and cartoons arranged by categories, and among the most common jokes are those identified as "Jewish jokes" or "Jew jokes." For the most part, the jokes are about Jews rather than jokes provided by Jews, and they fit the characterization of Jewish humor as deprecating material related to the characteristics and characters of Jewish life, often deriving from the legacy of persecution in Eastern Europe and the immigrant experience to countries in the West (see Ziv 1998, 12). Although jokes about Jews have been especially conspicuous as ethnic humor in Europe and the Americas in the late nineteenth and early twentieth centuries, the extent of websites in the twenty-first century as the Internet globalized is still surprising. One cause for amazement concerns the perception of Jewish jokes as "period pieces," related to their historical association with mass immigration in the early twentieth century rather than the assimilation of the twenty-first century.

Websites such as oldjewstellingjokes.com, jewishjokes.net, and awordin-youreye.com focus exclusively on the Jewish joke as a genre. The number of hits for "Jewish jokes" consistently is the largest among ethnic-religious categories outside of racialized "black jokes" and "Chinese jokes," and the figure has grown steadily since Smith's early inventory of ethnic jokes as an integral part of computer lore. An indication of the pervasiveness of Jewish jokes is a 2011 Google search that revealed the number of sites coming back as "Jewish jokes" or "Jew jokes" amounted to double the frequency of sites listed for Polish, Irish, Catholic, and Mexican jokes. With the emphasis in the discourse of the twentieth century over the effect of joking in oral and print circulation, questions remain for the twenty-first century about the role of technological mediation, such as what happens to the characterization of Jews as agents of joking when the category of "Jewish jokes" goes online in such a massive number of sites. Once pronounced dead (or at least out of oral circulation), Jewish jokes abound on the Internet, in citation if not performance. Does that mean the jokes enjoy a second, more robust life in digital culture than in oral tradition or photocopied lore? Broadly speaking, this query provides a basis for theorizing the shift of narrative communication in the twenty-first century from analog (face-to-face, oral, corporeally based) to digital (reliant on mediated communication by individual users) culture (see Blank 2009b; Bronner 2009; Howard 2011; Jenkins 2008; Turkle 2011). Indeed, what happens in the move from a backslapping rendition of a joke in-person to a text read on an Internet site, or from an inside joke to a video gone viral in e-mails and downloads?

One answer to the question of the ubiquity of Jewish jokes on humor sites is that the texts are essentially archived and then selected for oral reenactment or private amusement. Readers can imagine a process by which the texts are extracted from their performative social contexts and are posted, as if the webpage was an enormous bulletin board for passersby to browse. The Internet, then, is a massive storehouse rather than a stage for performance or a folk frame for play "just among us." In an archival transformation (or what some may see as a conversion experience), many webmasters take pride in, or show their technological mettle by, making available historic or formerly analog forms in long digital lists. Another view is that the Internet transforms folkloric genres by providing a different communicative medium and a novel play frame. From this perspective, digital media are not simulating or stirring a face-to-face interactive context; instead, they serve to redefine the social setting and reorganize the cultural frame, thus allowing users to create a fresh expressive form.

Although it is tempting to lump Jewish jokes together with the pervasive ethnic humor on the Internet, I focus on Jewish jokes because of their historical association with oral and print forms and the scholarly presumption that they should not grow in digital culture. Rising in oral tradition with mass immigration from Eastern Europe in the late nineteenth century, Jewish jokes enjoyed immense popularity on the theater stage as well as in print in the early twentieth century. With the assimilation of subsequent generations, repression of material that could be twisted into anti-Semitic barbs, and an aversion to self-degradation, Jews especially discouraged the circulation of Jewish jokes. With their heavy reliance on Yiddish terminology and references to the immigration period, Jewish jokes were often contextualized, and consequently distanced, as old, "classic," or relic humor (see Biro 2001; Eilbirt 1981; Minkoff 2005). Although many of the jokes were reportedly told by Jews to one another, many Jews became uncomfortable when they "went public" in print, and especially on the global Internet. Commonly based on the view that Jews are symbolic targets for ridicule and marginalization in host societies either because their social difference needs to be reinforced as they integrate or their minority status raises suspicion among members of the dominant society, the jokes inevitably raise the question of whether stereotyping and racism are evident.

As a group in a dominant Christian context that is not easily separated by physical difference, Jews both championed and were victims of humor that commented on their alleged physical differences and aspiring social status. Jokes could be considered high-context expressions because they demanded symbolic decoding with knowledge gained from being in a cleaved culture (Fischman 2011, 48). When presented by Jewish humorists, the jokes were intended for Jews to "poke fun at themselves," but they increasingly expressed concern that the narratives appeared malicious when told outside the group. A counterargument is that the Internet deflates the prejudicial impact of ethnic humor by rendering it in mummified form. Throughout this chapter, I contend that digital culture has made Jewish jokes visible, if not audible, by recontextualizing them from esoteric folk culture into an exoteric memory piece.[1] Just as oral practice can signal a baleful or benevolent intent, so does the Internet have an open "design," a visual frame for interactive discourse that affects the projection of anxiety and consequent communication of meaning on the fictive plane of humor.

THE FORM OF THE JOKE, JEWISH AND OTHERWISE

For the comparison of analog and digital versions of jokes to be valid, I should first establish that the forms are equivalent. Jokes usually take the form of brief, fictional narratives, usually told in the present. Complicating this description is the proliferation of joking questions (also called "riddle-jokes") that are often included in lists of jokes in Internet humor sites, as well as in oral performances. Listed as a "Daily Jew Joke" on a Facebook community page, for instance, is "What do you get when you lock 2 Jews in a room?," with the answer, "3 opinions."[2] It can also be rendered as a proverb by stating a condition and a result: "Two Jews, three opinions" (Telushkin 1992, 17). If "Jews" structurally constitutes a motifeme (a unit of action that is a variable building block of a plot or linguistic sequence), then other groups could conceivably fill the slot, as in a light bulb joke with the formulaic question "how many (group) does it take to screw in a light bulb?" (Dundes 1962, 1981). Yet a Google search for "two three opinions" comes back with hardly any variations of "Two Jews, Three Opinions," suggesting a Jewish rhetorical frame. Even those results that come back such as "two lawyers, three opinions" and "two economists, three opinions" refer to the primary use of the phrase in a Jewish context (Michaels 2006; Michaelson 2006).

In uttering the saying or spinning a story around "two Jews, three opinions," the question arises whether the characterization of Jews is deprecatory inside as well as outside the play frame of humor. The Internet can be a location to offer a textual interpretation on the characterization, suggesting a metafolklore of the Jewish joke, that is, traditionalized narrative that comments on a tradition. Although folklorist Alan Dundes suggested the term *metafolklore* in a pre-Digital Age for "oral literary criticism," the expectation of commentary, often interactive, on the Internet invites an expansion of metafolkloric discourse (Dundes 1966). For example, under the title of "Two Jews, Three Opinions," a rabbi online shares the following narrative:

A new rabbi comes to a well-established congregation. Every week on the Sabbath, a fight erupts during the service. When it comes time to recite the Shema prayer, half of the congregation stands and the other half sits. The half who stand say, "Of course we stand for the Shema. It's the credo of Judaism. Throughout history, thousands of Jews have died with the words of the Shema on their lips." The half who remain seated say, "No. According to the

Shulchan Aruch (the code of Jewish law), if you are seated when you get to
the Shema you remain seated."

The people who are standing yell at the people who are sitting, "Stand up!"
while the people who are sitting yell at the people who are standing, "Sit
down!" It's destroying the whole decorum of the service, and driving the
new rabbi crazy. Finally, it's brought to the rabbi's attention that at a nearby
home for the aged is a 98-year-old man who was a founding member of the
congregation. So, in accordance with Talmudic tradition, the rabbi appoints
a delegation of three, one who stands for the Shema, one who sits, and the
rabbi himself, to go interview the man. They enter his room, and the man
who stands for the Shema rushes over to the old man and says, "Wasn't it the
tradition in our synagogue to stand for the Shema?"

"No," the old man answers in a weak voice. "That wasn't the tradition."
　　The other man jumps in excitedly. "Wasn't it the tradition in our synagogue to sit for the Shema?"
　　"No," the old man says. "That wasn't the tradition."
　　At this point, the rabbi cannot control himself. He cuts in angrily. "I don't
care what the tradition was! Just tell them one or the other. Do you know
what goes on in services every week—the people who are standing yell at the
people who are sitting, the people who are sitting yell at the people who are
standing—"
　　"That was the tradition," the old man says. (Zauderer 2011)

　　"This is a joke," the rabbi affirms at the story's conclusion, but he connects the fiction of the joke to a disturbing reality with the metafolkloric
comment that "Jews tend to fight with each other, especially with regard
to matters religious and how they establish one breakaway synagogue after
another." The rabbi narrates the joke in the present and frames it as a distinctively Jewish type, but it has been traced to a nonethnic precedent in the
nineteenth century with the rabbi being replaced by a judge (Raskin 1992,
14–17). To be sure, the rabbi's narrative strategy is to engage his presumably
Jewish readers with a story, but he also acknowledges it as a way to deal with
what he calls a "troubling issue." He expects to arouse commentary on the
issue with the story because, in his words, "Recognizing that problems exist
is the first step in the healing process—not only between husband and wife,
but within the entire Jewish community as well" (Zauderer 2011).
　　Under the title "Two Jews Three Opinions," a non-rabbinical blogger visualized the joke by creatively using photo editing software to create
and subsequently post an image showing the backs of two Orthodox Jews

(identified by full beards and dark skullcaps). The blogger put in English callouts that viewers would read from left to right as one would read an English sentence rather than the Hebrew, which would be scanned from right to left.

The first one states, "It's a valid point but I must disagree." The second shows a cloud above a man who states "But you're the only one who has spoken so far." The blogger further clarifies that the intent of the blog is to "provide fun, healthy and constructive debate about Jewish issues" (Brad 2008). The reference that might be lost on non-Jewish viewers is the association of Orthodox Jews with an agonistic learning style in which students argue over interpretations of sacred texts. The implication of the cartoon, though, is that this style extends into daily life. The blogger featured the image's "joke" to promote feedback—indeed, heated "debate"— on a broad array of topics. Instead of seeing the screen as something to be passively read, he encouraged viewing the "frame" established by the "two Jews, three opinions" image as highly interactive.

The shared characteristic between riddle-joke, narrative, and image humor is the presence of a punch line. According to folklorist Elliott Oring,

> The punchline is a device that triggers the perception of an appropriate incongruity. It reveals that what is seemingly incongruous is appropriate, or what is seemingly appropriate is incongruous. In any event, the recognition brought about the punchline must be *sudden*. The punchline must bring about an abrupt cognitive reorganization in the listener. As such, the punchline is not a necessary element of humor but a literary device that characterizes the particular form of humor we label "joke." (1992, 83; italics in original)

I would add to Oring's characterization that the punch line can be a visual device as well as a literary one. In the image on the blog "Two Jews Three Opinions," the picture establishes that Jews are talking without a caption stating so. An incongruity is set up by the first Jew apparently arguing with another person, but the punch line is that he is arguing with himself. In the riddle-joke, the punch line is the answer to the question that brings an unexpected or incongruous statement. In the riddle-joke, the twist is often wordplay. In the visual material more common in digital culture, the convolution is conveyed visually either by an incongruity between what is seen and what is read or the fiction of the composed image and its reality. Understanding the punch line, or "getting" the incongruity of the joke, depends on a shared, typically unstated cultural understanding of the references in the text or image (Correll 1997). Although some strict structuralists might view the production of humor mechanically as the setup of the incongruity, my point for further analysis is that the cultural under-standing of references suggests a perceptual psychology to unpack meanings as well as identify processes of enactment. That a punch line falls flat and the teller responds with the apology "I guess you had to be there" indicates that participants in the play frame do not relate to the joke in the same way. If the listener or reader mutters "I don't get it," more than a miscomprehen-sion of the structural incongruity is implied. The suggestion is that the joke is not relevant (or even repulsive), and this situation raises questions about social perceptions and psychological issues often wrapped around the joke.

Both analog and digital cultural forms of jokes have punch lines, but a difference in ritualization can be discerned in oral performances. Someone may say "I've got a joke for you" at a place and time that the teller and listener perceive to be appropriate. Setting up a joking frame on a fictive plan outside of everyday time signals a play on forms, an expectation of symbols and associated references, and a ritualized sequence of narration and punch line that often invites comment or a reversal of listener and teller (see Douglas 1968, 370). The content, too, needs to be considered appro-priate, or the references understood, for it to be effective. If participants in a play frame perceive the joke as a joke with the expectation of it being brief, biting, and funny, the joke will be contextualized in the moment for teller and listener, and the separation in time and place as joking will allow for reordering or subversion of reality. According to anthropologist Mary Douglas, "Social requirements may judge a joke to be in bad taste, risky, too near the bone, improper, or irrelevant. Such controls are exerted either on behalf of hierarchy as such, or on behalf of values which are judged too precious and too precarious to be exposed to challenge" (1968, 366). All jokes, she observes, express the social situations in which they occur: "The one social condition necessary for a joke to be enjoyed is that the social group in which it is received should develop *the formal characteristics of a 'told' joke*: that is, a dominant pattern of relations is challenged by another. If there is no joke in the social structure, no other joking can appear" (1968, 366; italics added).

If the joke is not *told* online, then, is it, perceptually, a joke? On the Internet, the poster of the joke is probably not aware of a listener but nonetheless uses the design of the page to render the joke appropriate or implicates an audience. With most sites providing space for comments and ratings, the user expects a response, but it is fair to say that online the joker has more opportunity to joke and more leeway to post questionable material. The anonymity or disguise allowed by the new medium encourages broader participation because the risk of rejection is reduced. Thus, jokes posted online still depend on a contextualized appropriateness within the design of the electronic "page." In print, within the spate of joke books that appeared during the early twentieth century and, later, on the Internet, attention shifts from oral delivery to textual form.

An indication of the anxiety caused by the status of the Jewish joke is humor about its definition. Richard Raskin calls defining the Jewish joke a "risky enterprise" and cites an attempt to draw ethnic boundaries in the metafolkloric statement "A Jewish story is one which no *goy* [Yiddish for non-Jew] can understand and which a Jew says he has heard before" (1992, 181). Implying that the text of the joke is not as significant a marker as the response of the listener is another joke typically set in Eastern Europe that associates Jews with joking:

> You tell a joke to a peasant and he laughs three times: when you tell it; when you explain it; and when he understands it. A landowner laughs only twice: when he hears the joke and when you explain it. For he can never understand it. An army officer laughs only once: when you tell the joke. He never lets you explain it—and that he is unable to understand it goes without saying. But when you start telling a joke to another Jew, he interrupts you: "Go on! That's an old one," and he shows you how much better he can tell it himself. (Friedlander 2011; see also Olsvanger 1965; Raskin 1992, 181)

The story's setting raises a question of whether the Jewish joke is historically defined by the Jewish Old World and immigrant experience (Jason 1967, 49). As a type, it can be told, or posted, by both Jews and non-Jews, but there is typically a reference to a Jewish character or behavioral trait with roots in Eastern Europe. Writing in a folkloristic journal, Ed Cray (1964) tried to broaden the experience that informs Jewish jokes with the assertion that the joke is "one which intrinsically deals with the Jew and one which would be pointless if the Jewishness of a character were removed" (344). For sociologist Christie Davies, the key to the distinctiveness of the Jewish joke type is one of social boundaries that can be expressed positively or negatively, and, for that matter, orally or online: "Jewish jokes are unique in the way in which they refer explicitly to the problematic nature of the boundaries of a people and focus on the blurring of this boundary not by similar or related outsiders but by assimilating insiders" (1990, 309). The trouble with this perspective is that it does not address the perception of the joke's content or transmission. Fernando Fischman connects, for example, South American Jewish jokes (*chiste judío*) with their North American cognates by identifying key components of "a humorous narrative whose dramatis personae are Jewish and act according to socially shared stereotypical images—the Jewish mother, the greedy businessman, the stingy Jew" (2011, 48). Of significance to the perception of the historicity of the jokes is Fischman's observation that his informants generically classified the jokes as having immigrant origin. The label "Jewish joke" in this perspective suggests an emic category of an orally delivered deprecatory, humorous narrative, whether told by Jews or non-Jews, deriving from Jews' immigrant experiences of the late nineteenth and early twentieth centuries.

DEAD OR ALIVE? OBSERVATIONS ON THE VITALITY OF THE JEWISH JOKE

Noting the rapid rise of the Jewish joke in the nineteenth century as a distinctive historic genre, *Commentary* editor Irving Kristol proclaimed its demise, boldly declaring, "What we call Jewish humor is Yiddish humor" and "with the wiping out of the Yiddish-speaking communities, the creative source of this humor is gone" (1951). The American-born son of Yiddish-speaking immigrants from Eastern Europe, Kristol assumed that the Jewish joke was esoteric knowledge; it was a lore shared privately among Jews. This is not to say that Jews stopped telling jokes, but to Kristol, in post-immigrant America neither Jews nor jokes should be defined by the lore of the *shtetl* (Yiddish term for a small town in Eastern Europe). Formerly he claimed, "the European Jew, achieving self-consciousness in the Enlightenment, found himself at the point of intersection of faith and reason, in a comic situation he could only master with a joke" (1951). From Kristol's mid-twentieth-century vantage point, Jews had moved past arguing for their place in civilization and had joined modernity. In this agenda, he responded to the categorization of the Jewish joke by Sigmund Freud early in the twentieth century as "stories created by Jews and directed against Jewish characteristics" (Freud 1960 [1905], 111). Unlike Freud, who characterized Jewish humor as unusual because the narrator is the object of mockery rather than an "other," Kristol thought that Jews no longer wrung their hands with one another over the distressed "Jewish situation." Instead, he observed that Jews used humor as Americans generally did: to confront the challenges of modernization.

When Kristol suggests the end of the Jewish joke, he refers to the passing of the standard comic folktype of the bearded, backward Jewish immigrant on the vaudeville stage and in many joke books published in the late nineteenth and early twentieth centuries. He shares a displeasure with material that moved from private conversations among Jews to public consumption and misinterpretation. Well before Kristol's famous column, the Central Conference of American Rabbis (CCAR), in 1912, objected to the publication of the fast-selling publication *Hebrew Jokes*. The CCAR

> entered a strong protest, requesting the discontinuance of the publication and sale of the book, because of its vilification, and insisted that the jokes are not harmless fun, but dangerous libels. We regret to state that the firm in a letter received March 13, 1912, replied that it was at a loss to understand our criticism, and it assigned the conventional excuse of holding the Jew in high esteem, and of making him "the target of the same good-humored raillery as the Scotchman and Irishman." (Friedman 1912, 107)

The CCAR's Committee on Church and State observed "a large national movement" featuring the "Jewish comedian," often a non-Jew spouting jokes in a costume lampooning the orthodox Jewish immigrant from Eastern Europe. The theme of the jests often involved Jews in business as peddlers or merchants with non-Jews. The committee declared, "We are not supersensitive, but our pride must resent the burlesquing of the Jew, of his religion or traditions" (Friedman 1912, 103). Although recognizing that Jews had told such jokes among themselves, the committee bristled at the mockery of Jews in the popular culture movement of Jewish jokes to the stage and print.

If not accused of being supersensitive to ethnic teasing in the turn-of-the-century era, the same Jews who laid claim to a long folkloric tradition of the self-deprecating jest were accused of being humorless. The Chief Rabbi of England responded in 1893 with a "Defence of Jewish Wit and Humour." The sources he gave for the placement of Jews among civilized groups with a humorous repertoire was not in the earthy material of the Yiddish speakers from Eastern Europe but rather the ancient texts of *Midrash*, a compilation of homiletic teachings on the Hebrew Bible (Chief Rabbi 1893, 370–371). The Jewish joke repertoire reported among Jews in oral tradition primarily represented humor performed in Yiddish, which presumed a bounded social context and a reference to hardscrabble, oppressed life in Eastern Europe. Yiddish writers mediated anecdotes, jokes, and humorous skits into print and theatrical performances, but jokes were not widely collected as folklore (see Levitan 1911; Ravnitzky 1922). The Yiddish language, and especially the Yiddish accent in a host country's language, represented the expressive inflection of Jews set apart from non-Jews, and for many immigrants it signified amusement (Fischman 2011, 47–49). The language as a sign of minority or folk status also provided in commentaries a contrast to popular or mainstream American culture. In a 1913 story in *Survey* magazine, writer Viola Paradise reports that the typical Jewish immigrant goes to the theater for amusement where she "hears Yiddish jokes and songs and American popular music, and she marvels at the wonders of the moving-pictures" (Paradise 1913, 701). The historical association of Yiddish with the immigrant generation led to the presumption that as Jews became assimilated and lost their inflection the Yiddish humor would drop away in favor of the popular culture of the host society.

Despite the predictions of the doom of the Jewish joke by the mid-twentieth century, exoteric forms of humor identified as Jewish jokes enjoyed great popularity in oral circulation and print during the boon of ethnic jokes in the midst of the 1960s and the civil rights movement (see Blumenfeld 1965). Besides being reported in folkloristic field collections (see Baker 1986; Barrick 1970; Cray 1964; Dundes 1997), a spate of mass-market books under titles such as *The Official Jewish Joke Book* by Larry Wilde (1974), *Truly Tasteless Jokes* by Blanche Knott (1982), and *Gross Jokes* by Julius Alvin (1991) flew off bookstore shelves. Much of the content of these texts was not about the *schlemiels* (awkward, unlucky persons) and *schlimazels* (inept persons) of Kristol's Yiddish humor but the narcissistic, spoiled Jewish American Princesses and their doting, neurotic mothers of a post-immigrant generation (Dundes 1985). The theme of a group using commercialism to advance themselves despite social prejudice and physical obstacles became channeled into queries of the impact of success on ethnic identity and social relations epitomized by the nonnormative family and sexual mores. The new topics also included more comparisons to African Americans with whom Jews were connected as persecuted minorities (Boyer 1993). Moreover, the structure of civil rights-era texts appeared different. Instead of the joke being related as an episodic story, the new forms offered a humorous answer to a question, such as the opener of the "Jewish" chapter of *Truly Tasteless Jokes*: "What's the Jewish version of foreplay? Half an hour of begging" (Knott 1982, 19).

Although these books suggest that jokes were being silently read as relics of an earlier era, Henry Eilbirt, in *What Is a Jewish Joke?* (1981), insisted that the printed Jewish joke was still "an orally told genre." He argued that placing jokes on a printed page did not destroy their fundamental orality. "When we read them," he wrote of the jokes, "we are really listening to them in our heads" (Eilbirt 1981, 5). Folklorist Dan Ben-Amos countered that the Jewish joke, like many folkloric forms, is performed and therefore depends on physical delivery and an appropriate social context; they are, in his words, "communicative events" (1973a, 122). The social context to which Ben-Amos refers is an encounter between teller and listener of shared Jewish identity. Compilers of Jewish joke books from the 1960s and 1970s drew their materials from oral tradition, but, unlike the earlier period, they did not rely solely on Jewish tellers. Placing the jokes on the printed page encouraged a suspension of the social frames in oral performances. No longer framed as a communicative event "just between us," the printed joke drew more cognitive attention to the meaning of words rather than the contextualized inflected delivery or identity of the teller. Seeing the joke in print gave the text a fixity and permanence that it did not have in oral tradition. As reading material, the jokes encouraged individualistic, silent consumption.

The ambiguity of cultural effect as Jewish jokes moved from esoteric to exoteric expression became especially evident in the research of folklorist Alan Dundes, who documented the burgeoning technological mediation of Jewish humor through the facsimile machine and photocopier. Together with Carl R. Pagter, Dundes identified cartoons and texts distributed through the technology of reproduction that in the corporate "paperwork" empire appeared to contain more anti-Semitic sentiments, or at least relied on Jewish stereotypes, particularly commercial associations, as ethnic icons to convey their humor (Dundes and Pagter 1978 [1975]). For instance, he claimed that the Jewish American Princess cycle was not a Jewish joke per se, but that it used the symbol of the Jewish female to reference mainstream American society's anxiety over the effects of consumerism (Dundes 1985). Dundes in fact identified the "begging" joke as a joke told by Jews, but he differentiated their poking fun at "the alleged proclivities of Jewish women, either the Jewish mother or the Jewish wife" from what he called anti-Semitic folklore, or the ethnic slur of Auschwitz and other Holocaust jokes that Jews eschewed (1997, 20).

Along with other analysts, Dundes also implied that men were the primary transmitters of jokes generally, and ethnic jokes specifically, and further speculated that technological mediation such as the fax machine, often managed by women, allowed women to express more "complaints about the males with whom they live" (1997, 94; see also Mitchell 1985). In popular culture, the tendency toward insulting or transgressive humor by women and the spread of the joking context to non-Jews became evident in fame accorded to edgy Jewish comics, many of whom were women. Their uncivil use of sexual references and insults appeared to go over the line of genteel or gentile propriety for humorous effect. The humor performed in nightclubs or on comedy records countered the image of self-deprecating Jewish humor with a post-immigrant aggression (Del Negro 2010; Whitfield 1986, 246). In the Digital Age, the computer "joke machine" further altered the significance of gendered performance by removing or disguising the identities of posters. What appeared to rise in importance with the anonymity of posters was the transgressive act of joking and the textual focus on the content of, and response to, the joke.

Posters often leave clues with their monikers to their identities or the identities they want others to perceive. One psychological statement is the assumption of Yiddish labels such as *shmendrick* (neurotic bumbler), *kibitzer* (busybody), *noodnick* (nag), and *payats* (clown) to emphasize effectiveness as a joker. This association with Old World Yiddish characters (and more recent Jewish comedians such as Jerry Seinfeld, Rodney Dangerfield, and Woody Allen) owes to the attribution of joke telling as a distinctive Jewish trait. Echoing the sentiment of journalist Leo Rosten (1968), Elliott Oring (1983) interpreted the purported Jewish reliance on humor in everyday discourse as a turn from characterization of Jews in religious terms as the ancient "people of the book" to a modern secular classification as the "people of the joke." This ascription raises the possibility that the modern, post-immigrant popularity of the Jewish joke owes to the perception that Jews who tell jokes, or the jokes themselves, are supposed to be funny, at least in part because of their background of struggle, out of which they lampoon the disrespect they receive or their response of incivility. The Jewish persona can be perceived to set up a play frame in a workaday world. Although this perception underlines an ethnic difference, objectifying Jews as consumable entertainment, it nonetheless tethers Jews more closely to mainstream society as a group that shares in the everyday experience of a good laugh (see C. Miller 1993; Spalding 1976, xv; Telushkin 1992, 19–20).

Behind the imputation of joking as a Jewish trait is the view that as many material culture and religious practices of Judaism faded from view in twentieth century America, joke telling became a primary marker of Jewishness.

Although assimilated, Jews could disclose their ethnicity through the esoteric and linguistic references in jokes or the very fondness for telling jokes. If the idea of the Jewish joke is lodged in the topical context of European immigration to America, and to an extent in Western Europe, the modern Israeli experience was difficult to figure into the self-deprecatory, mobile world of the Jewish joke. Some commentators claimed that "Jewish humor got lost in transit to Israel," that at least Jewish humor in Israel as part of a majority, nationalistic culture is not self-aimed and universalized (Nevo and Levine 1994, 126; Saper 1993, 81; see also Telushkin 1992, 173–184). They argue that Israeli humor was nationalistically lodged rather than being associated with Jews globally.

In sum, the Jewish joke in its narrative form could be identified through at least seven different thematic criteria:

1. A historical reference in humor to the experience of East European or Yiddish-speaking Jews (see Katz and Katz 1971; Spalding 1976, xiii–xiv; Ziv 1998).
2. The use of humor to deny harsh conditions and to find advantage in disadvantage (See Eilbirt 1981, 277–278; Spalding 1969, xiv).
3. The delineation of what is special about Jews in contrast to others, often stressing the uniqueness of Jewish society and culture, including reference to Jewish communal characters (turned into folktypes) such as the *rebbe* and *rebbetzin* (Yiddish terms for an esteemed rabbi and his wife, respectively), *chazzan* (Yiddish for cantor), and *shames* (Yiddish term for synagogue sexton). The distinctiveness of Jewish society also is conveyed with reference to religious traditions such as the *bris* (circumcision for boys), reciting the Shema prayer, and synagogue worship (see Cray 1964, 335–343).
4. The criticism by Jews of other Jews, often with the implication that Jews could criticize themselves better than anybody else (see Spalding 1969, xvi; Telushkin 1992, 17).
5. The use of humor as a kind of parable to elucidate a moral and teach a lesson. Related to this use is the textual or intellectual content of the joke related to the cerebral or inconspicuous nature of Jewish character. In Kristol's (1951) view of what Jewish jokes are *not*, for instance, Jewish humor contains "no

pranks, no slapstick, no practical jokes—nothing that reduces
the spiritual and human to the mechanical."

6. A propensity for using joke telling to manifest social differentiation, particularly of the wings of Judaism such as Orthodox,
Conservative, and Reform. In this view, the fact that Jews
tell jokes about each other demonstrates not so much self-
hatred as the internal segmentation of their society (Ben-Amos
1973a, 129).

7. A concern for stereotypical Jewish attributes or collective cultural personality such as answering questions with questions,
concern for money, argumentativeness of Jews among themselves, and a propensity to joke (Nevo and Levine 1994, 127).
Folktypes of community characters such as the *yenta* (talkative
female busybody), shlimazl, and schlemiel mark esoteric versions of Jewish traits, whereas in exoteric versions the identification of the Jew (often in contrast to other ethnic types of
"black man" and "Chinaman") signals behavioral stereotypes.

Although the emphasis in oral performances of Jewish themes had been
on the historical context of immigrant and merchant life, the rise of print
versions of Jewish jokes influenced a referential move to the last theme of
stereotypical Jewish attributes or collective cultural personality. An implication of this move was that Jews were in fact less recognizable as an assimilated
group in host countries. The play frame of the jokes, especially when contextualized by popular culture, appeared to mock Jewish foibles and implied
the maintenance of a Jewish identity defining individuals and the solidity of
their community. In so doing, the jokes raised a question of whether *Jewish*
was a significant ethnic or even racialized category of modern life.

In the nineteenth century, Jewish advocates were concerned that a purported lack of humor among Jews discredited them from being part of an
advanced civilization. Efforts in print and on stage were made to promote
an ethnically distinctive humor among Jews to merit joining progressive,
modern countries (Oring 1992, 116–121). In the twentieth century, a collective humorous tradition associated with the past could be read as a sign
of integration, but it ran the risk of fueling stereotypes that erected barriers
between Jews and non-Jews. Scholars pointed out the decline of the Jewish
joke as more than a loss of *Yiddishkeit*; they correlated this decline with
Jewish mobility out of separate communities and the subsequent loss of

Jewish social bonds (Golden 1965, x; Telushkin 1992, 125–141; Zeitlin 1997, 17–24). Jewish communal leaders still worried about the persistence of anti-Semitic humor but also postulated that with the increase of tolerance for, or deracialization of, Jews in middle-class society, the Jewish joke would go the way of stigmatized blackface minstrelsy (see Rubin and Melnick 2006, 17–48; Telushkin 1992, 21–25). The remoteness of the Yiddish-speaking community from Eastern Europe also contributed to the erosion of the dialect story, a mainstay of the post-immigrant Jewish generation. However, for many observers, the dialect joke was not Jewish anyway because its reliance on the immigrant malapropism could be located among many groups (Brandes 1983; Bronner 2006). These signs could be read to mean that the Jewish joke engine would stall on the global superhighway of the future-oriented Internet in the twenty-first century. Instead, posting of Jewish jokes by all measures has accelerated in digital media (Berger 2006, xii; Davies 2011, 4; Schachter 2008, x; Serracino-Inglott 2001).

Jewish humor, even for the unassimilated Orthodox, is hardly remote or esoteric on the Internet (see Heilman 2006, 184). With a quick search, millions of jokes can be obtained. Although true for humor generally, the *Jewish Daily Forward*, the largest national Jewish newspaper, saw fit to feature a news story on the growth of sites for Jewish jokes. "From riddles and one-liners to satires and comic strips," the article proclaimed, "the Internet's trove of Jewish humor goes on and on." The author viewed the trend positively with the comment, "This is instant gratification at its best, funnies at your fingertips" (Solomont 2005). Nonetheless, he carefully noted those sites, such as Bangitout (bangitout.com), constituting "a place where Jews can laugh at themselves." The jokes selected to exemplify Bangitout, as in other sites such as *A Word in Your Eye* (awordinyoureye.com), referred to revealing Jewish identity in popular culture: "How do you know you are at a Jewish Thanksgiving meal? Leftover vegetable kugel [baked casserole, usually with potato] is suddenly titled 'stuffing.'" According to *Jewish Daily Forward*, the Jewish Humor Yahoo! Group (http://groups.yahoo.com/group/JewishHumor) was especially adept at poking fun at modern Jewish life, and one could note larger issues that referenced the recession at the time (an exemplary joke was "Why did the man getting an *aliya* [an honor to come to the platform in synagogue] say his name was Sarah bat Moshe? He's having financial trouble and put everything in his wife's name.")

The Jewish Telegraphic Agency (JTA), the main international Jewish news agency, also took notice of the transmission of Jewish humor on the Internet but expressed more worry about whether this humor in an open, public medium would be perceived negatively. The Digital Age story pointedly raised the question "What is the line between lighthearted parody and wicked satire? Between being 'good for the Jews' and 'bad for the Jews'?" (Klein 2009). Although not a new question aimed at non-Jewish appropriation of, and even Jewish production of, humor for a wide audience, the query took on a new immediacy because, according to the JTA article, in the twenty-first century, "people hang out . . . on Web sites." Rather than the image of the silent reader taking in a joke book, on websites users produce and consume, and the result is often folkloric. An indication of the interactive process is in the response to the circulation of one video based on jokes about Jews eating Chinese food on Christmas. When asked for the source, a viewer commented, "Oh my cousin from Argentina got it from his uncle in Israel who sent it to his doctor in California" (Klein 2009). I now turn my analytical attention to the placement of Jewish jokes on websites in the twenty-first century where users in digital culture live, work, and play.

THREE SITES OF THE JEWISH JOKE IN DIGITAL CULTURE

Whether or not the Jewish joke continues to be told in the twenty-first century, it is arguably more evident than ever before because of the global visual medium of the Internet. A key feature of the Internet in digital culture is the ability to retransmit material without necessarily taking the role of "teller." The "forwarding," "retweeting," or "reposting" of humor allows for a distancing of the teller from the material (see Frank 2009; Hathaway 2005; Perz 2009). Users might even reinforce this transmittal objectivity with the introductory comment (or subject line) of "FYI" (for your information) or "thought you'd be interested." Although mechanically the computer eases the process of transmittal by taking away the pressure to perform, the question remains: Why do so many users choose Jewish jokes to transmit, especially non-Jews who, after all, constitute the vast majority of computer users? One possibility is that the perception of Jewish jokes as historical artifacts or non-racialized material takes away for some users the stigma of joke texts. For many users, Jewish jokes are not as highly charged as the other major sources of ethnic humor in African American and Chinese material. One could also point to symbolic reasons for their circulation: many of the attributes of characters in Jewish jokes are visible in commercial culture (an obsession about money), feminization (in the roles of the Jewish mother and the Jewish American Princess), and the witty or creative individual struggling in a dominant society (see Baker 1986, 148–155; Dundes 1985; Foxman 2010; Reik 1962, 66–74).[3] These characterizations relate to the mass culture that acts as a foil for many computer users working within a transgressive play frame. In choosing the Jewish joke, users can project their concerns about massification represented by the computer to an external source that is relevant to their status. Indeed, many sites for Jewish jokes online differ from earlier print sources by having fewer references to the shtetl folktypes and more to the ordinary figure in a larger society who feels unjustly marginalized.

Even if this symbolic explanation holds, the spread of Jewish jokes online still seems curious in light of predictions of the decline or obsolescence of the defensive, self-deprecating Jewish joke and dialect story. Often torn from a performative context, Jewish jokes online (even more than books that have connections to an author or editor) convey ambiguous meanings. As Elliott Oring points out, a website for humor is more like an archive than a repertoire or an event, but it is an influential one because of its visibility in digital searches (2003, 129–130). Oral tradition operates editorially; jokes become transformed or eliminated from a repertoire (139). In a face-to-face communicative event, jokes frequently invite a comeback and a narrative exchange. Jokes can be customized and selected for specific social conduits. In oral tradition, observers have assumed that the lines between anti-Semitic or exoteric lore could be clearly distinguished from esoteric or Jewish humor. Online, many joke sites labeled "Jew jokes" are actually hate sites while others are presented in conjunction with ethnic humor sites (Billig 2001; Weaver 2011). The division appears to signal a new era and definition for the non-performative Jewish joke.

To identify varieties of the frames or designs used for Jewish jokes in digital culture, I will discuss three of the leading Jewish joke sites in an effort to identify patterns in online communication of ethnic humor and Jewishness. With digital culture, it is prudent to not only contemplate the intentions of a Jewish joke—if that is what the genre can be called—but also the response of a remote and disembodied viewer. A broader thesis than Freud's self-deprecation postulate based on the Jewishness of joke tellers' needs testing in online communication—especially because of the uncertain relation of a narrator to the subject, and the removal of context in drawing attention to a text or image.

One analytical strategy is to adapt anthropologist Gregory Bateson's (1955, 1956, 2000 [1972]) contribution of frame theory to explain transgressive play. According to frame theory, the Jewish joke online can be viewed as metacommunicative by referring to an inherent paradox of its framed or stylized play characteristic of structural incongruity: messages in the play frame deny the very rules that make play possible. People listen to jokes because they accept the idea that the material is located in time and place within reality but will subvert that reality in the end. The fragile play frame is especially critical for jokes because the action of joking may often be interpreted as offensive and aggressive. As I have previously discussed, Internet sites foster metafolklore because of their interactive and visual features and therefore use metacommunication to provide a discourse of meaning in the absence of a "real" material and social context.

In the physical frame of the computer screen, Jewish jokes online are arguably not about the Jewish joke. As metamessages, they use the ambiguity of the Internet frame to question Jewish joking and, ultimately, Jewishness as a category between reality and fantasy. Social actors who cognitively establish boundaries or symbolic oppositions of allowable "play" and "not play" construct frames. When the stylized actions of a group are challenged, the frame may be used to ask if this is play and confront the need for, and meaning of, the play in relation to behavior outside the frame (see Bronner 2010, 2011; Mechling 2008, 2009). The Internet poses this kind of challenge because the actors involved may be unrevealed to one another and do not constitute a group in the usual sense, or the ability to restrict a frame within the Internet's openness presents an obstacle to social construction.

For the purposes of a frame analysis, let me proceed from the most textual to most contextual of popular Internet sites featuring Jewish jokes. Jewishjokes.net is the top ranked Jewish joke site retrieved from Google searches. The compiler is anonymous, but the site conveys its Jewish context by its welcoming rhetoric of "Shalom," its traditional blue and white color scheme, and a variety of Jewish networking links including the Jewish online dating and social networking sites JDate, JewishSingles, and JewSchool. Whether as an editorial statement or a sign of Jewishness, the prominent image next to the welcoming message is of a bearded, tallit-wearing man beckoning the viewer with his index finger in one hand and a pair of scissors in the other. When I asked a college-level class what this figure represented, my Jewish students recognized him as a *mohel*, a specialist for Jewish ritual circumcision, while the non-Jews thought of him as an "old country" stereotype.[4] The difference was significant because the Jewish students interpreted the figure to signal the site to contain insider jokes relating to Yiddishkeit, whereas the non-Jewish students anticipated stereotypical or anti-Semitic material, especially related to the traits of financial stinginess and ethnic difference. Gender was not as much of a predictor of perception as religious-ethnic identity.

Under the "add a joke" tab, the site invites password-protected members to contribute jokes and then subject the texts to ratings. The joke tellers therefore are identified, although they can use monikers that disguise their ethnic background. In the listing of the latest jokes, Jewish references can be discerned from screen names such as "moish" (a nickname for the Jewish biblical patriarch Moshe or Moses), "funnyJew," and "alte_kaker" (literally, in Yiddish, "old shit" and idiomatically a "geezer") while there are other participants whose identity remains masked through less revealing handles like "Tony," or "chihuahualady." Still, viewers scrolling through the lists get the impression that overall these are Jewish jokes from Jews. The pre-established categories for humor listed in alphabetical order are "American Jewish, Blue-Ish Jewish," "British Jewish," "European Jewish," "Food," "General Jewish," "Health," "Israeli," "Jewish Mother," "Rabbi," and "Yiddish."

Jewishjokes.net presents a user-influenced voting forum that displays the site's top ten rated jokes on a scale of 1 to 5 (5 represents "very good" while 1 stands for "very poor"). The only perfect score is surprisingly not awarded to a joke in narrative form. It goes to a humorous image deriving from *The Simpsons* that depicts a scene of Krusty the Clown walking his dog through his old neighborhood, which also happens to feature store windows with advertisements for a barber, "Fantastic Schlomo's: Payos Trims Two for One" (referring to bargain rhetoric of "two for one" on an ultraorthodox Jew who has earlocks, or *payos* in Yiddish), and the grocery store product "I Can't Believe It's Not Trayfe" (a parody of a commercial advertisement for the margarine I Can't Believe It's Not Butter). All of the other jokes rated in the range of "4" are narratives involving Jewish denominationalism, Jewish figures such as rabbis, or Jewish/non-Jewish relations, often in an Old World context. Many of the low-rated jokes are under the "Israeli" category. The lowest-rated joke, for example, required esoteric information on the double meaning of falafel as food or as pendants on a soldier's uniform:

There are two Israelis in the front of a car and an American in the back. One
Israeli says to the other, look at that man and his falafels. So the American
says, falafels, where? I am hungry.

Without the knowledge of Hebrew slang, the joke falls flat. The content
of the joke indicates a low-context frame because the knowledge necessary
to appreciate the humor does not permeate the social conduit. The site dis-
tances narrator and viewer by not allowing comments on individual jokes,
but it implies that humor can be key to social networking by facilitating the
e-mailing of posted jests to a "friend" and receiving jokes by e-mail.

 Close behind jewishjokes.net in popularity is aword-
inyoureye.com. Like Jewishjokes.net, it rhetorically references its Jewishness with its welcoming message of
"*Mazeltov*, you have arrived at the best website for Jewish
jokes and Jewish humour available today." The home page
screen is multicolored but contains no visual icons. The site has the look
of an archive with enumerated sets of jokes. But unlike Jewishjokes.net,
awordinyoureye.com has a clear backstory and moderator behind its production. The site began in 2000 when David Minkoff, a Jew from London,
England, established the site to share "what [he] feel[s] are the best Jewish
jokes around." He claims oral sources for his jokes, including schoolmates,
family, friends, co-workers, the changing rooms at the Maccabi football
club,[5] friends at his Israeli dance class, and his rabbi. Minkoff does not identify his sources but implies that his Jewish jokes in fact represent Jewish tellers. As of January 2012, the site contained over 2,525 jokes organized into
135 sets of several jokes under the categories "Jewish Jokes," "Naughtier
Jewish Jokes," "Kosher Lateral Thinking," "Material for Speeches," "Jewish
Jokes for Children," and "Non-Jewish Jokes."[6] With the framing device of
designating Jewish jokes by what they are not, one notices that the three sets
of Jewish jokes mostly concern modern institutions or situations such as
finance, education, marriage, and health. A few about priests act as a coun-
terpoint to the rabbi jokes contained within the Jewish jokes.

The establishment of humor outside the Jewish play frame by aword-
inyoureye.net also brings up another rhetorical strategy in the presentation of the jokes. Minkoff insists that the jokes' selection be made on the
basis of their funniness but couches them in nostalgia for a past world of
Yiddishkeit. From the site, he published two joke books in 2005, with the
Yiddishism of "Oy!" as the lead title. His introduction in the first volume

nostalgically connects the Jewish joke to life in the Jewish community and a past age:

> I grew up in a Jewish household (my father was a kosher butcher and poul-
> terer) so I was surrounded by Jewish culture. I started collecting jokes from
> the age of thirteen. Don't all boys get a book on Jewish customs and folklore
> as one of their Bar Mitzvah presents (as well as umbrellas, a *siddur*—or prayer
> book—and fountain pens)? (Minkoff 2005, ix)

His pride in the number of jokes compiled on the site insists on the value of the Jewish label while also representing the relic nature of its community in modern life.

More so than the previous two sites, oldjewstellingjokes. com takes advantage of the visual aspect of the Internet's capability to upload and subsequently stream videos.

The site contains videos of Jews over sixty years of age telling jokes. Although not all the jokes relate to Jewish topics, they associate Jews with being funny because of their heritage, their culturally induced delivery, or their collective personality. Animated tell-ers set against a plain white background are introduced by klezmer music associated with Yiddishkeit. Belying the site's modern look, however, is the notion that the prime transmitters of the Jewish joke are "old people." The performers are presented in contrast to "digital natives," who are assumed to be young, assimilated, and cosmopolitan rather than ethnic and non-tech-nologically oriented (see Prensky 2010). The aged performers often inflect their stories with a Yiddish accent and conclude with a laugh track, thereby reinforcing the Jewish joke as a product of nostalgia.

The producer, director, and editor of Old Jews Telling Jokes is Sam Hoffman, who garnered notice with assistant directorial credits behind mass-market hits such as *It's Complicated* (2009), *The Producers* (2005), *School of Rock* (2003), *The Royal Tenenbaums* (2001), and *Dead Man Walking* (1995), among others. Hoffman describes the twenty-first century beginnings of the site in his hometown of Highland Park, New Jersey, with twenty of his father's friends and relatives. Emphasizing the narrative of the Jewish joke, he cast people he thought could "tell a good story." Hoffman decided that no joke teller could be younger than sixty because he "wanted a lifetime of experience to infuse these jokes" (2010, viii). He filmed individu-als in technologically advanced studios in Los Angeles and New York City. Within a year, he claimed that the jokes had been seen 6 million times and had gone viral, which, he had to explain to the pre-digital tellers (labeled "digital immigrants" by Prensky [2010]), was a "good thing." Implying the metamessage of the Jewish jokes within the play frame, Hoffman notes that on the archival, instantaneous Internet, the videos represent the performative memory of Jewish jokes. According to Hoffman, Jewish jokes as old jokes, "get passed around and around, sometimes for decades. The jokes themselves become time capsules, revealing the fears and anxieties and celebrating the joys of all aspects of life, including its end" (viii). In his book (2010) describing the success of the website, Hoffman proceeds from immigrant-era topics of the Jewish mother and coming to America to modern themes of the suburbs and retirement in Florida. The last two subjects exemplify the representativeness of the broader pattern of commercialism, individualism, and modernization with Jewish symbolism.

As if to question the vibrancy of Jewish culture with the fading of the Jewish joke, Hoffman ends his book with jokes about death. An exemplary joke in Hoffman's collection refers to the transition of authentic Jewish artifacts to nostalgia in the post-Jewish context. Considering the title of the site, Old Jews Telling Jokes, the opening line is startling—"The old man is dying." It goes on from there:

> He calls his son into his bedroom. "Sammy," he says, "I can smell all the way up here that your mother is downstairs in the kitchen, baking rugelach. You know that your mother's rugelach is my favorite thing in the world. I'm sure that this will be the last thing I'll ever eat. Would you please go downstairs and get me some?"
> Sammy leaves the room. Five minutes go by. Ten minutes.
> Fifteen minutes later, Sammy returns to this father's bedroom. Empty-handed.
> "Sammy," the old man says, "where's the rugelach?"
> "Pop," Sammy says sheepishly, "Mom says they're for after the funeral."
> (Hoffman 2010, 225)

In an esoteric version, the rugelach is for the *shiva*, a seven-day period of mourning in Jewish tradition (see Lowitt 2006; Platt 2011; Rozakis 2007, 92). The food is associated with Eastern European cuisine, and the joke uses this detail for the significance of nostalgia as the younger generation contemplates the passing of Sammy (in oral versions, the character is often rendered as the *zayde*, or grandfather). The old man, and his Yiddishkeit, is a thing of the past. His pleasure of eating rugelach has been transferred into a symbol by the dominating Jewish mother of the New World for the broader society. The mother reverses the expectations of evoking memory with a future orientation characteristic of modern culture.

In one featured joke, at the closing of *Old Jews Telling Jokes*, the text appears to make a reference to the listing of jokes on the Internet. The joke raises the question of whether an archived joke still has life. In the metamessage of a joke about jokes, folklorists will recognize a migratory narrative adapted for a Jewish, or modern, context:

> This guy goes to prison. He's very scared. The first day he's eating lunch, and when lunch is over he sees one of the inmates get up on the table and say, "Thirty-two!" and everybody in the whole place laughs. And then he says, "Sixty-eight!" and people are roaring. The new prisoner says to the guy next to him, "What's going on?" The guy next to him says, "Well, you know, we've all been here so long, we've heard all the jokes. We've memorized them, so we don't have to retell them. We just say the number, and people remember it, and then they laugh." Well, this guy just thinks that's terrific. So he spends the entire next year memorizing and practicing all of the jokes. He's finally ready and he gets the nerve to try it. He stands up on the table and shouts, "Fifty-five!" Dead silence. He can't believe it. He thinks for a moment and says, "Seventy-four!" Again the room is completely still. The other inmates stare at him. He starts to panic. So he picks the surefire one. He says, "One hundred and three!" Nothing happens. He goes back to his seat. He says to the guy next to him, "What happened? What went wrong?" The guy says, "Well, some people can tell a joke, and some people just can't." (Hoffman 2010, 237; [Michael] Miller 2010; see also Barth 1987, 70–72; Dundes 1989, 34)

One might question how this narrative is a Jewish joke if there is not a single reference to a Jew or Jewish object. I have collected variants of this joke with the punch line/motifeme of "some people can tell a joke, and some people can't" in other high-context settings (such as a hunting camp or college dormitory). Indeed, the joke emphasizes the importance of oral delivery, but placed within the context of Old Jews Telling Jokes, it additionally questions the passing of a Jewish community in which "we've all been here so long, we've heard all the jokes." The new guy cannot replicate the fantasy of the jokes or the reality of their experience in community. The website constructs a play frame on the site with old Jews who are presumed to be funny to create symbolic distance between old and new, and therefore creates a paradox of a figure being connected to a group while being disconnected from its heritage. The new guy can recall the action but cannot maintain its practice.

Simcha Weinstein, author of *Shtick Shift* (2008), thinks that the Jewish joke of yore may be gone because of its struggle with the past need to disguise one's Jewish identity. In his view, a "twenty-first century humor" has emerged with the Internet that honestly and often brutally declares narrators' Jewishness as an attitude rather than as an appearance, belief, or practice. Referring to Jon Stewart and Sacha Baron Cohen as popular, edgy performers who do not tell Jewish jokes but act "Jewishly," Weinstein claims that these "performers are firmly rooted in reality—or at least a twisted sense of reality that includes themselves in their parody of anti-Semitism. All very post-modern" (2008, 33). Considering that the Jewish joke originally appeared as a response to oppression, in the context of the Digital Age, he asks, "what happens when the oppression largely disappears?" Weinstein's claim is that Jewish humor with its shtick of neurosis from the burdens of being rich and famous projects anxieties of being American. Jewish success is narratively used to reference the paradox of America being the wealthiest and most powerful nation in history while suffering at home and abroad. This pattern of symbolizing Jews as success-oriented Americans may have been presaged by the Jewish American Princess joke and the comical figure of the neurotic, feminized, "nebbish" Jewish male as commentaries on American consumerism and feminization (Dundes 1985).[7]

A way to categorize the paradoxical perception of the Jewish joke's metamessage in emerging digital play frames of the twenty-first century is in the concept of *allosemitism*. The term emphasizes perception of otherness in the Greek root of *allos* for "other" rather than hostility or anti-hostility toward Jews. Sociologist Zygmunt Bauman characterizes the consumption of expressive material about Jews as affectively ambivalent, especially in a modern environment of tolerance, meaning that while use of the material can show either positive or negative emotion that is "intense and extreme," it contains evidence of the opposite (Z. Bauman 1998, 143–144; V. Weinstein 2005, 497–498). According to Bauman, the emerging psychology of allosemitism refers to the "practice of setting the Jews apart as people radically different from all the others, needing separate concepts to describe and comprehend them and special treatment in all or most social intercourse—since the concepts and treatments usefully deployed when facing or dealing with other people or peoples, simply would not do" (Z. Bauman 1998, 143). The possibility in this usage is that "the Jew" in the postmodern or Digital Age becomes a cognitive category for a non-racialized Other, a type close to, or actually part of, the normative culture, but one that needs differentiation, or at least projection onto the category of "the Jew" from one's own social and economic anxieties about a differential identity within mass culture.

The dark side of projecting Jews as a broadly American malaise is apparent in the use of joke sites by hate groups to criticize moral decline and multiculturalism in America. The "Jew Jokes" site at http://www.nazi-lauck-nsdapao.com/jew-jokes.html is sponsored by the neo-Nazi NSDAP (the Foreign Organization branch of the National Socialist German Workers Party) based in Lincoln, Nebraska. In making the rhetorical move from "Jewish" to "Jew" in its adjective for the jokes, the site is establishing the Jew as a racial type possessing physical differences rather than an ethnic background. The site emphasizes joking questions similar to those found in *Truly Tasteless Jokes*, but they are framed in a succession that follows more traditional racial slurs such as "Why is the rhinoceros jealous of Jews? Jews have bigger noses." They may also include propagandistic, anti-Semitic messages such as "What caused the Jew's biggest problem? The greatest man who ever lived, Adolf Hitler." The site verifies Elliott Oring's contention that humor may appear on the Internet but that its enactment or performance is not an unconscious sublimation of aggression as is often interpreted in oral tradition; instead, such humor is in fact deliberately and consciously used to exaggerate hostility (Oring 2003, 42–43, 129–140). The play frame and its metamessages of paradox break down in hate group sites because their design rarely mentions laughter or a concept of a fictive plane. Unlike the other sites, Jews are depicted not as integrating into society but as being in need of removal. According to rhetorical critic Simon Weaver, the racist site operates on the logic of exclusion and segregation, based on the observation of threat (Weaver 2011, 421). More paradoxical is the arrangement of jokes around the observation of integration and inclusion, similar to oldjewstellingjokes.com, that rhetorically employ allosemitic strategies of simultaneous inferiorization and aggrandizement to bring out the difference of the otherwise hidden minority group.

Although not all humor sites are as overtly anti-Semitic and exclusive as the Jew Jokes site, but many do manipulate their presentation in popular search engine results by framing their sites' content as humor to lure in visitors and incite racial hatred. Exemplifying the humor of hate is Racist-Jokes.info, set against a solid black background. The site's home page prominently displays its proud slogan: "The face of Hate on the 'net!" Like the Jew Jokes site, Racist-Jokes.info again concentrates on joking questions and cartoons with stereotypical icons to "spread the hate," as they put it. The home page leaves little doubt about the illiberal agents of its creation when it clearly states that their provision of "jokes based on race" owes to the fact that "we're racist" (Weaver 2011, 418). The jokes are not categorized by content but by the group—"Jews," "Arabs," "Gooks," and "Spics." In addition, a strong theme of homophobia runs through much of the content, along with support for what Simon Weaver categorizes as "the hard right, white power, neo-Nazism and the Ku Klux Klan" (2011, 418). Trying to normalize the site's content, the designers include a traffic rank of over .5 million visitors spread across the globe. To be sure, these "visitor counters" rhetorically reinforce the acceptability for visitors to peruse the profane content found on the website. Moreover, a high visitor count also helps to validate the site's very existence by creating an illusion of vernacular authority regarding its contents' acceptability as a legitimate storehouse for controversial or hate-inspired joke repertoires.

APPROPRIATING THE JEW IN DIGITAL JEWISH JOKES

My survey of popular sites with Jewish joke content demonstrates the importance of the Internet in establishing a Jewish narrator to evoke an esoteric experience even as the texts tend toward an exoteric understanding of the material. Being in an open cyberspace, however, such sites still appear to struggle with the potential for conveying a stereotype to an audience that may not share the same frame of reference. One way that such sites often deal with this virtual dilemma is to couch Jewish jokes as nostalgia for a past era and people. Without the Jewish narrator and in the absence of narrative, the Jewish joke online appears unsublimated and contemporary. Hence it conveys more clearly anti-Semitism on hate group sites and even on normalized humor sites that decontextualize jokes as metafolklore about American or modern conditions. Online, Jewish humor often comprises jokes without Jews and arguably is not about Jews. In contrast to Sigmund Freud's view of "stories created by Jews," the Jewish joke online engages the transgressive qualities of cyber-modernity and signals a change in the Jew as a cultural symbol in the twenty-first century from forms consistently expressed in the nineteenth and twentieth centuries. Jewish joke sites display the paradoxical features of allosemitism by appropriating the figure of Jews full of Yiddishkeit and implicating them as the everyman lost in postmodern mass culture, a dumpy or neurotic character who is both reveled and reviled.

Theodor Reik (1962), who elaborated on Freud's (1960 [1905]) ideas on Jewish projection in humor of self-degradation, theorized a psychology of Jewish joking based on the isolation of Jews in society and their wish for integration. Reik observed that many joke tellers intentionally operate in the region "between fright and laughter" to deal with difficult subjects (1962, 233). In a compact play frame, the effective joke evokes unconscious alarm that is weakened by sharing social anxiety (equated with feelings of guilt) with the listener by the time the punch line rolls around. Reik speculated that the "intensity of response" to Jewish jokes, at least among Jews, owes to the "severity of Jewish moral notions, by the strict inhibitions and suppressions induced by religious education" (234). More than other jokes, he contended, Jewish jokes presuppose a "certain emotional solidarity." In other words, the modifier of Jewishness suggested a communal connection in the midst of alienating or individualizing forces of modernization (see Spalding 1969, xiv). In Reik's psychological take on oral performances of esoteric Jewish humor, "the telling of Jewish jokes also has the unconscious aim of cementing the bond that was originally founded on certain common values, and on the awareness of the Jewish isolation within the nations in which they live" (1962, 236). Countering Irving Kristol's disdain for Jewish jokes gone public, Reik editorialized that Jewish jokes spreading to widening circles of non-Jews should be read as social progress because the possession of the jokes in their play repertoire meant that boundaries had been broken down. Attitudes of self-hatred hypothesized that a "masochistic-paranoid attitude" as a result of a concealed desire to suffer (so as to remain a community was at the root of Jewish humor) would also be absent in such a future scenario (see Booker 1992; Falk 1993; Gilman 1990).

The explosion of Jewish jokes in digital culture plays out a process in which non-Jews appropriate Jewish jokes because of what psychologist Patricia Wallace describes as their provision of "socioemotional thaw" to the isolating "chill" of individualized, often alienating work on the computer (1999, 18–19; see also Bronner 2009; Smith 1991). Jewish jokes are not alone as expressive material in this process, as folklorist Paul Smith observed at the dawn of the Digital Age, but the symbolism of Jewish jokes regarding secluded, de-enlivened individuals negotiating between integration into a large society and retaining a sense of group-ness is psychologically compelling in response to anxieties of a growing digital culture. To be sure, Jewish jokes online still can serve the purposes of bigotry and hostility, but the dominant frame for digital play refers to the symbolic acquisition of

Jewishness as a way to access group-ness in a commercial, mass culture. The Internet has also facilitated the visualization, as well as virtualization, of Jewish identity for Jews troubled by a loss of community. Jewish jokes with their socioemotional reference to Yiddishkeit have reemerged online even more than on the street or the stage to address the tradeoffs of assimilation and commercial success. Despite Kristol's obituary, the Jewish joke in the twenty-first century has not yet been laid to rest.

NOTES

1. I use the concepts *esoteric* and *exoteric* in the sense suggested by Franz Boas of a cultural process involving the movement of specialized knowledge within a community (esoteric) to a dominant society (exoteric). See Boas (1902, 1938). William Hugh Jansen's (1963 [1959]) problematic usage of the terms refers more to relative expressive content: esoteric is a group's folklore about itself and exoteric is a group's folklore about other groups. See Bronner (1986, 109–110).
2. This particular joke can be found at the Daily Jew Joke Facebook page (http://tinyurl.com/dailyjewjoke), posted on 23 October 2010.
3. An indication of this thematic shift is a relative absence of six jokes identified as "classic" in Richard Raskin's *Life is Like a Glass of Tea* (1992). With the exception of the Jewish mother joke (taken from Wilde's *Official Jewish Joke Book* [1974]) in Raskin's list, the classic jokes involve religious themes of rabbinical characters questioning relationships of humans to God. Raskin cites publication histories of the individual jokes but does not chronicle their circulation on the Internet.
4. A mohel is a Hebrew-Yiddish term for a Jewish ritual specialist trained in the practice of brit milah (circumcision for boys eight days after birth as specified in Genesis 17:1–4). The anxiety over circumcision of the penis and the view that the bris is a distinctive mark of Jewish identity have led to a large number of jokes in Jewish tradition and is possibly the reason for the website using the figure as a symbol for Jewish humor generally. For example, awordinyoureye.com has a separate page for "bris, circumcision, mohel jokes" (http://tinyurl.com/87k7bb). The "naughtier" versions are visually represented in red type, in contrast to the tamer jokes in black. Jewish students also thought the Yiddish pronunciation of the figure sounded funny: "moyel" (perhaps because it sounds similar to the English word "mole" or a Brooklyn accent pronouncing girl as "goil"; a comic title for a song, for example, is "I Lost My Goil to a Mohel and Now I'm All Cut Up). Most of the jokes involve wordplay such as the confusion of "castration" and "circumcision" or variable meanings of "cut" and "tips." For example, riddle-jokes that were familiar to my Jewish students were "Why did the mohel retire? He just couldn't cut it anymore" and "Why did the rabbi want to be a mohel? The tips were good." One mohel joke about the Internet requires esoteric knowledge: "What is the proper blessing to recite before logging on to the Internet? Modem anachnu lakh. One Jewish context for this joke is the reference to many blessings for everyday activities in Jewish tradition. Another is the familiar blessing of gratitude Modim anachnu lakh (We shall thank you and recite your praises / For our lives which are entrusted in your hands / And our souls which are deposited with you / And for your miracles which are every day with us / And for your wonders and

goodness at every time, evening, morning, and afternoon). In relation to my thesis about commentary in the jokes about commercial mass culture, the replacement of "modem" for "modim" represents the replacement of God with the machine in modern digital culture.

5.   Maccabi football clubs are Jewish soccer organizations. They take their name from the Maccabees, a Jewish rebel army who took control of Judea in the second century AD. For an example of a London Maccabi football club, see http://www.londonlions.com.

6.   The site was active in the period I checked between December 2010 and January 2012. In that time, Minkoff added 140 texts and included a banner stating, "The 135th set of Jewish jokes was added on 22 December 2011."

7.   The demasculinized Jewish man as a *nebbish* (from the Yiddish for a fearful, scrawny, or unfortunate person) is often portrayed as dominated and intimidated by women, although he might be smart. Often in the modern American context, the Jewish nebbish is equated with the technological or educated nerd. See Brod (1995); Desser (2001, 278).

7

From Oral Tradition to Cyberspace
Tapeworm Diet Rumors and Legends[1]

Elizabeth Tucker

TWENTY-FIRST CENTURY AMERICANS LIVE IN A COMPLEX, FAST-MOVING society. With free-flowing information from the Internet, television, and radio, it can be difficult for people to distinguish fact from fiction. At times of crisis, rumors and legends articulate borderlines between safety and danger, health and illness, and boredom and excitement. Sociologist Tamotsu Shibutani defines rumors as pieces of information that help groups solve problems (1966, 227). According to folklorists Gary Alan Fine and Bill Ellis, some rumors about immigration, terrorism, trade, and tourism are *"too good to be false"* (2010, 5; italics in original). These rumors express anxieties about globalization, emphasizing threats to established beliefs and perceptions. Organ-theft rumors, for example, express resentment of powerful nations and concern about children's vulnerability. Legends make rumors more persuasive through their development of exciting, controversial story lines that seem to have a kernel of truth. Folklorist Linda Dégh explains that legends debate belief: "Short or long, complete or rudimentary, local or global, supernatural, horrible, mysterious, or grotesque, about one's own or someone else's experience, the sounding of contrary opinions is what makes a legend a legend" (2001, 97). Besides expressing anxieties and concern about truth, legends show how we adapt to uncertainty in our global economy.

Tapeworm diet rumors began in the 1960s, when people wondered whether swallowing a tapeworm would make them slender and attractive without any exercise or reduction in food intake. In the late 1960s, promoters of a weight-loss candy called Ayds told stories about people who had

DOI: 10.7330/9780874218909.c07   150

lost massive amounts of weight by eating two pieces of Ayds candy with a hot drink before meals ("Ayds Diet Candy" 2003). During this same time period, people enjoyed sharing legends about famous-but-foolhardy doomed dieters and jokes about cute but obnoxious tapeworms that demanded food. These rumors, legends, and jokes did not specify the tapeworm's scientific names, but we should recognize the two names most applicable to diet rumors and legends: *Taenia solium* (pork tapeworm) and *Taenia saginata* (beef tapeworm). This chapter will trace patterns in tapeworm diet rumors and legends from the 1960s to the present, exploring how digital folklore expresses the shift toward fear of a country where health and safety threats arose in 2009. I will also examine tapeworms' symbolic significance as monstrous, voracious creatures that express a societal code.

My interest in tapeworms began during my first research project as a college professor. In "The Seven-Day Wonder Diet: Magic and Ritual in Diet Folklore" (1977), I analyzed some amazing and disgusting legends circulating among middle-aged women and college students in upstate New York who worried about their weight. Among these narratives, the most horrifying legend described a tapeworm crawling out of a woman's nose while she lay in bed next to her husband; she had swallowed a tapeworm in an effort to become thinner.[2] This legend reflects Americans' interest in quick weight loss during the 1960s and 1970s. In 1977 I found that many female dieters dreamed of quasi-magical changes, of shapeshifting from unsatisfying bodies to beautiful Cinderellas.

Since the early 1990s, when many people began to use the Internet, diet rumors and legends have proliferated. Quick and easy access to information has fed dieters' desire for rapid bodily transformation, encouraging them to expect awe-inspiring weight loss with very little waiting time, but it has also made them ask more questions and heightened their awareness of danger. The Internet has made it possible for users to read and send messages while watching videos and working on projects. This simultaneous involvement in multiple media has added intriguing layers to the process of rumor- and legend-sharing that has existed orally for so many years. As Henry Jenkins explains in *Convergence Culture* (2008), active participation in new and older media has caused a cultural shift that brings together both innovative and traditional forms of communication.[3] Media scholars James Hay and Nick Couldry (2011) identify four ways that the term *convergence* has been used, including one that applies to communication about tapeworms: "as a technological hybridity that has folded uses of separate media into one another"

(473). Before turning to examples of media uses, I will consider the symbolic resonance of tapeworms, which makes them powerful and complicated.

WORMS' SYMBOLIC MEANING

Why have tapeworms fascinated legend tellers and listeners for such a long time? Like other "bosom serpents" analyzed by legends scholar Gillian Bennett (2005), tapeworms protrude from the body in a shocking, inappropriate way. Some narratives, such as the legend in which a husband sees a tapeworm crawl out of his wife's nose, have phallic resonance. A phallic interpretation is supported by the worms' gender in legends: either "it" or "he," but never "she." Here is a story that folklorist Anne Kimzey (2010) shared with me:

> I vaguely remember a tall tale about a tapeworm cure. You are supposed to fast until you are extremely hungry and then sit at a table with your mouth open and a delicious plate of food in front of you. Eventually the tapeworm will get impatient, travel up through your digestive system, and stick his head out of your mouth in search of the food. You are supposed to be ready with a pair of scissors and cut his head off. Then the tapeworm will die and you will be cured.

Male tapeworms like this one insist on being fed. Some cures tell us that the only way to kill them is to behead them; others recommend strong medicine of various kinds.[4]

In the context of legends and rumors, the tapeworm has power because it is a *monster*: a scary, disgusting, and mysterious beast that lurks within hidden body cavities. As such, it can be a formidable antagonist. Freudian analysis of the monster's dynamics suggests interesting possibilities. Anthropologist David Gilmore notes that "the monster represents an amalgam of opposing psychic energies, not just id but an alliance between id and superego. Surrounding the threatened ego, the composite monster unites the chaotic danger of the id and the punishing superego, the alpha and omega of the mental apparatus" (2009, 18). The strength of this composite character helps to explain its impact on those who tell and listen to legends.

Since the tapeworm wants to eat everything it can find, *right now*, it represents the id, which wants immediate gratification. However, this is not the only aspect of the Freudian psyche that the tapeworm fits. This little beast, which resembles a tape measure, becomes a gatekeeper for fat-building calories and therefore represents the superego. It represents not only individual control but also American culture's intense focus on slimness and youthfulness.

To a significant extent, the tapeworm represents the "hungry self" identified by the feminist author Kim Chernin (1994) in her work on women's struggles with eating disorders. Chernin states, "Most of us would prefer to think of our suffering with the female body as vanity, to hide generational problems by the counting of calories, to express in the code of inches and pounds the severe, persisting doubt, even after decades of feminist thought, about the role of women in our culture" (xv–xvi). She suggests, "The female body has a story to tell. In its hunger, its hidden shame, its shadowy sense of guilt, there is the still as yet not fully articulated indictment of our culture's treatment of women" (xv). Chernin's point about vanity is an important one; there is more to the quest for a new body than exaggerated focus on one's own beauty. Many of the tapeworm rumors and legends that I have collected come from women who feel anxious about their appearance. Societal pressure to look thin and attractive gives the "code of inches and pounds" authority.[5] Originally explained in relation to the mass media, the process also applies very well to the Internet (Hay and Couldry 2011, 476–477). As an enforcer of the code of inches and pounds, the tapeworm may impress Internet users as a good way to transform the body, even though tapeworm ingestion may cause severe health problems.

EARLY TAPEWORM RUMORS AND LEGENDS

The beginning of tapeworm diets in the United States is shrouded in mystery, but evidence suggests that people swallowed tapeworms to lose weight in the early twentieth century. A primary source has confirmed the use of tapeworms for dieting during the 1920s: a woman I know told me that her mother ordered tapeworms by mail during that time period. I cannot, of course, be sure that the product she ordered actually contained tapeworms, but the daughter believed that it did. Besides this statement, and others that I have seen online, there is pictorial evidence of early use of tapeworms (or medicine identified as tapeworms) in dieting. A number of current websites on tapeworm diets include a reproduction of an old-fashioned magazine advertisement for "sanitized tape worms"; the original advertisement can be found in the Museum of Questionable Medical Devices in the Science Museum of Minnesota. Not all people with an interest in tapeworms wanted to get thinner to improve their appearance. Laura

Hillenbrand explains in her acclaimed book *Seabiscuit: An American Legend* (2002) that some jockeys of the 1930s swallowed tapeworms in order to stay thin enough to win races. Apparently this method worked pretty well.

During the mid-1960s, when I was a teenager, people joked about thin individuals having tapeworms. From 1964 to 1966, members of my family in Colorado Springs, Colorado, told my thin younger sister that she might have a tapeworm and suggested that she should offer sandwiches to the tapeworm. I was not very thin myself and wondered whether a tapeworm could offer a quick and easy diet solution. My friend and fellow folklorist Janet Langlois, who also lived in Colorado Springs as a teenager in the 1960s, told me that she enjoyed hearing her father tell his favorite joke about a hungry tapeworm that craved lemon cookies (2010).[6] Another female friend of mine who grew up in Connecticut told me she had heard in the 1960s about an affluent dieter who had swallowed tapeworms at a clinic in Switzerland. Tapeworms ate the wealthy dieter from the inside out and she died. This is certainly a horrible death but also, from the standpoint of those who are not particularly wealthy, intriguing and entertaining.

 Barbara and David Mikkelson's *Urban Legends Reference Pages*, better known as Snopes.com, has been tracking the veracity of legends since 1995. One of Barbara Mikkelson's insightful essays, "As the Worm Squirms" (2006), summarizes and interprets tapeworm diet legends in relation to the life and career of the famous opera singer Maria Callas. Mikkelson explains that Callas loved to eat raw steak and liver, from which she probably ingested tapeworm eggs. Although legends attribute her illness to dieting, no evidence suggests that this was the case. Mikkelson notes that many Callas legends end with her losing the ability to hit high notes because of her pursuit of slimness through the tapeworm diet. "Such flourishes," she suggests, "remind us that vanity rumors are often employed to humble women who aren't much liked or are seen as having attained high positions they did not merit" (Mikkelson 2006). Even though Callas died in 1977, people still tell legends about her unwise dieting. A female friend told me this version in the fall of 2010:

> I know how Maria Callas got rid of her tapeworm. She didn't eat for a while. Then she lay down with a bowl of milk, and it came out her mouth. I was under the impression she did it a couple of times. It worked, but when she lost her weight, she lost her voice. The moral of this story is: it's okay to be a heavy opera singer.

My friend's story ends with a kinder message than other versions of the Callas legend deliver. Instead of castigating Callas for her foolishness in pursuing a dangerous diet, this story gently suggests that opera singers should not worry too much about their weight.

More recent tapeworm rumors and legends focus less on fame and more on the horrors of tapeworm consumption, which has become increasingly feasible for everyday Internet users. Anyone with a computer can access websites that display lurid color photographs of tapeworms and tell grisly stories about what happens when a person ingests them.

WORMS ON THE WEB

On the World Wide Web, it can be difficult to distinguish actual information from legend-related material; of course, the boundary between fiction and truth has always been one of the legend's most intriguing characteristics. Blurring this boundary has become a form of play.[7] There are many carefully constructed websites that mock medical and commercial websites in entertaining ways. Rythospital.com (2008), for example, presents images of pregnant men and ads for a drug called Rivitalex that limits sleep to twelve minutes per night. There is a sub-genre of fake websites devoted to saving nonexistent or inappropriate animals, such as the site called Save the Endangered Pacific Northwest Tree Octopus from Extinction! (1998). The website for the Save the Guinea Worm Foundation (2010) proclaims, "Save the date! August 7 is International Save the Guinea Worm Day!" and invites fans of the guinea worm to become "Preservers" who will save the species from extinction by hosting the worms in their own bodies. Anyone who has heard stories about the ravages of guinea worms, as I did while living in West Africa, will not want to join the "brave group of men and women volunteers [who] host living guinea worms in a valiant effort to preserve the species." This is a good parody of "cause" websites, though.

During the past several years, there has been much playful web activity related to tapeworms. On YouTube we can find such videos as "The Evil Tapeworm" (2008), "Tapeworm in My Bathtub" (2007), "Monsters Inside Me: Pork Tapeworm" (2010), and "Colonoscopy Demonstrating a Moving Worm" (2008).[8] Comments on these YouTube videos show that viewers find them to be "gross" but interesting. These videos identify the tapeworm as a dangerous creature and highlight the incongruity of its appearance in familiar bodily and domestic spaces.

To explore how tapeworm diet legends have wiggled their way into Internet dialogue, I read all the comments on tapeworm diets on a number of popular websites, including Diets in Review, Museum of Hoaxes, and MiniMins. The first two sites are American; the third is British. Both Diets in Review and MiniMins evaluate popular diets and offer support to participating dieters while Museum of Hoaxes examines "dubious claims and mischief of all kinds" (2011). Extensive comments appear on Diets in Review, where I first noticed a contrapuntal pattern: one or more eager, enthusiastic comments about the tapeworm diet followed by several negative responses. In the negative responses lay the legend-related content. Such comments as "Where can we find this incredible pill???" and "Can someone please email me on how I can buy a tapeworm" inspired such responses as "This is the STUPIDEST diet I've ever heard of" and "This is absolutely ridiculous—insane." Some writers wrote brief comments while others went into more depth, narrating horror legends or creating horror-legend parodies.

Many horror legends have signaled dangerous foods, medicines, and other commercial products, so we should not be surprised to find legends of this kind arising in Internet comments on tapeworm diets. These narratives tell the sad and shocking story of a female dieter who, eager to fit into smaller clothes, swallows tapeworm eggs and dies horribly. Several tellers of this legend cite a 2003 television show on the Spike TV channel, *1,000 Ways to Die*, as their source, showing that the tellers participate in multiple media forms ("Die It"). One female Diets in Review commenter tells this story:[9]

> The woman who tried the diet died. She lost 60 pounds. Was on the phone braggin about her weight loss. Then suddenly felt ill and passed out while still on the phone. "A diet to die for." The tape worm chewed holes in her liver, intestine. Lungs and heart . . . She reached her goal to ware a size 4 dress!! At her funeral!!! (2009)

In other variants of this legend, the dress size and other details differ, but the warning against vanity, as in the legend "The Fatal Hairdo," which describes a young woman dying of insect bites under an elaborate hairdo, remains the same (Marchalonis 1979, 267–278).

Some commenters' personal narratives follow legend patterns in focusing on extreme damage to internal organs. Here is an excerpt from a long personal experience story narrated by a woman who suffered from worm infestation:

> I was rushed to the hospital with a burst appendix. When they brought me to the hospital to remove it, the doctors found that my appendix burst because it was literally swarming with worms along with everything else in my body, liver, kidneys, and intestinal track. If my appendix hadn't burst when it did and I hadn't been open up the doctors said I would have died. (Diets in Review.com 2009)

The narrator of this dramatic story depicts worms as dangerous, deadly creatures and does not assign any blame to the worms' host. While the story delivers no overt moral message, it makes readers focus on the horror of being overwhelmed by worms.

Other postings on diet websites stand on the borderline between legend and legend parody. This one from a commenter named "Ellen" describes a sister's death:[10]

> My sister, Lacie, tried this diet because she thought she was overweight. She WAS 14 years old and was supposed to be turning 15 yesterday, April fools day. She was a meer 98 pounds, underweight for her age. She ate some Beef Tapeworm larvae without us knowing. She died about 3 months after they started eating her body alive. She weighed about THIRTY EIGHT pounds when she died. It does cause people to lose weight, but with a COMMON side effect. DEATH. Almost everyone Dies from this diet. If your stupid enough to kill yourself, try it. (Diets in Review 2010)

While Ellen sounds serious and worried about others who might succumb to tapeworm infestation, the mention of April Fool's Day suggests that the narrative parodies previous horror stories. Most of the other parodies on diet websites clearly mock dieters, as seen in a brief comment from a male participant on Diets in Review:

> I truly loved this I lost like 60% of my body fat and I have still not gained it back although it may have to do with the fact I now live in a mental clinic for the mentally retarded and they only feed us 2 servings of jello a day. (2010)

Like the story about Lacie, this one identifies the tapeworm diet as a stupid plan to follow. Even though it has a scornful, jocular tone, it delivers a moral message in its own humorous way. And like many other contemporary legends, it entertains the listener with quirky humor while making a serious point.

"MEXICAN PETS"

Since January of 2008, many web comments on tapeworms have focused on a YouTube clip from the "Diet Fads" episode of the television show *E! Investigates* (2008). The video, "Cocky Tapeworm Diet Expert," had garnered 91,908 hits by January 2011. The diet expert is Garin Aglietti, proprietor of a clinic in Mexico and administrator of a website called WormTherapy.com that has provided information about obtaining tapeworm cysts. "In recent years," *E!*'s narrator states in the video, "the tapeworm has been banished to the black market." Aglietti explains that tapeworms, illegal in the United States, come from parts of the world that do not have access to sanitation or medicine. "An African tapeworm that gets to eat an American diet just couldn't be happier," he proclaims while smiling broadly. His sharp contrast between Americans' safe medical procedures and the third world's dangerous conditions has contributed to circulation of rumors and legends.

Ever since Jan Harold Brunvand's book *The Mexican Pet* was published in 1988, readers in the United States and other countries have been familiar with the legend of a visitor to Mexico who buys a sewer rat, thinking that it is a dog. The legend of "The Mexican Pet" suggests that living conditions in Mexico are much worse than those in industrialized nations. The clever seller of sewer rats succeeds in persuading the tourist to buy a pet, giving that tourist a source of disease and danger. Brunvand's documentation of this popular legend eloquently demonstrates Americans' uncertainty about perils that they might unwittingly acquire in a comparatively undeveloped country.

Keeping "The Mexican Pet" legend in mind, we can gain a better understanding of responses to the *E!* YouTube clip. In July of 2008, "Carolyn," a member of MiniMins, started a comment thread titled "The Tapeworm Diet (Eeeww!!)." The thread began with this message:

> Hi everyone! Just read about the most gross diet ever, the TAPEWORM DIET. A clinic in Mexico sells tapeworms at £500.00 for weight loss. You swallow a cyst from a cow's inside (it's a pink pill!) and it becomes a tapeworm, which attaches itself to the small intestine, and digests up to 40% of your food! After 3 months you swallow another tablet to kill the tapeworm and you poo it out (it looks a large brown slug!) A UK hospital consultant had this warning: "A tapeworm will take in some of the food you eat, but it also ingests vitamins and nutrients important to the body's wellbeing. Common side effects include abdominal pain, weakness, headache, nausea,

constipation, diarrhea and vomiting. It may also cause intestinal perforation. I do NOT recommend this as a form of weight loss."

A string of comments appeared very quickly. These comments ranged from short expressions of disgust such as "OMFG!" (an initialism for "Oh My Fucking God") and "Nooooo . . . YUK YUK YUK!!!!" to longer statements such as "I've heard of [the tapeworm diet] before but I didn't think anyone would be stoopid enough to actually pay. It's so dangerous not to mention yukky!" Commenters' use of capital letters eloquently expressed their horror and disgust. Like many other messages that appear on Snopes.com, these create a horror scenario that people would want to avoid if possible.

Of all the comments on this part of MiniMins, two seemed especially noteworthy. The first expressed an aversion to Mexico: "I've heard of that before but had no idea it was available through a Mexican clinic!!" The second comment compared tapeworm treatment to a well-known film: "its nasty, how could people have some think like that in side em XP[11] / its like some think out of aliens lol."[12] Referring to the 1979 movie *Alien*, in which a horrifying creature pops out of actor John Hurt's abdomen, this comment suggests a commonality between extraterrestrial monsters and the tapeworms obtained in Mexico. The word *alien* provides the obvious link: people use the term in reference to creatures from outer space, or illegal immigrants from south of the U.S. border. Violation of borders (either bodily or territorial) seems to produce great anxiety.

GLOBAL CRISIS

In March of 2009, a global health crisis began to develop: 60 percent of the population of town of La Gloria in the Mexican state of Veracruz came down with a mysterious form of influenza. On March 17, the first case was confirmed as the H1N1 virus, also known as "swine-origin A," or, in the vernacular lexicon, "swine flu." Early in April, the first case in the United States was confirmed. American students who had travel plans to Mexico worried about contagion; the number of tourists in Mexico abruptly diminished. On April 27, the European Union advised its members not to travel to the United States and Mexico. Gradually, the H1N1 virus spread throughout the world. By early May, many U.S. schools were periodically closing in an effort to contain or prevent the spread of the virus. On June 11, the World Health Organization declared a global pandemic.

So how did the H1N1 flu crisis affect people's perception of health-related trips to Mexico? On a number of websites featuring comments on tapeworm diets, the level of anxiety increased. The Museum of Hoaxes' site forum, for example, included a relatively calm user comment on January 13, 2009: "Tapeworm infections pose a serious public health problem in many less developed countries due to poor sanitation conditions. So special awareness is required for facing this disease." On March 22, a more agitated user comment appeared: "hey.. DO NOT BUY THIS PRODUCT I SAW THIS SHOW 1000 [WAYS] 2 DIE AND LATER THE TAPEWORM WILL OUTGROW U." Both the upper-case letters and the telegraphic tone of the comment connote worry. Another comment from April 19 suggests that various rumors about the effects of tapeworm ingestion were spreading: "you people are sick! tapeworm can give you headache, confusion, and hydrocephalus! you never learn until you get one!" At such a time of global concern about the H1N1 virus, worries about tapeworms were also increasing.

On July 22, "Alyssa" posted a narrative about a tapeworm acquired in Mexico to the Museum of Hoaxes site:

> Yes I have seen this happen to people too! I've also seen an episode where an older man got the tapeworm parasite from visiting mexico. For YEARS he never knew he had the damn thing until one day it decides to come out his rectum, his wife tries to help and is literally pulling out the worm and its never ending and takes a long time! the guy went on medications for basically the rest of his life because he was so infested, and there was no guarantee when the worms would completely be out of his system. GROSS obviously his case was unfortunate, and you people are actually doing this on purpose. My words for you people are IDIOTS with no common sense! (Alyssa 2009)

Although Alyssa identifies this story as "an episode," it clearly conforms to the structure of the tapeworm horror legend. The story presents a scenario very similar to that of the legend I collected in 1977 in which a tapeworm crawls out of a woman's nose as she lies next to her husband in bed. While the story is much the same here, the gender roles are different. Here the tapeworm protrudes in a phallic manner from the husband's rectum and his wife tries to pull it out. Like other legend characters whose lives are ruined forever, this man "[goes] on medications for basically the rest of his life." The nightmarish tapeworm infestation takes place because of a trip to Mexico.

Further attention to the tapeworm diet arose on the Internet following an episode of *The Tyra Banks Show* on November 9, 2009. Presenting information about Mexican clinics that offer tapeworm treatment for would-be dieters, the show introduced several specialists on the subject. One of these experts was none other than Garin Aglietti, who showed a video demonstrating how he and his associates obtain worms from cows in Africa. Reactions to the show on the Internet expressed consternation. Blogger "BLACKberry," who recorded a live blog of the show, wrote, "Garin sells his tapeworms in Mexico because he can't do it here. I wonder if there's a Tapeworm Flu" (2009). BLACKberry's notes highlight both the illegality of tapeworm treatment in the United States and the recent spread of the H1N1 virus. The semi-humorous quip regarding "tapeworm flu" creates a connection between the two subjects of concern, both of which seem to come from Mexico. In addition, the blogger expresses anger about the video's indication that tapeworms at the clinic in Mexico come from "Africa, that big city between the Atlantic and Indian oceans": a vague, disrespectful attribution of origin.

Other Internet postings following *The Tyra Banks Show* also raised questions and sought to revive old rumors. One such rumor arose in a query from "Nathan" in the forum UADDit on December 30, 2009:

> Recently, Tyra Banks discussed the tapeworm diet. The tapeworm diet is exactly what it sounds like. A person ingests a tapeworm, and loses weight because the tapeworm is taking nutrients away from them. Essentially, the tapeworm diet is a diet without any reduction in calories, or exercise. I heard a woman died from the tapeworm diet, what happened to her?

Since Nathan does not mention more specific information, he seems to have heard a rumor about death by ingestion of tapeworm. A response to his question clarifies the presence of clinics in Mexico and states, "Never heard of a woman who died from the tapeworm diet but I'm not surprised if it happened, the tapeworm diet is extremely dangerous" (Nathan 2009). As with many other posted comments about tapeworm diets, a warning to avoid danger is the main message.

Like "The Mexican Pet," rumors and legends about tapeworms acquired in Mexico emphasize gruesome contamination. In the context of the global health crisis in the spring and summer of 2009, stories about people with terrible tapeworm infections reflect agonized uncertainty. When a mysterious disease spreads quickly, people worry about unknown sources of contagion. No matter where they appear, tapeworms represent small but powerful monsters; these monsters' violation of the body's interior space horrifies people who hope to stay safe and healthy. In narratives about Mexico, a country previously featured in numerous contamination legends, this kind of violation seems especially frightening. Switzerland, where glamorous tapeworm swallowers of the 1960s allegedly met their deaths, has a different status as a fully industrialized country. There is, however, a major similarity between tapeworm legends from both places. As Gary Alan Fine and Bill Ellis observe, "People—wealthy or impoverished, modern or traditional—must interpret complex worlds in which truth is often cloudy or opaque" (2010, 198). How can any of us be sure that we are doing all that is necessary to stay safe? One of the messages of tapeworm legends is that even if we do our best, we may not find the right answers to a conundrum that is puzzling us.

VIRTUAL LEGEND TRIP

Sometimes Internet research requires person-to-person contact. In April 2010, a year after H1N1 spread throughout the world, I made some telephone calls to ask for information about weight-reduction methods advertised on the Internet. Besides hoping to gather interesting information for my research, I wondered if I could find an effective weight-reduction method. Years of sedentary academic work had not made me any thinner than I had been in the 1960s, when people joked that my younger sister might have a tapeworm. Although I did not think that a tapeworm diet would be safe, I was eager to learn how this process worked. Therefore, I sought information as both a researcher and a consumer. Those of us who conduct research also function as consumers in our daily lives. Usually my consumer inquiries do not have a close relationship to my research, but in this case they did.

I decided to get in touch with Garin Aglietti, whose interview on *E! Investigates* had drawn people's attention to tapeworms imported from the third world.[13] Having confirmed that he in fact *did* own a worm therapy clinic in Mexico, I called the worm therapy website's number—1-888-898-WORM—and explained that I wanted to gather information about weight-loss methods.[14]

"How much weight do you want to lose?" Aglietti asked.

"About fifteen pounds," I replied. "Where would I go to get tapeworm therapy?"

"You'd come to our clinic in Tijuana," he told me. "We treat many illnesses there: asthma, psoriasis, Crohn's disease, and others."

"Would I have to stay at the clinic long?" I asked.

"No," he replied. "You'd come in the a.m., get inoculated, and be on your way later in the day, and you could stay overnight in San Diego."

"Isn't tapeworm therapy dangerous?" I asked.

"It works pretty well," he told me. "I've done it a couple of times myself."

"Can I get rid of the tapeworm after it helps me lose weight?" I asked.

"Sure," he answered. "It's important to kill it at the right point. You kill the worm, you've lost ten to fifteen pounds. You'd be surprised how unrealistic some people's expectations are. Some people hear about our site from a friend and want to lose eighty pounds. They're almost *never* happy."

After some more conversation, I asked, "How much does tapeworm therapy cost?"

"About $1,500 to $1,800 for one or two organisms," he told me. "We grow them in cows."

After our telephone conversation ended, I considered how people learn about worm therapy. Some find information on the Internet while others come to the clinic because friends have told them that tapeworm therapy causes quick, massive weight loss. There is a "friend of a friend" (FOAF) effect here: people talk with friends (or friends of friends) and then hope to undergo a sudden reduction in size. Their expectations fit the pattern of "miraculous transformation" that I had found in my earlier research on diet folklore. Aglietti had encouraged me to have that kind of hope myself when he told me, "You kill the worm, you've lost ten to fifteen pounds."

My other discovery was that Aglietti encouraged potential clients to view worm therapy as an intriguing challenge. Toward the end of our conversation he told me, "If you have that pioneering spirit and don't mind harboring a worm, this method can work for you." "Pioneering spirit" sounded brave, patriotic, *American*. The phrase "harboring a worm" reminded me of some of the language on the Save the Guinea Worm Foundation website, which encouraged visitors to think about saving an endangered species by offering their bodies as hosts. The emphasis on risk-taking and bravery could appeal to dieters, especially young people wishing to prove their courage. As legend scholars have demonstrated, the desire to test one's courage has motivated many legend trips by teenagers (Dégh 2001, 253; Ellis 2004). Both young people and adults may feel a need to prove their bravery; alternatively, they may reject worm swallowing as a dangerous, foolish thing to do.

Tapeworms, associated with hunger and self-regulation since the early twentieth century, have become story characters that get people's attention quickly. Evoking laughter, disgust, and horror, stories about tapeworms gross out listeners. These stories continue to be powerful in our complex Internet-based culture, which lets people perform multiple tasks online and through older media. Through the Internet, television, radio, and word of mouth, people can tell stories, applaud and criticize each others' stories, watch and create videos, and buy and sell products. Such communications constitute a form of technological hybridity that epitomizes convergence. They also reinforce the societal code of inches and pounds identified by Kim Chernin (1994, xv–xvi): a code that has flourished in this era of heavy Internet usage.

Internet marketing has shown people that worms are not just parasites needing a cure; they may also offer a cure for excess weight. In 2009, the popular television show *House* aired an episode (titled "Teamwork") portraying worms as a quick but unusual means of regaining good health. Will worms become part of home medicine chests in the future? As medicine and technology move forward, rumors and legends will give us answers to that question and others.

NOTES

1. I thank Janet Langlois, Jan Harold Brunvand, Faye and John McMahon, Suronda Gonzalez, and Anne Kimzey for their helpful discussion and contribution of information and stories about tapeworms.

2. Jan Harold Brunvand includes that text in the "More Dreadful Contaminations" chapter of his book *The Choking Doberman* (1984, 111) along with a comparable legend from Ronald Baker's *Hoosier Folk Legends* (1982).

3. While writing and revising this chapter, I find myself doing the same kind of old-and-new media multitasking that Jenkins's *Convergence Culture* describes: checking business-related and personal e-mail, picking up "snail mail" from the mailbox, watching videos sent by friends, taking a break to watch part of the popular film *Couples Retreat* (2009), listening to my son tell a legend that he heard at his workplace, and pushing the "like" button to show appreciation of a witty comment posted on Facebook by this book's editor, Trevor J. Blank.

4. Other tapeworm cures have been noted by folklorists working with African immigrants in the United States. Felicia R. McMahon (2007) told me about Sudanese traditional cures for serious illness caused by tapeworms. It is important to note that while Americans pursue tapeworm ingestion as a means of weight loss, the Sudanese and other West Africans view tapeworms as causes of illness requiring cures.

5. This code expresses itself through the process of media communication elucidated by cultural theorist Stuart Hall (1980).

6. A long "shaggy dog" joke about a tapeworm that likes hard-boiled eggs and lemon cookies can be found on the website jokebuddha.com under the title "Recent Tapeworm Jokes" (2010). This joke belongs to the "Stories about Animals and Humans—Miscellaneous" category (B400–B499) in Jan Harold Brunvand's "Classification for

Shaggy Dog Stories" (1963). Shaggy dog stories are usually long, drawn-out, and silly, with punch lines that make listeners both laugh and groan. Not all jokes about tapeworms are shaggy dog stories; some take the form of relatively brief, humorous descriptions. One of the earliest humorous descriptions of a tapeworm appears in George Horatio Derby's *Phoenixiana* (1856).

7. Indeed, play is intrinsic to human behavior; cultural historian Johan Huizinga (1955) identifies humanity as "playing man." Brenda Danet, author of *Cyberpl@y: Communicating Online* (2001), explores the inherent playfulness of Internet communication and culture. Danet explains that her book reflects "the spirit of adventure, fun and experimentation that accompanied explorations in a new medium and the ways that it shook up old norms and expectations" (4). She recognizes the importance of the research of Sherry Turkle, whose *Life on the Screen: Identity in the Age of the Internet* (1995) helped scholars understand how much people enjoy presenting themselves playfully on the web. Since *Life on the Screen* was published, it has become clear that people not only enjoy playful self-presentation as individuals but also have a wonderful time creating websites that represent nonexistent institutions.

8. Since completing my initial draft of this chapter, some (but not all) of the YouTube videos I observed have regrettably been removed from the site and are no longer viewable via the hyperlink information provided in this volume's master reference list. This is an unfortunate risk with documenting online media.

9. All message board verbiage is quoted as written, complete with misspellings.

10. In an effort to protect the identity of Internet commenters, I provide pseudonyms in place of their actual names or handles (hence my use of quotation marks upon first introducing an informant).

11. "XP" is an emoticon symbol meant to convey a grossed out/disgusted or vomiting facial expression. Turned 90 degrees clockwise, the image of an individual with tightly closed eyes and tongue hanging out is more easily identifiable.

12. A similar comment on tapeworms in comparison to *Alien* appeared on the Diets in Review site in December of 2009.

13. Although Aglietti's WormTherapy.com website provided information about ingestion of tapeworms and other worms through the spring of 2010, it currently offers information about hookworm and whipworm therapy with no mention of tapeworms.

14. A year after my conversation with Aglietti, in April of 2011, I started losing weight through the Jenny Craig weight-loss program, which offered weekly counseling sessions and online support (Jenny Craig Weight Loss Program 2011). After five months, I lost twenty pounds.

8

Love and War and Anime Art
An Ethnographic Look at a Virtual Community of Collectors

Bill Ellis

THE CONCEPT OF FOLK GROUPS HAS BEEN CENTRAL to academic folkloristics for many years. Originally, such groups were assumed to be illiterate,
preliterate, or simply not as literate as the academic elite who studied them.[1]
Alan Dundes boldly challenged this stereotype in 1965, declaring that "folk
groups" could be "any group of people whatsoever," so long as they shared
some common factor and developed traditions that gave their communities individual identity (1980, 6–7). "The folk" could include professionals, college professors, and even the most elite of scientists and engineers.
Since then, folklorists have tried to banish the stereotype of "the folk" as
the poorly educated topic of elite research, but, sadly, old habits of thinking
are difficult to break. With the emergence of the Internet, most Americans
now spend a considerable amount of time, both on the job and in leisure,
keeping in touch through the medium of typed text transmitted among
computers. Nevertheless, folklore theory stubbornly tends to define "folk
groups" as networks of people who meet face-to-face and share information
through spoken word and body language alone rather than through the
more sophisticated means of electronic media now in fashion. Yet such a
preference revives the old ethnocentric stereotype of "folk" meaning "ignorant" and implicitly condemns the discipline once again to the study of
obsolescent communities rather than to those that are vibrantly alive and
active in our midst.

David Pierpoint (screen name Sith Krillin), a Colorado PC technician and anime fan, created Anime-Beta, an online forum for anime art

DOI: 10.7330/9780874218909.c08   166

collectors, in April 2002.[2] Today it continues as a well-visited and cohesive virtual community. This chapter explores the multifaceted dynamics of symbolic interaction within this group, in which I have been actively involved since October 2004. Made up of a wide range of members, mostly in their late twenties and thirties with professional careers, the "Betarians" (as they refer to themselves) represent a lively group, passionate about their hobby but generally polite and respectful to each other and newcomers. Even so, the things they collect are not just rare but unique, and so anime art becomes, I argue, a type of fetish in both an imaginative and a social sense. Ownership means absolute possession of a specific, emotionally significant event in the narrative created by using the object. For this reason, possessing such an object invests the owners with equivalent social power among those sharing the same reverence for that narrative. No wonder competition among collectors is intense; yet the Anime-Beta community, with a few important exceptions, has remained relatively cohesive over time. What distinctive social customs account for this paradoxical camaraderie among highly competitive individuals, deadly enemies as an auction's close time approaches, but mutually cooperative fellows otherwise? I argue that the two instincts—competition and cooperation—are in fact not mutually exclusive but inextricably linked in a way common to many dynamics in folklore. I propose that they are mediated through a factor that I call "restitution," a social means of resolving the tension that the competitive act creates in a way that is seen as beneficial to the collectors' community at large.

After suggesting how pre-Internet folkloristics could be extended into the virtual realm, I briefly introduce the field of anime art collecting and provide a short history and demographic overview of the Anime-Beta community. I then examine the dynamics of this virtual community with the help of discussions posted on the forum and in personal surveys I have conducted, identifying the key values and tensions that characterize anime art collectors in general and draw them together as a group. Finally, I look in at several serious disagreements within Anime-Beta that led to public "flame wars" and observe what means were used to restore the group's sense of shared identity.

In so doing, I intend to not simply establish that Anime-Beta is a folk group motivated by the twin laws of innovation and conservatism, for the participants in this and similar web-based groups already know and feel this.

Rather, I intend to show how a close examination of the way this community's identity is performed and negotiated can give us insights into the social dynamics that keep such groups cohesive and viable. Restitution is a powerful cultural tool, one that allows individuals a carnivalesque license to be competitive and self-centered in building a collection while at the same time remaining on courteous terms with other enthusiasts who share their passion for the art. To some extent, this dual tension affects all self-aware communities, with the ambitions of its active members threatening to cause internal splits at the same time the desires of others to keep peace can succeed to the point that the group simply becomes uninteresting. For communities to work, the books need to balance: individual accomplishment needs to be valued but social power must be buffered with generosity to other collectors. When the balancing act works, the result can be intensely therapeutic to members and identity strongly felt. Using Richard Bauman's (1971) insightful concept of differential groups, I examine how this identity is *performed* by the members of Anime-Beta and suggest how restitution may well be a dynamic that helps unify other kinds of folk groups, virtual and traditional.

ONLINE COMMUNITIES AS FOLK GROUPS

American culture, as in many parts of the world, has been transformed by near-universal access to the Internet, either through computers or increasingly by smartphones. The primacy of oral discourse has given way to a new form of discourse that uses typed text rather than the spoken word, although often with distinctive typographical and nonverbal features that mimic body language and voice intonation. Within a few years of the emergence of e-mail, listserv networks developed around a wide range of interests, using a common server to reroute a member's message to fellow subscribers. And as the World Wide Web developed strategies for hosting bulletin boards, still more specialized groups formed around these as well.[3] The process continues, with Facebook and similar social networking mediums creating tightly focused groups that communicate with each other in an esoteric way. Nevertheless, many folklorists have found computer-mediated communities of minimal interest to the discipline, even though such communities clearly illustrate social principles that folklorists have observed in groups dominated by face-to-face oral discourse.

Some of this hesitation derives, understandably, from reliance on theoretical positions that were developed prior to the widespread use of computer-mediated messaging. Dan Ben-Amos's revolutionary definition of folklore as "artistic expression in small groups" called it a form of "communication [that] takes place in a situation in which people confront each other face to face" (1971, 12–13). As Trevor J. Blank notes, this qualification confuses the matter (2009b, 4): is the essence of folklore its content or the medium used to communicate it? Blank might also have noted that Ben-Amos had pointedly removed "oral transmission" from his definition. Insisting that "authentic" folklore is passed on only through "pure" illiterate social networks, Ben-Amos contended, was destructive to scholarship because it ignored "the real social and literary interchange between cultures and artistic media and channels of communication" (Ben-Amos 1971, 14). Nevertheless, Ben-Amos followed this bold statement by insisting that an item of folklore performed on television or printed in a book "ceases to be folklore because there is a change in its communicative context" (14). However, as Blank notes, defining folklore in terms of the medium of communication, purely and simply, means that such theories become obsolete as soon as new media, beyond the vision of the 1970s, become a mundane part of life for new generations (Blank 2009b, 6).

To begin with, one needs to define the characteristics of a folk group in terms that are independent of the media by which they interact and use for artistic expression. Assuming that technology is destructive to folklore, as Dundes (1980) argued, unintentionally reverts to the old notion that folk groups are in some significant way more primitive than the fully empowered elite. If folklorists truly accepted this idea, he noted, then folklore—along with its academic study—would pass into oblivion as the peasants of the world became educated and learned to use the latest technological tools (Dundes 1980, 6). But in reality, folklore was constantly emerging among all groups, urban and rural, lower class and elite, and the development of new media of communication stimulated and did not discourage the process. "So technology isn't stamping out folklore," Dundes concluded, "rather it is becoming a vital factor in the transmission of folklore and it is providing an exciting source of inspiration for the generation of new folklore" (1980, 17).

So what should scholars consider the primary factor in defining what kind of community can fruitfully be discussed as a folk group? One possibility is to focus on the role played by social networks in folklore transmission, as described by Linda Dégh in collaboration with her husband, Andrew Vázsonyi (1994 [1975]). Reacting to naïve notions that folklore passed through a culture in a random, homogenous way, Dégh and Vázsonyi

showed that in fact tightly knit conduits of specialists conserved most traditions. Certain individuals, they observed, are drawn to certain traditions—
tales, for example. Others may find such stories trivial or forgettable, but
those who find them appealing seek them out and collect them. Such storytellers, Dégh and Vázsonyi inferred, share a similar personality type, learn
their repertories from individuals of similar personality types, and pass them
on to still other congenial persons. So folklore, they conclude, involves the
formation of social networks of informants who specialize in and commit to
the preservation of a certain type of lore (Dégh and Vázsonyi 1994 [1975],
208–209). Gary Alan Fine (1992) later tested and refined their work in his
study of adolescent Little League baseball players, whom he found to circulate rumors and legends selectively along observable networks of friendships
and common interests.

But do all web-linked networks constitute folk groups? At first, the idea
seems dubious: since the emergence of virtual forums and e-mail listservs,
many networks have developed around common interests ranging from
politics to crafts. While one could say, following Dégh and Vázsonyi, that
all participants share a strong interest in a given topic and contribute information relating to it, does that in itself make their online interactions folklore? In most cases, individuals who subscribe to such online services arrive
bearing none of the traditional tokens that folklorists have used in the past
to define "folk." As Richard Bauman (1971) observed, "the folk" has often
been used to call attention to factors that unify a group in a superorganic
way, a tie that exists among all members independent of their conscious
sense of themselves as a group. These factors typically include ethnicity, religious training, occupation, age, or kinship (35). But typically, members of
virtual communities have few of these factors in common: scattered across
the globe, they bring a diverse range of ages, jobs, and backgrounds to the
group. Few of them have ever met face-to-face. Is a common interest and a
habit of regularly checking each others' messages enough to define them as
a folk group?

If these factors were all that linked such communities together, one
might well hesitate. But as Bauman points out, folklore is not "so much
baggage" that the group carries along abstractly with them through time and
space (1971, 33). One may share ancestry, or age, or kinship with other people and still choose not to participate in the same traditions that they preserve, or even be aware of them. Thus, Bauman has noted that within a society that shares many of the same cultural products, a diversity of *differential*

identities will form, in which a diversity of self-aware groups may form. To understand how we forge and maintain these identities, he stressed, one must look not at passively shared knowledge but rather at "particular relations and events" in which the performance of folklore makes such identity consciously felt. Such events do not take place exclusively within the group but are also performed in the sight of a larger populace, making one group's identity felt by contrast and perhaps even conflict with others who may be similar in interests and membership. Thus, Bauman observed, "folklore may be as much an instrument of conflict as a mechanism contributing to social solidarity" (1971, 38). By analyzing folklore as *action* rather than as content or membership, he concluded, researchers would "find the true locus of the interrelationship between the folklore and its bearers" (38). In much the same way, Dorothy Noyes has more recently (2003) argued that a "community" (a term she finds more apt than the more abstract "group") is a *felt* reality that is repeatedly enacted through individual performances and collective action (27–29). To that extent, she concludes, "identity is a performance" (28).

To summarize, a folk group is not a superorganic state of being, defined by its demographic status or the media with which its members communicate. Likewise, folklore cannot be subsumed by a preexisting list of "folk genres" studied by scholars in the past or the allegedly preliterate nature of its content. Rather, a folk group consists of the sum total of many self-conscious choices by individuals to interact in a distinctive way, and these observable acts constitute the *performance* of community. The most objective and beneficial way to study such folklore, as the most forward-looking folklorists in the pre-Internet days have suggested, would be to look closely at how and why individuals choose to participate in social networks such as Anime-Beta and at the particular situations and events that provoke the most participation, particularly at times when conflict and aggression are involved.

The specific subject matter of this study, moreover, has been anticipated by a number of important studies. By 1977 Alan Dundes had already identified folklore about computers as embodying the impact new technologies were having on the contemporary American world (1980 [1977], 17). The material he presented here, and in the various collections of "urban folklore from the paperwork empire" compiled with Carl R. Pagter (1978 [1975], 1987, 1991, 1996, 2000), challenged old conceptions of folk groups by showing that jokes, legends, and folk art were in common circulation among business professionals, academics, and computer programmers.[4] Similarly, Linda Dégh boldly asserted in *American Folklore and the Mass Media* (1994) that folklore disseminated through print or broadcast media remained folklore. She argued strongly against the notion that traditional discourse had been "contaminated and destroyed" by the influence of television and newspapers (10). By pointing out that gifted narrators had always combined material from oral and print sources, she further showed that the notion that folklore was properly the domain of illiterate cultures was inaccurate and short-sighted (21–22). And in proposing that there were forms of folklore that remained folklore, even when transmitted in print and televised form, Dégh went beyond even Ben-Amos's (1971) revolutionary redefinition of folklore.[5] Finally, Camille Bacon-Smith's 1992 ethnography of the intense subcultures that developed among fans of popular television series (such as *Star Trek*) present many of the dynamics that developed in the following decade among enthusiasts of Japanese anime. Her description of "circles" illustrates the process of differential identities nicely, especially as she notes that there may well be a number of these operating simultaneously among the followers of a given TV series.[6]

It is certainly true, as Brunvand (2004) and others have observed, that the availability of the Internet has facilitated the circulation of lore in radically novel ways. Many legend texts, he notes, are now "frequently forwarded" in verbatim or near-verbatim fixed texts rather than being recomposed through oral discourse. Certainly the assumption that Internet communications are closer to print mass media than to orality has deterred many folklorists from investigating the area closely (see Blank 2009b). And yet semioticians like Brenda Danet (2001) had no trouble in locating and documenting complex computer-mediated traditions of play, ranging from folk speech and impromptu games to sophisticated forms of folk art among the first generation of Internet users.

Likewise, Bruce Mason (2007) convincingly demonstrates the folk group status of the Middlesbrough List, a virtual community devoted to the fortunes of a British football team.[7] While conceding that participation in such a group involved a host of solitary acts, Mason finds that the interaction among widely dispersed supporters of the team mimicked many real-life festive events and allowed people to engage in highly social conversations, even when individuals were dispersed across many continents. Participants in such networks were hardly limited to geeky loners; like the members of any face-to-face folk group, their passionate interest in a single topic (the Middlesbrough football team) united them. Consequently, members generated a strong sense of communal identity through folk speech and shared esoteric knowledge and tolerance for the quirky and distinctive behavior of individuals in the group. Thus, the lively nature of virtual communities relies on the successful negotiation of social rules. These rules need to be orderly and consistent enough to make most participants (especially the occasional and passive members) comfortable about visiting, listening, and posting a comment once in a while. Yet they also need to leave room for playful chaos. Mason adopts a fruitful analogy from the Middlesbrough List: a successful virtual community is like a pub in which regulars become known for their quirks and special talents but where many others feel welcome to drop in and enjoy the social atmosphere.

The Anime-Beta community, however, is affected by a twist that makes it quite different from the Middlesbrough List. A common desire to see their team prevail united Mason's web-based participants, whereas members of Anime-Beta are divided by competition among themselves in matches where only one forum member can emerge triumphant. In addition, only one person at a time can possess unique artworks, so every victory is essentially an ultimate one. So the anime art-collecting community is distinctively different from other virtual groups, in both its core values and the social dynamics that mediate relations among members. Before discussing the strategies it has developed to maintain unity, therefore, it is necessary to first explore the reasons for collecting animation art and the incentives for collectors to socialize with each other in this virtual environment.

METHODOLOGY

I have been an active participant in the Anime-Beta forum since registering in October 2004. Like many collectors of this sort, I began as a solitary enthusiast, picking up art from a recent anime series (*Cardcaptor Sakura*) that had interested me because of its sophisticated use of folk materials.[8] Before long, I was communicating via e-mail with other such collectors, who recommended Anime-Beta as a convenient place to learn more about the fine points of animation art. Throughout my years as a Betarian, I have been an active participant in a number of threads dealing with topics controversial among collectors, which have at times prompted several dozen responses. These threads remain permanently archived on the forum site, and so I started by retrieving examples that discuss demographics or contentious issues in collecting animation art. Notable among these threads were several notorious "flame wars"[9] in which Betarians became sharply divided in opinion to the point where moderators eventually had to intervene and "lock" the thread, thus preventing any further discussion on the topic.

A second source of information on the Anime-Beta community is the forum's "Memberlist," which serves as a complete tally of all individuals who have registered on the site from its founding to the present. While the site contains no direct links to individuals' private identities, it does often include volunteered demographics such as age, gender, and place of residence. However, registration does not require one to disclose demographic information, and many members do not disclose such data in order to avoid having personal information accessed and abused by identity thieves or stalkers. The member listing does include continuously updated records of how many posts each member has contributed as well as the most recent time in which he or she last visited the site. The forum also used to have a statistical site that gave a snapshot of how many members have logged in during the last twenty-four hours as identified by their correlating screen names.[10] Accessing this information allowed me to identify key members who have been active in the community for five years or more as well as those who were currently the most active in visiting and posting.

On January 7, 2010, I announced my intention to write an ethnographic report about the anime art collectors' community in a prospectus posted on the blog associated with my online art gallery.[11] This received several positive responses from other collectors active in the Anime-Beta community, and, in time, I focused my attention on this group. A little over a year later, on February 21, 2011, I formally approached the Anime-Beta community, requesting permission from active members to discuss their social interactions in an academic publication. I also gave members the opportunity to opt out of the study by requesting that they contact me if they did not wish to be included in the study.[12] While no one asked to be excluded, I have cleared all quotes or references to individuals discussed herein before finalizing my draft. So, in collaboration with fellow participants in the Anime-Beta community, I present user screen names (or "handles"), discussion contents, quotes, themes, and site data (except when specified otherwise) unmodified from the way they appeared in their online context.[13]

MEETING THE BETARIANS IN CYBERSPACE

Japanese animation, or *anime*, began as a popular culture indigenous to that nation, but during the 1980s, many popular series were adapted into versions in major European languages and broadcast on children's cable networks in Europe and North and South America. In the English-speaking world, the major breakout occurred in the mid-1990s with the production of dubbed versions of *Sailor Moon* (1995) and *Dragon Ball Z* (1996), followed by the international popularity of the *Pokémon* series (1998). The overall fan base for anime grew rapidly in the United States from 1994 to 2004[14] and remains at a stable and economically significant level.

From the beginning, Japanese animators used a process similar to that developed by North American firms, particularly Fleischer Studios. Senior artists first work out the outlines of the animated scenes through key drawings, capturing the start and end points of the characters' motions along with extreme or significant moments along the way. Junior artists then design the *in-betweeners*, additional images that link the key moments together smoothly. During the classic period, these sketches were traced by hand on the back of transparent plastic sheets, but in the 1960s, this time-consuming process was eliminated with the help of a modified photocopy machine.[15] These sheets are called *cels*, a shortened form of *celluloid*, the type of transparent plastic used in classic animation.[16] Artists working from directions provided by the studio then fill in the printed outlines. In the end, these cels are photographed one by one against a hand-painted background, and, with the addition of effects and a soundtrack, this footage becomes the final broadcast form of the anime. These sketches, cels, and backgrounds constitute the animation art that fills enthusiasts' collections.

For many years, animation art did not provoke much interest among collectors. The numbers of cels used to make even a short subject were prodigious, and studios lacked both the storage capacity and the interest to preserve them. In the early days, the art was even cleaned off the plastic sheets so they could be reused. Animation employees were allowed to take home art they liked, and gift shops at Disneyland sold cels for minimal prices as souvenirs. This began to change in 1984 when New York auction house Christie's held a special auction of classic Disney cels that had been preserved by a former employee. Much to Disney's and the auction house's surprise, the lots sold for unprecedented prices, and Disney, taking the lesson to heart, began hosting a series of "The Art of . . ." auctions hosted by Sotheby's. Good examples of American animation art, particularly from classic Disney productions such as *Snow White and the Seven Dwarfs* or *Fantasia*, now might sell for tens of thousands of dollars.[17] By contrast, in Japan, anime remains a disreputable industry, and adults interested in the material are disparaged as *otaku*, a derogatory term used by Japanese to imply a socially isolated person whose interest in anime (or another hobby) is obsessive.[18] Hence, the market for animation art within Japan is modest and has actually experienced its most significant growth outside the country. Most pieces of anime art sell for under $100 and top out around $2,000 to $3,000. The newly emerged interest in anime, combined with affordable prices, attracts a wide range of enthusiasts who find it possible to put together collections from well-known anime series quickly and with relatively little expense.

Computer-based networks of anime art collectors formed relatively early during the emerging interest in anime among young people. The first really influential message board devoted to anime art collecting, Animanga, was launched in May 1997 as a sidelight to a website dealing in cels and other anime-related merchandise. However, the more recently founded Anime-Beta has proven to be uniquely durable in comparison to other virtual communities focused on anime art collecting.[19] The core group of Anime-Beta's community originally became acquainted through a short-lived forum called Anime-Alpha, which went live in 2001. The discussions were primarily centered around art from the series *Dragon Ball Z*, and then grew to include other series like *Sailor Moon* that were gaining popularity among youngsters through syndication on the Cartoon Network channel at the time. Unfortunately, this community proved unstable. Anime-Alpha's webmaster became embroiled in a personal dispute with a number of members. In the end, several people were banned (i.e., blocked from participation) at the webmaster's discretion, and when their fellow participants spoke up for them, they found themselves banned as well. The dissident group formed Anime-Beta as an alternative, registering 54 members in its first month (April 2002) and 175 members in its first year. Most of the remaining active members of the original forum gravitated over to the new group. Before long, Anime-Alpha ceased to exist.

The newly coalesced group at Anime-Beta grew quickly and remained much more stable than any of its rivals. According to records maintained on the website, new members joined steadily for several years, with 2006 marking the high point (198 new members). From 2007 on, the rate of growth slowed markedly, with only 36 new registrations in 2011. The slower rate of joins, combined with the attrition of older active members, has been noted with some concern by long-time Betarians. Nevertheless, activity remains brisk among collectors within the Anime-Beta community, and it has become the chosen meeting place for enthusiasts in this field: "Simply put, this forum is THE place to discuss and learn about anime production art," Macron One (M 31) commented.

Who are these Betarians? One would expect them to match the fan base of anime itself, which is rather young: a recent survey indicated that three-quarters of anime fans were twenty-five or younger and had been introduced to the genre by age fifteen (Kinsella 2009). But in fact, most collectors join Anime-Beta during their mid- to late twenties, with a significant number being thirty years and up. New members often commented on this maturity in responses to my survey (see appendix B). One such newbie,[20] theultimatebrucelee (M 21), commented that "members here are generally more organized and advanced in life, life style (income, knowledge, point of view, opinion) and are more respectful towards each other." He added, "probably age in general plays a large factor." Another new member, Sky Rat (F 28) also stressed the group's sophistication: "I continue visiting Beta because there are a lot of really experienced collectors there so I continually learn things and if I have any questions there is usually at least one person there who can give me some insight."

When the forum was founded in 2002, long-time members recall, males were the dominant gender, but by 2004 females had become the majority.[21] The female contingent grew from 52 percent to 56 percent in 2005, to 65 percent in 2008, and to 69 percent by 2011.[22] Members who describe themselves as "married" have always been outnumbered by those describing themselves as "not married," though the difference has lessened over time. Married members numbered only 25 percent in 2005, but this faction increased to 39 percent in 2008 and to 41 percent in 2011. A thread asking, "What do you do for a living?"[23] inspired answers describing a wide range of professions. Some members, especially younger ones, shared that they either attend college or hold entry-level positions in customer service, waitressing, and factory work; but most Betarians told of working in professional occupations that require higher education, such as financial brokerage or medicine. The forum's respect for members' privacy does not permit a more specific description, but it seems clear that Betarians are predominantly female, mostly unmarried, typically in their mid-twenties to thirties,

well educated, and in professional careers. Like the adopted social rules of
Anime-Beta, community members take their chosen hobby very seriously.
Certainly they are quite different from the shy, self-isolated, naïve Internet
addict negatively characterized by critics of otaku.[24]

Anime-Beta members engage in a healthy mix of activities. Enough
posts take place so that there is always something new on the site, but not
every member feels obligated to be conspicuous.[25] In fact, the overall health
of the forum depends less on how often the most vocal members posted
comments as on how many people continue to check in regularly and pay
attention to the discussion. On this front, despite the apparent drop in
activity, Anime-Beta remains in good health.

WHAT BRINGS COLLECTORS TOGETHER?

One explanation is self-evident: the art itself, of course. If the objects
collected are unique and distributed through a limited number of auction
sites and dealers, then serious enthusiasts will inevitably encounter each
other again and again; in time, they are bound to recognize each others'
specific interests and tactics. Some of this involves self-interest; indeed, the
more one knows about one's rivals, the more alertly one can outsmart them
during a sale. Still, the forging of relationships among collectors is beneficial
to the hobby itself. Collectors sell as well as buy. ReiTheJelly (F 27) describes
Anime-Beta as "a natural podium for people hawking their goods," adding,
"It allows me access to personal gallery sales which I otherwise wouldn't hear
about, and it also offers me the opportunity to reach hundreds of people
whenever I have items for sale."

Other members attribute their lasting interest in the community to the
hobby-specific information that is regularly shared in discussions, particularly warnings about deceptive sellers. Naturally, authenticity is an essential
issue in the art collecting community. While forgeries are not as common
in anime art (mainly because prices remain too modest to justify the labor),
occasional instances of fakery do occur and are discussed at length within
the community forum. Beyond discussing or alerting peers of potential
fraud, members also utilize the forum to ask technical questions about the
fine points of anime art and its conservation. As a result, one member might
learn a useful piece of information by reading posts, and another might gain
status by showing his or her expertise. The user JWR (M 53) confirms this:
"It is important to share information. I have learned a lot about the in's &

out's of this hobby from reading threads here and likewise have been able to add things that I have knowledge and experience in."

In short, Anime-Beta attracted collectors because it was an effective conduit for knowledge specific to anime art. Dégh and Vázsonyi (1994 [1975]) made quite similar points about storytellers who shared an intense interest in collecting and conserving certain types of narratives. There is an important difference, however: anime art is an artifact of the mass media and not a type of folk art created by an artisan using traditional subjects or means of fabrication. So a network that focuses on preserving and appreciating anime art is different in kind from a conduit that shares ballads or folktales. Also, the knowledge generated by collectors on how to find, display, and conserve art does not at first seem to constitute folklore, as much of it is derived from the practice of professional archivists and librarians. Yet if we accept the premise that social networks mediated by computers can (potentially) be as binding and cohesive as those that use print and broadcast media, clearly the anime art–collecting community can become just as valid a folk conduit as any studied by Dégh and other traditional folklorists. What is necessary, however, is to discern which activities are most controlled by the interplay between individual choice and the formalization that takes place as the members of the community develop and maintain common values. We must keep in mind Bauman's insistence that folklore research needs to be based not on abstract generalities of what folklore is and what it is not but on observed interactions that present the relevance of enacted traditions to people in a direct, empirical way (1971, 33).

The nature of collectors' impulse to collect has been examined by a number of intellectuals, notably cultural critic Susan Stewart (1993) and communication scholars Brenda Danet and Tamar Katriel (1994). Stewart observes the compulsive need of collectors to impose some pattern of organization on the items they collect, cataloguing them or arranging them elaborately in display cases. She argues that while individual items, or souvenirs, are metonymic replacements for significant moments in history, the collection is a metaphor for the individual's perception of the world. While a souvenir captures a moment of historical time, a collection is an expression of *classification*, an attempt to transcend the realm of temporality by making all time simultaneously present in a microcosmic way (Stewart 1993, 151). In so doing, she continues, the objects are removed from their original contexts and are given a new, often playful significance within the collector's world (156). Superficially, this suggests that hobbyists are often motivated by an irrational desire to amass quantities of seemingly trivial objects, classify them in self-generated hierarchies, and display them neatly as a means of imposing order on a small part of their disorderly lives.

Such criticism may at times be valid: hoarders are obsessive in a self-destructive way. But Stewart draws a distinction between irrational collectors who simply accumulate goods for their own sake and true collectors who consider the systems they generate as more important than the individual objects themselves (1993, 154). And indeed, considering collectors as obsessive pack rats, like similar stereotypes leveled at otaku and members of Internet communities, ignores the sources of passion that drive such communities. Danet and Katriel (1994) concede that some collectors can be obsessive organizers; however, they argue that the order-focused approach to collecting ignores the very factors that most collectors identify as the source of their passion. These include the unpredictable course of finding and acquiring objects and the ways in which the objects, once acquired, serve as "a springboard to fantasy" (Danet and Katriel 1994, 24–29).

Paradoxically, then, the pleasure of collecting requires a continuing tension between rational and irrational emotions. This tension, begun in the suspenseful process of collecting anime art, is perpetuated through owners' intensely personal connections to the art objects they own. Both sources find the anthropological concept of *fetishism* central to their analysis of these strong emotions. In its strict anthropological sense, a fetish is a power object created in an unofficial magical or religious practice, but by extension it can mean any tangible object that embodies a single, intensely meaningful experience (Ellis 2003, 18–19).[26] Marxist, psychoanalytical, and postmodern critics appropriated the term for a very wide range of meanings, but the more focused anthropological sense is germane to the collector's instinct, especially if the objects sought after are not just rare but unique, representing moments of time in a much cherished work of art. As Stewart comments, "the object's position in a system of referents . . . and not any intrinsic qualities of the object . . . determines its fetishistic value" (1993, 163–164). That is, for some enthusiasts, the primary value of the collected object does not reside in any intrinsic value but rather in the way it allows the owner to link to some intensely meaningful historical or creative act—in much the same way that the collector of sports paraphernalia would find the most value in owning the actual baseball that was involved in a memorable moment in a championship game.

Anime art collectors do accept the need to keep their collections well organized, but their passion for the hobby comes from a much more disorderly emotion. Danet and Katriel (1994), relying more directly on social science research, give more emphasis to the way fetishism tends "to attribute the features of living beings to inanimate objects" (29), which likewise honors the dynamic quality that hobbyists find in their most cherished finds. Remembering that animation art is a way of giving an illusion of life to a series of still images, it is predictable that anime art collectors tend to see their objects as having a life of their own. So the process of accumulating a gallery of such objects relies on and indeed encourages a rich appreciation of imaginative links, making the Betarian mind a more complicated place than Stewart's (1993) order-based approach might at first suggest.

According to Danet and Katriel, collectors tend to use five root metaphors to explain their fascination with the objects they collect:

1. Collecting is hunting.
2. Collecting is therapy.
3. Collecting is passion, desire.
4. Collecting is a disease.
5. Collecting is supernatural experience. (1994, 36)

Danet and Katriel contend that the first, third, and fourth metaphors are the most common. Collectors often refer to the "thrill of the hunt" to describe the intense excitement and pleasure associated with tracking down and acquiring a piece of art; rhetorically, this also suggests the collectors' awareness that "the hunt" is capable of turning dangerous, becoming an obsession or even an addiction. Conversely, Danet and Katriel observe that the second and fifth metaphors, collecting as a relaxing and calming pastime with spiritual or quasi-religious overtones, are less common. To test Danet and Katriel's (1994) conclusions, I asked Anime-Beta members to propose a metaphor for their love for anime art collecting. However, I did not offer the five root metaphors at the outset so that the comparisons offered would be original and specific to the Anime-Beta community. Betarians' answers did fit into Danet and Katriel's five root metaphors, but with interesting variations.

First, I found that Betarians *did* frequently invoke metaphors to describe their love of collecting cels or other anime art as a kind of hunt. JWR (M 53) was the most explicit: he described collecting anime art as "The thrill of the hunt followed by the joy of 'bagging and tagging' the rarest of beasts, the

A1 End."[27] The hunting metaphor neatly combines the competitive pastime of the sport, in which hunters have to match wits not only with their wily quarry but with their rivals, who see the event as a chance for bragging rights with the help of luck, craft, and a little treachery. But hunting involves both aggression and the willingness to take life, and in many cases risk one's own life. In fact, as we will see, there are times when "war," rather than the relatively benign "hunt," is the more apt metaphor to describe the tensions raised within the Anime-Beta community. For this reason, it is significant that more often members described *nonviolent* forms of hunting, which might better be termed *searches*, *challenges*, or *quests*. Key member jcaliff (F 36) said:

> It's like going to estate sales . . . you have to dig through piles of crap to find something worthwhile that gives you a sense of accomplishment when you finally find it.[28]

Another key member, GuyvarIII (M 28), compared the activity to "buying an incomplete jigsaw puzzle" that led the owner both to appreciate the beauty of the individual pieces but also wonder how they fit together into the whole. Both the "estate sale" and "jigsaw puzzle" images mute the competitive aspect of the activity at hand: here the challenge is to not best a rival collector but develop the mindset needed to discern the value in a mass of otherwise worthless materials, or the pattern implied by the decontextualized objects one obtains.

In addition, on more than one occasion, respondents used Danet and Katriel's third and fourth root metaphors, calling fellow Betarians "passionate" about their hobby. Cordelia (F 30) commented that it was "like eating warm chocolate fudge with vanilla ice-cream" while duotrouble (F 39) added (with a "grinning devil" emoticon) "you know what they say about chocolate."[29] At times this passion has verged into becoming what many collectors allude to as an "addiction." This metaphor is sometimes invoked humorously as a festive celebration of collectors' willingness to surrender to the unpredictable, deeply emotional, and therefore exhilarating elements of the collecting world. But in truth, some collectors have gotten themselves into serious financial straits by overindulging in their "habit"; they find that the intense pleasure of winning or owning objects with such intense psychological significance leads them into an unhealthy addiction, in which they find themselves desiring one wish list item after another.

This was dramatized recently on Anime-Beta in a thread started by gonzai (F 48), a key member, who announced that she was considering "making a gynormous[30] purchase" and started a light-hearted poll on how she would raise the money: hang out at the local red-light district, cancel her heat and electrical service, or buy cases and cases of ramen.[31] The first responses took the thread as facetious: star-phoenix (F 29) commented, "Definitely know how you feel, and definitely went with the Ramen! I have done that before quite a few times ["smiley" emoticon]." But as the thread developed, members began to add seriously concerned messages, noting that a diet of ramen noodles could lead to malnutrition and urging the starter of the thread to consider the purchase carefully if it really did mean a sacrifice of money needed for food and shelter. This led gonzai to return, reassuring everyone that she did not seriously plan to invite her granddaughters into a cold house. Yet even she conceded that one of her previous purchases had been a financial hardship: "As much as I loved the artwork, it set me back for quite a while . . . Ate my share of ramen at that time." And star-phoenix added that she had once refrained from purchasing art for an entire year in order to pay off a major acquisition. "I am just as horribly addicted as the next person here!" she concluded, adding, "It takes a lot of self control!" Certainly most forum members acknowledge that the chance to make an important purchase can be both an opportunity for peak pleasure and a dangerous surrender to emotion with long-term consequences.

Most importantly, while Danet and Katriel assert that the "collecting is therapy" metaphor is "the least likely . . . to find expression in discourse about collecting" (1994, 40), I actually found it to be the *most* common metaphor espoused by the Anime-Beta community. In addition, I frequently found this metaphor colored by the fifth root metaphor, "collecting is supernatural experience," for anime art enthusiasts frequently express deeply spiritual rationales for their enthusiasm. In a thread discussing the underlying motives of collectors,[32] nene (F 24) volunteered:

> For me, the cel usually sparks up a good memory and I associate that good feeling to the cel everytime I look at it. Owning that piece is like creating a piece of magick and subsequent purchases in the same field are similar to continuing to build on that positive magickal energy.[33]

Such metaphors are founded in the liminal status of the objects collected, which gain power by being representations of transformative fantasies set in imaginary worlds. So seeking and possessing much-desired pieces of anime art is, for collectors, a way of training imagination in a manner that they find both therapeutic and spiritually fulfilling.

There is a paradoxical tension here: participation in fantasy has long been seen as an isolating pastime in which individuals retreat from their real worlds and instead indulge themselves in imaginary ways, in a way that ultimately makes them less and less able to socialize with others. Yet as anthropologist John L. Caughey (1984) observes, imaginary experiences are a normal part of most people's everyday lives, and they have immediate impacts on their real world conduct and social relations. To assume that fantasy is intrinsically trivial, he asserts, "is in itself a cultural myth" (29). In fact, many cultures (especially in Asia) creatively use imaginary worlds to work through internal problems. Western cognitive therapists also use such strategies to encourage individuals to restructure negative self-images, Caughey documents, "with reportedly major effects on waking mental health and social relations" (1984, 252). As child psychologist Claire Golomb (2011) concludes, fantasy worlds are themselves liminal realms, both real and unreal. They are unreal in that they are set in a faraway time and location, but in content they relate "problems and conflicts that all children face" and are grounded in dynamics that are at once familiar and safely projected into a nominally "unreal" world (Golomb 2011, 159). Folklorists Yvonne J. Milspaw and Wesley K. Evans (2010) make a similar point about the fantasy worlds generated by participants in role-playing video games. The world in which participants place themselves is not a wholly imaginary one with randomly determined rules but rather a realm in which real-life problems are made visible in a lucid, simplified way (211–212).[34]

So the distinctive popularity of the "therapy" and "supernatural" metaphors shows that members of the Anime-Beta community feel themselves as sharing a deeply felt personality type and engaging in a communal form of storytelling that they find enjoyable and individually and socially beneficial. This, more than the mere opportunity to learn about or purchase artwork, is the "common factor" that participants share. And so Anime-Beta, in its deep emotions, is in fact quite similar to the network of storytellers studied by Dégh and Vázsonyi (1994 [1975]), as both personality types instinctively form a tightly knit folk conduit that values the therapeutic and transformative value of imagination. A closer look at the interactions among members suggests ways in which this "therapy" works.

"SPRINGBOARDS TO FANTASY": COLLECTING AS COLLECTIVE THERAPY

Why should anime art collecting be seen as therapy? One reason is that the most competitive side of collecting naturally takes place in isolation, as enthusiasts seek out desirable items and then lie quietly in wait to win them at the lowest possible price. But in a healthy personality, an isolating factor creates an equal and opposite desire to socialize with other collectors. So in a paradoxical way, the very intensity of the hobby's competitive side encourages intense partnerships among those who share the same interests. A second isolating factor is the nature of the material collected: it is subject to "intrinsic vice," or the tendency of art made from inexpensive media to deteriorate if not stored carefully. Thus, collections are typically stored in controlled environments, out of direct light, and are infrequently put on display, even in the owner's home. When one adds that even the most popular anime series remain relatively unfamiliar among the general American population, it is evident that collecting anime art can be personally very energizing yet intensely isolating at the same time.

An informal poll held on Anime-Beta in February 2008 showed that about three-quarters of collectors had never shown their collections to more than twelve people in all, with 44 percent admitting that they had shared their treasures with at most just four other friends. In the thread that accompanied this poll, members repeatedly mentioned their frustration at not being able to explain to others why these art objects were so valuable to them.[35] One key member of Anime Beta, jcaliff (F 36), feels this alienation strongly enough to include the conclusion of a Shel Silverstein children's poem in her signature:

> Hector the Collector loved these things with all his soul,
> Loved them more than shining diamonds, loved them more than
>   glistenin' gold.
> Hector called to all the people, "Come and share my treasure
>   trunk!"
> And all the silly sightless people came and looked . . . and called it
>   junk.[36]

For this reason, collectors find it psychologically reassuring to participate in a community that implicitly understands and shares their intense interest in the objects they seek out. Members who lack "real-world" friends who understand what makes anime art special find it especially important to maintain social ties with fellow collectors. "Many friends don't understand the interest in anime or cels," Goldknight (F 36) comments, "so I like that I have this place [Anime-Beta] to come to and discuss all the aspect of this fun hobby and not feel self conscious about it."[37] Such contacts among enthusiasts often develop into close alliances and long-lasting friendships, making the community stable in the long term.

In many cases, participants had been members of other online groups before registering on the forum. I asked members to explain their loyalty to Anime-Beta rather than gravitating to other available options. Most responded that they considered the participants on the forum to be "old friends" rather than simply fellow collectors. "I have been able to meet many nice people that I still keep in contact to this day from 2003," star-phoenix (F 29) comments. Key member blueheaven (M 33) adds, "I figure if [old friends] can find the time to drop a thought every so often, then so can I." Participants who find significant others who share their interests may more easily resolve this tension, but those who lack such face-to-face contacts may naturally seek out a virtual community like Anime-Beta in order to fulfill their psychological needs. For example, even a couple who shared their enthusiasm for the hobby with each other under the joint screen name Angelic-Lair (M 34 and F 27) add, "we still seek feedback from others [on the site] and we can't get that in the 'real world.'"

Comments such as these reflect a hunger for social interaction and a willingness to tolerate the friction caused by the hobby's competitiveness in the interest of a common good. Goldknight (F 36) made this clear: "People come and go, but the dynamic remains the same. There will always be a bit of conflict with so many different personalities and nationalities, but the goal remains the same." pixie_princess (F 32) gave a remarkably balanced description of the virtual community that had developed around the forum:

> It may sound sort of goofy, but in most cases there exists a certain amount of comradery between groups of users. We have common interests in so far as series that we enjoy (at times) or anime genres as well as the shared interest in animation art. A large portion of the folk here are pretty friendly, and most seem honest. It's such a small community and most of the time there is at least something interesting being discussed.

In short, by sharing a common factor (passion for collecting anime art), the members of Anime-Beta generate the intimacy and personal relationships among themselves that folklorists have shown to be integral to the self-generated identity of a folk group. Such groups form because they embody positive social and psychological functions for their members, so it makes sense that collectors would find the mutual reinforcement of an online community therapeutic. In other words, collectors may hunt in solitary, but they seek out and enjoy the collective support of the group.

The metaphors offered by other collectors point to a second way in which the activity was internally beneficial: by providing what Danet and Katriel call a "springboard to fantasy" (1994, 29), the art objects encourage owners to use their imaginations in a richer, more fulfilling way. Such images highlight the essentially liminal quality of the art objects. For instance, Macron One (M 31) explains, "It's like going backstage and getting a chance to meet and greet my favourite movie stars." Of course, a movie star is a real person with liminal qualities whose performance allows audience members to indulge their imaginations by participating in the make-believe action of the film. But a cel is a physical object, not a real person, and so the metaphor in fact represents a redoubled fantasy idea: two-dimensional anime art is like a three-dimensional human being who enacts a fictional three-dimensional character on a two-dimensional movie screen. In much the same way, Susan Stewart saw the attraction of an individual souvenir as being a "partial double," or metonymic reference to an object that was part of a larger experience—for example, a ribbon from a corsage worn at a memorable romantic evening (1993, 136). And yet a cel is an especially potent souvenir as it evokes a "partial triple" metonym based on the liminal qualities of the image. A cel or sketch is a flat object that projects a strong sense of three-dimensionality through commonly used artistic strategies of perspective and foreshortening. A photographed image of it is projected onto a movie screen—another flat object that acts as a window into a fictive three-dimensional world that is often realistically portrayed through clever cinematography and special effects. Both use visual tricks to engage the viewer's imagination, which in turn opens a doorway into a fantasy world created in collaboration by the artists who create the image and the audience members who allow themselves to be engrossed[38] or emotionally captivated by the narrative.

Many other Betarians related their interest to an enjoyable memory of engagement with a specific moment in the anime narrative. irmgaard (F 30) likened looking at a cel to "rereading a passage I particularly liked, was moved by, or thought was well done, in a story I enjoyed or found interesting. I can appreciate it just by itself; but it also alludes to the larger piece as well, bringing back pleasurable memories." Other cases emphasized the context of the aesthetic experience. "It brings out the kid in me!" exclaimed eyes0nme19 (F 25), adding, "Art collecting is like saying I don't want to grow up." Cordelia (F 30) called a cel "a keepsake for [her] memories." On the one hand, possessing a cel from a memorable scene elicits the same response as when she watched the episode for the first time, and at the same time it "reminds me of my student days . . . watching the anime with my sibling and talking about it with friends . . . happy times." So the successful acquisition of a desired piece of anime art is liminal in several ways: it mimics a window into an alternative world; it provides a vivid reminder of an especially meaningful moment in a much-loved story; or it incites an intensely vivid memory of childhood. Here again, Stewart's comments on the souvenir are relevant, for she notes that we normally use such objects to evoke a voluntary memory of childhood—not, to be sure, one's historical past but "a childhood voluntarily remembered, a childhood manufactured from its material survivals" (1993, 145).

"LIKE CREATING A PIECE OF MAGICK": ANIME ART AS FETISH

Anime art objects are not simply images to be appreciated for their color, composition, and perspective but are opportunities for nostalgic reflection and creative use of imagination. This reaction is strikingly similar to psychological studies of children exposed to various types of popular media, including action-oriented cartoons and classic fairy tales (see Singer and Singer 2000; Valkenburg 2004). The latter, researchers found, elicited a distinctively different reaction: subjects became "silent, very subdued and self-absorbed . . . the fairy tales seemed to have touched the children's inner concerns and left them in a pensive mood" (Golomb 2011, 163). Anime plots, like those of classic folktales, act by identifying psychological problems and conflicts faced by children (and many adults), so collecting objects that exercise the owner's imaginative abilities in the same way can be logically recognized and repeatedly used as a form of therapy.

Danet and Katriel (1994), while noting that collectors use metaphors of supernatural experience less frequently than others, quote a number of examples that relate to the magical realms invoked by anime plots: collectables "cast a sort of spell" or "bewitch" the would-be owner. Such comparisons "call up associations of positively toned transformation," they conclude, evoking travel "outside of the ordinary frame of experience" (48). It is not surprising to find such metaphors more frequently among anime art collectors, for a cel embodies a concrete bit of a story that viewers are supposed to imagine taking place in a fantasy world. Obviously, one cannot physically enter the magical world of Sailor Moon and share her adventures. But one can, in a very real sense, *own* Sailor Moon by actually possessing one of the images that was in fact used to create the popular series.[39]

In this sense, animation art is a liminal object serving as a "doorway," the literal meaning of the Latin root. The collected objects are both ownable artifacts as well as objects of imagination, inviting their owners to use their creative powers to revisit the original contexts of the collected objects. A flat object made of plastic and paint, a cel nevertheless provides a doorway through which its owner can enter an imaginative world. The physical object undergoes a semiotic transference of symbolic value and subsequently reminds the viewer of its context within the original anime series in which it appears. Indeed, many collectors are obsessive about locating "their cel" by identifying the episode and scene number in which it appears. But in a more imaginative sense, seeking out their cel also allows owners to pretend or fantasize as though they were actually a part of the anime plot.

The anime itself is a liminal realm that invites viewers to identify with the protagonist. The plots of many anime series include references to Japanese and Western fairy tales in a way that signals that they, too, are exploring psychological issues in the same ways (Ellis 2009).[40] Folklorist Nicoloe Farrell (2009) in fact suggests that one reason the long-running series *Inuyasha* proved so popular with youngsters is that it introduced a wide range of previously unfamiliar, exotic cultural motifs within a fairy tale structure that had "a sort of universal, cross-cultural appeal" (244–245). Folktales captivate audiences because they have the power to embody psychological conflicts faced by many people; anime enlarges that power by introducing new kinds of characters with magical capabilities. Logically, then, it makes sense as to why many people—adults as well as adolescents—find engaging with anime fantasies to be deeply therapeutic. Protagonists in anime plots are often placed in dilemmas that they must overcome—not through physical prowess but through understanding emotions and achieving maturity.

In tangible, purchasable form, anime artwork symbolizes a meaningful narrative about its origins, evolving significance, and physical journey into the present. A play frame lets the cel's possessor comprehend values that would otherwise be difficult to grasp by using the object's place in a larger, implied narrative to influence social relationships (Ellis 2004, 19). Likewise, the fetishistic qualities of anime art are made stronger when the character collected is one that its owner can use imaginatively as a kind of avatar while seeking to overcome real-life challenges. Sui Kune (F 24) makes this point clearly:

> Cel collecting to me is feeling like I'm closer to the character in question. The main character I collect is really close to me, since I have a similar chronic illness. I can't even describe how good it feels to have pieces of her, and of history from the show.

In a long, expressive post, key member cutiebunny (F 30) makes a similar point even more directly. She compares collecting anime art to "Being something that, currently, I cannot be," then elaborates:

> I collect a lot of artwork from titles that incorporate spiritual elements into their characters and/or plot. I gravitate to characters that, through suffering, overcome their limitations and, spiritually speaking, evolve.
>
> But, at least right now, I can't do this. I work in a line of work that, in its most absolute sense, is destructive . . . If you internalize your emotions, you'll die. I can't tell you how many good coworkers I've seen die from stress related conditions in my seven-odd years at [my position].
>
> I look at my gallery, often, at work. I gaze at the images of Sailor Moon as she struggles against evil, or maybe of Sakura[41] as she uses another card to save the day, and I see genuine instances of good triumphing over evil. It calms me. It gives me a goal in life, that, once I'm able to retire, to be the person that I really want to be and not the one that, for the sake of employment, I have to be.

cutiebunny combines the "therapy" analogy with the "supernatural experience" root metaphor that Danet and Katriel (1994) felt was less common among other hobby groups. But it makes sense that this comparison would appear among anime art collectors. Anime does in fact regularly incorporate mythological elements, showing characters in contact with mystical beings, and even incorporating the deities from other cultures in a kind of mythological *bricolage*. So in some ways, collectors' fascination with certain characters and plots suggests the recent popularity of Neo-Pagan religious circles whose members form personally significant mythologies by using elements from a wide range of traditions, both ancient and modern. Folklorist Sabina Magliocco (2004) argues that the religious experience of such groups is not simply a form of cultural tourism but serves to reclaim "traditional ways of knowing that privilege the imagination" (97). Like

Caughey (1984) and Golomb (2011), Magliocco argues that imagination is not opposed to rationality but is central to maintaining psychological health since it "possesses its own inner logic that complements or enhances linear thought" (2004, 97). In short, using anime art in a therapeutic way allows collectors to expand their imaginative grammar,[42] thereby enhancing their abilities to use their imagination in profoundly transformative ways.

Others adapted the "hunting" or "questing" metaphor in an explicitly spiritual direction, turning the activity into a mythological or even a religious vocation. When I first proposed the "metaphor" thread on Anime-Beta, star-phoenix (F 29) at once exclaimed:

> HAHA! I can probably name one of the theoretical metaphors right now with my answer right here. For me it is like finding the lost city of Atlantis!

Atlantis is not only a reflection of an ancient Greek myth but also a lively motif in contemporary New Age beliefs and adventure stories, notably Jules Verne's *Twenty Thousand Leagues Under the Sea* (1870) and The Walt Disney Studio's 2001 animated film *Atlantis: The Lost Empire*. So comparing the search for anime art with finding the much-sought landmark makes the quest both epic and a kind of pilgrimage.

Another newer member, Benoit Spacher (M 32), began his metaphor by factually describing one goal of collecting—to gather and preserve primary documents from this genre for the future—but then plunged off the springboard into mythic imagery, referring to a "golden era" of animation art and saying that curators were "in fact some kind of century's end savior."[43] This time, the allusion is to an anime series in which the protagonist attempts to preserve some semblance of society from the surrounding ruins and chaos. Spacher felt this scenario was a good analogy to the way in which anime art collectors attempted to gather and conserve the scattered artifacts of the final era of fully hand-drawn animation, in the expectation that later on they would come to be valued by museums and art historians as having both artistic and cultural integrity.

So collecting is not just personally fulfilling to its participants but also a kind of magical quest, even a holy cause to find and preserve artifacts of tremendous significance and internal energy. The loner may be successful in hunting rare beasts, fighting fierce battles, finding treasure in unexpected places, solving vexing puzzles, and discovering lost cities—all motifs integral to folktales in all cultures, I might note. But to become a "savior," one must have a community to save. The hero must be recognized and admired for his or her prowess, not merely envied as the possessor of great fortune. And so in realistic terms, the "hunt" merges into a collaborative quest, in which the community shares in the thrill of victory. One person gains possession of the art object but in turn shares it with others and encourages others to fulfill their own quests. Such metaphors, of course, exaggerate the importance of anime art for effect, but in doing so, they affirm that they are fetish objects, invested with the aura of the fantasy from which they form a part, and that they are socially powerful objects.

"BLACK HOLE COLLECTORS": POWER AND RESTITUTION

Regardless of how expensive or inexpensive it may be, every piece of anime art is unique, making it an autographic object (see Douglas 1994, 12). While some examples of popularly collected objects may be extremely rare, they all exist as a group of copies. So while a collector who obtains a rare stamp or sports card in a desirable condition may be considered "lucky" or fortunate by uninitiated peers, the nature of the hobby is such that always other collectors possess an identical object. To this point, anthropologist Mary Douglas (1994) notes that some collectors are not satisfied with a nice item: they seek out *the* item—a one-of-a-kind object that gains its charisma from its origins in a moment of creative power that is artistically or historically important, or both. The most exclusive part of collecting sports memorabilia deals not just with autographs of famous athletes but with the objects—bats, balls, and uniforms—that players "actually used" during a moment or event perceived to be of symbolic importance. In such cases, the particular object's physical presence at a specific place and time invests it with a kind of magical power. As Douglas asserts, "Control is at stake in both issues," and so autographic rituals and objects are more strongly perceived as being genuinely *possessed* by their recipients (1994, 14–15). For this reason, an especially beautiful cel from a significant moment in an anime series becomes both an object of desire and a source of potential discord. The magic that resides in it for collectors also involves significant risk. The competitive nature of anime art collecting, carried to an extreme, can be destructive to the sense of mutually supportive community that is central to collectors' groups.

Mindful of the occasionally contentious effect of anime art collecting, participants in the Anime-Beta forum have developed a keen sense of what sorts of behaviors are discouraged. An interesting thread titled "What's your cel collecting pet peeve"[44] articulated many such behaviors. Clearly, buyers expect to conclude deals on favorable terms and take possession of their artwork quickly; sellers expect potential buyers to make reasonable offers, not haggle excessively, and pay up promptly. Authenticity and condition of artwork are (as in any field of collecting) central to the price, so a seller who sells an item that is not an actual studio product or is damaged in some way (even unintentionally) is quickly outlawed. But dishonest practices such as these would cause tension in any collecting situation, whether or not a community exists. Likewise, Betarians are like most virtual communities in quashing threads started by a member attacking another participant. Such "trolls" are quickly accused of "flaming" and asked to stop or risk being banned. In such cases, moderators may intrude publicly, locking threads by preventing any additional posts or even issuing temporary or (in egregious cases) permanent bans. But in most cases, the matter is handled behind the scenes, through personal messages between moderators and the offending parties that are not shared with the membership as a whole. In some cases, the participants are simply asked to "take it outside" into a special forum called "The Speakeasy." This is hidden from most members' sight and left free from the usual interference from moderators, so especially frank discussions can continue unimpeded until the participants feel that they have vented their concerns.

Other netiquette issues are more distinctive to collectors: it is bad form, for instance, to call attention to a "live" auction, even if one is not bidding, because publicizing the event would surely draw the attention of a wider range of bidders, driving up the final price for the eventual winner. So when Mandarake, a major Japanese auction service, holds one of its regular "Big Web Auctions," a thread begins with scanned images from the advance catalog, followed by some very general and carefully worded remarks on the overall quality of the goods for sale. Then a tactful silence is held until the end of the auction, when a burst of discussion allows Betarians to comment on the most spectacular items and (when one is lucky) crow over a hard-won victory.

Finally, many of the peeves mentioned in the Anime-Beta forum deal specifically with how the unique nature of a collectible item can challenge the anime art collector's community. Obtaining a unique object such as a desirable cel is an act of appropriation, a "capture" in a real sense since now no one else in the world can have it. Collectors who repeatedly brag about high-end acquisitions naturally draw resentment to themselves, as their actions disrupt the equilibrium of their subculture. If not checked, this imbalance has the potential to fatally divide the community. The unusual solidarity of Anime-Beta is therefore based on the principle that a good competitor is one who balances good fortune in collecting with a willingness to make *restitution*.

My adoption of restitution in an ethnographic sense derives from literary critic George Steiner's (1975) use of the term to explain the success of some translations of literary works over others. When the ideas in a text are extracted from their original linguistic setting and presented in a different language, an inevitable loss of meaning occurs. In an analogous way, too, a single piece of anime art—when extracted from the total process—is decontextualized to the point that it no longer, in and of itself, can stand for the original moving image. Steiner holds that this can be made up through a conscious recreative act, using linguistic choices that are impossible in the original language but add new dimensions to the work that are only available in the new language. In an analogous way, when anime art collectors add a cel or sketch to their collections, they can call attention to artistic elements in the image or relate it to the overall plot in a creative way that would be impossible in its original context, where it appears for only a fraction of a second. In either case, Steiner explains, the adaptor

> endeavours to restore the balance of forces, of integral presence, which his appropriative comprehension has disrupted . . . By virtue of tact, and tact intensified in moral vision, the translator-interpreter creates a condition of significant exchange . . . There is, ideally, exchange without loss. (1975, 302)

Steiner's approach, he admits, was inspired by the anthropological writings of Claude Lévi-Strauss, which suggest that "dynamic equilibrium" in cultures is achieved through exchange of material goods, verbal art, and women.[45] In other words, in a social sense, each selfish act requires a counteraction that benefits the community. "All capture calls for subsequent compensation," Steiner concludes, but "both formally and morally *the books must balance*" (1975, 303; italics added).

The concept of restitution can readily be applied to the activities of anime art collectors in more ways than one. Those who obtain fine pieces of anime art are seen as untactful, perhaps even lacking in moral sense, so an activity born in solitary action threatens to become even more isolating. But if collectors find a means of compensating other collectors in a way that "balances the books," then this system of taking and giving keeps the community in continual turmoil, which paradoxically stabilizes it as a whole. Collectors accept self-interested actions as part of their world, but courteous members of Anime-Beta are more readily forgiven their occasional acts of treachery.

A number of collectors allude to the concept of the "black hole collector," a derogatory term for a collector who purchases art but refuses to create an online gallery that displays it. As a result, a desirable, unique art object simply disappears from sight when such a collector acquires it, much as a star vanishes forever when sucked into the grip of a massive astronomical black hole. A similar derogatory term, "hoarder," refers to collectors so devoted to collecting art from a certain series or of a certain character that they insist on acquiring any and all such items as they become available to purchase or bid on.

Clearly, hoarding, and the mostly negative perceptions associated with it, makes the term a contentious one when invoked to describe other collectors' purchasing habits. Key member nene (F 22) complains that collectors tend to use the term too loosely, "as though a select few people have coined what they believe to be the maximum number of cels someone can own before they own too many." She suggests that this tendency alone could lead some collectors to become black hole collectors, to keep from making themselves vulnerable to envy and criticism. However, another key member, beatrush (M 27), counters that some collectors justify their reputation as hoarders. He recalls a specific bidder who frequents online auctions who "has literally a bottomless wallet" and insists on buying up every cel from a given series. "It is also almost next to impossible to outbid this person . . . unless you are willing to shell out a fortune[46] to do so," he concludes. Similarly, Keropi (M 45) wryly alludes to another collector who regularly outbids others for premium cels from a particular series:

> Well . . . his desire to pay just overwhelmed the rest of us. What can we say? We just didn't want it badly enough compared to him. Congrats to him even if he is a Black Hole Collector (TM). Lol ☺ .[47]

Keropi's observation ends with three common linguistic markers intended to ward off negative responses. The "(TM)," or "trademark," pokes fun at use of the term "black hole collector" as a common "name brand" of collectors that many members of the community use, not just the poster. The quasi-oral "Lol" or "laugh out loud" concludes the comment with a self-deprecating chuckle, which, along with the common "smiley" icon, signals "Don't take my use of that term too seriously." All of these, as Danet (2001) notes, denote playful, "speech-like" forms of communication that are forms of folk speech, implicitly recognized and understood by Keropi's readers (see also Fernback 2003). Unquestionably, the forum's discussions about hoarding indicate a wide range of opinions about the subject; by weighing in on the topic, contributors rhetorically reinforce the community's expectation that collections be shared in some way while also revealing a nervous acknowledgment that the core issue here provokes considerable tension within the community.

The hoarding and black hole collector images suggest that there are boundaries beyond which members of Anime-Beta know that they should not trespass without providing restitution. Creating an online gallery is, for Betarians, the simplest and most common way of doing so. This option has been available since August 2001, when Texas computer technician and anime enthusiast Jason Nolasco created Rubberslug (RS), a website to display scanned images of his cel collection. The site grew rapidly in scope after he expanded it into a place where other collectors could upload their belongings using a simple menu.[48] While some enthusiasts prefer to design their own websites with customized display options, RS remains the preferred place for anime art collectors to show off their holdings. A digital gallery publicly acknowledges ownership of specific items but gives others the opportunity to view scans of the art. Some curators of these digital galleries go well beyond this expectation, providing a kind of restitution in the form of elaborate commentaries, including links to online sources of informa-

tion on the series and its creators. From a collector's point of view, adding commentary to a gallery image often essentially compensates for the decontextualization of the image from its original place in the action. For this reason, many online galleries give information relating to the cel's original context, such as the episode and a brief summary of what is going on in the scene in which the cel appears. At times such galleries become tribute sites for certain anime series.[49]

On one level, the terms "hoarder" and "black hole collector" do not refer to a specific strategy of collecting anime art but to a lack of moral vision. The Betarians acknowledge the many different styles of collecting and many valid approaches. Indeed, they often clarify that the intention of their comments does not mean that everyone is "obliged" to carry out restitution in this way; they concede that valid reasons exist for accumulating art from a given series and/or not publicly displaying it. In a critique of the use of the terms "hoarder" and "black hole collector," Sylia (F 27) states rather bluntly:

> not meeting up to your personal standards doesn't mean that someone doesn't love what they get and deserve to have it as much as anyone else. I think that people use labels sometimes to imply that some collectors aren't as good as others . . . I understand people feeling sad that they might not be able to see the art again for a while if a collector there doesn't go public with it, although "public" for most people here tends to mean Beta, RS or some similar place. I don't recall the centre of the world ever having to be the predominantly western gathering of collectors that are these two websites.

Even combined with Betarians' willingness to back off their positions, Sylia's comment still acknowledges how strongly the members of this particular virtual community expect restitution to take place. That is, a collector who purchases for personal gratification alone may have perfectly good reasons for doing so and may even, for all we know, participate in a community of animation art collectors that sees conspicuous consumption as a token of social status. If such a venue exists, as Sylia's skepticism suggests, then it would be as valid a community as Anime-Beta. This, however, confirms Bauman's (1971) point that folk groups do not form spontaneously because of interests and activities held in common; rather, they develop differentially, based on values developed and reinforced within particular communities. In other words, a black hole collector is not likely to become or remain a member of Anime-Beta because that person's actions conflict with the key expectations of that community. And so the process of balancing collecting in private with maintaining an online gallery in public is a way of choosing to perform identity that is central to the continued vibrancy of the community.

"ALL'S FAIR IN LOVE AND CEL COLLECTING": COLLECTORS AT WAR

Another common peeve of the Anime-Beta community involves a practice that was more common when the community was relatively new. For a time, collectors would post threads informing fellow Betarians that an item they coveted had come up for auction. In such threads, the poster would typically ask for other collectors' support in "going for it," which was meant to imply (or sometimes openly request) that other collectors interested in the same series should refrain from bidding so that the inquiring collector would be successful in acquiring a wish list item.[50] The system worked well when there was an implied reciprocity: if one backed off from one auction in favor of a fellow Beta member, it was assumed that the person who benefited would be willing to do the same for another collector at a later auction. As a result, community members had only to compete with outsiders, and the final selling price was often lower than it would have been if other Betarians had posted bids.

However, the system was prone to abuse and unpredictable conflicts. When Anime-Beta was first opened, it organized its discussions by specific series that were being actively collected. A key member, duotrouble (F 39), recalls that several "elitist" groups of collectors felt that "If you weren't one of the few members always posting there and buying cels [from that series], then you were almost instantly snubbed." One particular anime series, she adds, became the focus of a small, aggressively competitive group.[51] As a result, the wish list favor was not widely reciprocated, and tensions began to grow. cutiebunny (F 30) recalls,

> When I first joined AB, there were many . . . collectors [for this series]. Every week, a Yahoo Japan seller . . . would list new cels [from that series] for auction. And, invariably, there were always one or two members who would claim that the auctioned item was their "absolute wishlist" and expect all others to back off. I think what surprised me the most was not only were other collectors oblivious of this weekly tradition, but would gladly stand aside so that the same two collectors could win the item.
>
> This was the one thing that I wanted to change. I knew it would take a lot of funds to do so, and having a job with a lot of overtime put me in a good position to challenge the two collectors. I also knew that, by challenging these two women, that I would gain a bad reputation. But, it was worth it to me. By sniping[52] and using different deputy services to jack up the prices, I was able to end these collectors' monopoly.

The wish list system, then, proved to be intrinsically unstable, resulting in increased competition at times rather than mutual benefit. While it seemed to honor the principle of restitution, collectors did not always reciprocate the advantage given by backing off from an auction and so those who requested the favor became suspected of being hoarders.

This instability led directly to one of the rare flame war events that challenged the unity of the Anime-Beta community. The controversy began when a relatively new member started a discussion thread calling attention to an especially desirable cel that had appeared on the Japanese auction site Yahoo Japan. An older and more established member at once invoked the wish list system, posting the message "I really want it." After some initial jockeying, the first member appeared to back off in favor of the senior collector. However, as the auction's end approached, she reconsidered and placed what turned out to be the winning bid. As a result, she found herself the target of several angry personal messages blaming her for violating the other bidder's confidence and breaching the community's social rules. Discussion continued in the unmoderated Speakeasy but boiled over into the public threads, prompting one of the moderators, gonzai (F 48), to try to settle the storm by providing some perspective:

> You all may be very surprised at how much this actually goes on without your knowledge. I know a couple people who have won absolutely fabulous cels— ones I would love to ogle in their galleries, however, they hide them cause they don't want to have people send them hate mail because of it. It's pretty sad that collectors need to feel that way.
>
> It's a hobby. You win some, you lose some. Get over it and move on. There's more great cels out there to be had . . . I know, cause I have been on the losing end of that battle many times, and to the same person—who happens to be a wonderful friend of mine. For as upset and as hurt I get at the time, I would never let that stand in the way of my friendship with her, and I would never expect others to be upset with her either. Sorry guys, all's fair in love and cel collecting.

As noted, Danet and Katriel found the "collecting is hunting" metaphor to be the most commonplace image in hobbyists' discourse (1994, 38). It is also the one that most embodies potentially negative tension. A hunter, like a soldier, is trained to kill, and the image embedded in the practice of what anime art collectors term "snipe bidding" is that of a sniper sending a well-aimed bullet through a mortal part of his or her prey—or perhaps through the vitals of the other bidder! Therefore, the moderator's summation—"all's fair in love and cel collecting"—also implies that the hobby often threatens to become, on some level, a form of war rather than a recreational hunt or quest.

This is not to say that the primary goal of collecting is to gain one's objective at any expense, including making resentful enemies out of fellow collectors. But it does embody the heightened tension that gives collecting and many other pastimes their special zest. Framing the activity as a hunting or combat situation acknowledges that the hobby contains an element of risk combined with the need for heightened awareness of many factors that may go for or against the determined collector. For this reason, many

anime art collectors watch as auctions for particular items count down to
the critical last minutes, prepared to fight off rivals. And because Japanese
auctions automatically reset the end time whenever a bid is lodged within
the final five minutes, the final battle can be intense and protracted. Thus,
the wish list custom on one level appears to favor the bidder by limiting the
unpredictable factors that can stand in the way of success. But in so doing,
the custom compromises one of the most important factors that Danet and
Katriel rightly observe makes any form of collecting so enjoyable: "the sus-
pense collectors live with, even relish" (1994, 39).

The forum moderator's reaction underscores the unstable nature of collectors' communities. Members are expected to be extremely competitive in
the quest for the most desirable items but nevertheless remain friends (or at
least respectful to each other) in the wake of a contentious auction. When
this uneasy peace breaks down, the process of reciprocity is publicly broken
as well. The customary ritual following a heated bidding competition calls
for the winner to post a scan of the much-desired cel along with commentary. But if doing so would open the new owner to attack, as the moderator
notes, the item may remain "hidden" and thus no restitution occurs.

Despite the moderator's intervention, the discussion over the disputed
auction continued to provoke increasingly sharp exchanges among members
until the same moderator locked the original thread a day later. While both
bidders in the center of the controversy remained active members, several
other prominent Betarians departed for good, an event remembered with
regret even several years later. As a result, members rarely mention the wish
list custom in Anime-Beta's public threads, and usually in a critical way.
Longtime member jcaliff (F 36) singles out the practice by calling attention to

People who post things like, "look at this amazing auction! I hope I win!"
We all know how that turns out if that person loses, especially to someone
else in the community since . . . some folks assume that they have some kind
of God-given right to own a certain cel. Or the drama that ensues if someone else from here wanted to bid. Or then someone who might have never
noticed that particular auction decides to bid for it. For Pete's sake, don't create competition for yourself. Don't post about it until the auction is over.

Yet the wish list practice does continue behind the scenes, as Betarians
admitted in responses to the private survey I circulated. blueheaven (M
33) sums up the "best fellow collector" as someone who "helps others find
their dream cels." ReiTheJelly (F 27) likewise notes that many of her colleagues do send private messages to fellow collectors, alerting them to items

their colleagues might desire. Significantly, she also observes that the sender might not actually consider the collector he or she notifies to be a "friend." Nevertheless, she adds, such gestures are not uncommon as "Keeping good spirits between members is essential."

So restitution is a more complex group dynamic than it first appears. Anime art draws collectors for many reasons, some of them intensely personal. Because the most desired items are autographic in nature, the competition over them is "to the death," with one collector gaining ultimate control and the other feeling an absolute defeat. Remembering that such art objects are fetishes and that they wield psychological power for the owners and for those who desire them, these contests necessarily have an emotional impact that noncollectors may find difficult to appreciate. However, the Anime-Beta community formed from people who understand full well the private motivations that fuel individual collectors' involvement in the hobby. In fact, this constant contact with fellow collectors who value such feelings is one of the most therapeutic elements of the online community. Betarians know that this common feeling cannot be eliminated without destroying the link that binds the community. But competition cannot be eliminated from the perspective either: it is part of the special spice that makes the activity of collecting so engrossing. Keeping both in balance enables Betarians to engage in a carnivalesque "celebration of the irrational" that affirms their common passion for anime art. Order enables disorder; illogic affirms shared values. Behaviorally and emotionally, the books balance.

CONCLUSIONS

The Betarians are a mutually reinforcing "family" of people who share and understand a passion known by relatively few people. This passion may be based on personality type, with individuals strongly drawn to anime's fairy tale qualities. Or it might be more aesthetic in nature, recognizing and valuing the human creativity that goes into hand-drawn animation. A final paradox is that the objects that inspire such passion are so physically fragile that they cannot be shared with more than a handful of close friends. In any case, the solitary nature of the hobby creates an equal and opposite desire to form tenacious social ties with other enthusiasts bitten by the same collecting bug. Once in contact, however, anime art collectors need to find ways to manage their intense emotional attachments to the objects they collect and the social reality that, as unique objects, cels can only be possessed by one unique owner.

Anime art is fetishistic in more than one aspect: historically important because of its place in creating a cherished narrative and at the same
time providing a liminal doorway into the content of the narrative itself.
As with any fetish, an element of magic surrounding objects of anime art,
and if their ownership invests one with social power, serious social risks are
involved as well. Hence, the process of social restitution has come to be integral to the long-term stability of the Anime-Beta community. Otherwise,
as George Steiner warned (though about a different intellectual enterprise),

> We come home laden . . . having caused disequilibrium throughout the sys-
> tem by taking away from "the other" and by adding, though possibly with
> ambiguous consequence, to our own. The system is now off-tilt. (1975, 300)

Restitution, with virtual communities as with translators, is a means of
bringing the social system back into a stable balance—not by challenging
collectors' basic instincts to seek and capture objects that attract them but
rather by allowing them to reimburse the community in some way that is
felt to be equitable. Displaying, cherishing, and properly conserving the art
is one means. Being generous to other collectors, particularly newcomers,
is another (especially if it shows a willingness to step back and allow others to build collections rather than add to one's own). A potential hoarder
becomes a valued "sharer" by becoming tactful in acquiring art and generous in sharing information, by being ruthless in auctions and polite in public discussions, and by being willing to value other collectors' collections as
highly as one's own.

So the Betarians share a common passion for the artifacts they collect
and also for the larger body of information that they share with each other.
Their involvement in anime and the imaginative world that it projects is
one common factor that draws them together. But more fundamentally,
they share an identity not as anime art collectors at large but as members of
Anime-Beta—a reference group that shares values, beliefs, and background
knowledge and uses a self-generated system of codes and signs for social
interaction.[53] More to the point, the group is keenly aware of its differential
identity and proud of the values that have kept it—alone among the public
forums—active and healthy for more than a decade. Through such a give-
and-take process, the Anime-Beta community has given chatty "regulars,"
curious "occasionals," and invisible "lurkers" a strongly felt identity—much
like any folk group. For indeed, there is nothing here that is necessarily *created* by the participants' use of the Internet to form these links. Noyes (2003)

concedes at the end of her discussion on the folkloristic concept "group" that the enacted rituals create a kind of fantasy of a community in "perfect reciprocity and equality." Yes, in lived history, conflicts still eat away at this image of perfection. Still, she concludes by reminding us that life is not a video game, that "the face-to-face village community is a salutary reminder that life is still material" (Noyes 2003, 34–35). Certainly so. And if so, then we can expect to see dynamics like restitution in equal power among groups who still form and struggle to stay unified through oral communication and physical interaction. People, after all, remain people, whether they are mediated by the spoken voice, the print media, the photocopy and fax, or the new media of the Internet.

Deadly Whispers (F 31), one of the forum's moderators, nicely captured this insight in a comment. She admits that like many of the original members who left Anime-Alpha to form Anime-Beta, her interests have changed with time. In fact, they have evolved to such an extent that she now rarely watches anime and no longer collects the art. If she were no more than a regular member, she concedes, she would probably not visit the site except to occasionally contact old friends. As one of the "owners" of the forum, however, she feels a stronger obligation: "I visit the site and help maintain it for the members. As long as someone is there, using its resources and posting in its threads, I will keep the board running." But why?

"The people," she simply replied.

NOTES

1. Elliott Oring (1986) gives a good overview of this controversy.
2. A thread informing Betarians of Pierpont's tragic death in 2003 at age 33 (due to a traffic accident) remains archived on the Anime-Beta website. "Sith Krillin," Anime-Beta Gen2, started by DbzGirl88 on 11 April 2003, accessed 9 July 2011, http://tinyurl.com/sithkrillin.
3. Danet (2001) gives a lucid and thorough survey of the emergence of playful and "speech-like" features in a variety of Internet-mediated modes of communication during the 1980s and 1990s (13–34). See also Fernback (2003).
4. The second-to-last of these anthologies, *Sometimes the Dragon Wins* (Dundes and Pagter 1996), contains some computer-circulated lore but mainly deals with material disseminated by fax machines.
5. Nevertheless, even Dégh balked at the suggestion that participants in Internet-mediated groups constituted a valid conduit for traditional knowledge. In *Legend and Belief* (2001), she argued that interactive typing on a keyboard for "an unknown audience" is not a genuine folkloric act, which, in her perspective, depends on live, face-to-face interaction. (114).
6. Like Dundes and Dégh, however, Bacon-Smith did not extend her innovative work

into web-mediated lore. While she notes the importance of privately published fan magazines in focusing the activities of these circles, she, too, describes a period just before the emergence of the Internet, in which her circles mainly interacted through face-to-face meetings at conventions and house parties.

7. The professional sport called "football" in the UK is known to Americans as "soccer." However, as Mason's discussion uses the usual British name, I have retained it in my discussion of his argument.

8. See Ellis (2009). This essay was presented at the Modern Language Association meeting in December 2001, so it reflects my early interest in the folklore content of manga/anime.

9. "Flame war" refers to a section of an online discussion in which a disagreement between two members leads to repeated exchanges of abusive and insulting messages.

10. During one of the periodic restructures of the site in June 2011, this feature, along with many others, was discontinued without explanation.

11. Sensei, 7 January 2011, "A Plan for an Ethnography of Cel Collectors," *Sensei's Den of Senility* (blog), accessed 9 July 2011, http://sensei.rubberslug.com/gallery/weblog. asp7 January 2011.

12. "Doing some ethnographic observations: The Next Stage," *Anime-Beta Gen2*, started by Sensei on 21 February 2011, accessed 29 June 2011, http://tinyurl.com/43sma7v.

13. Screen handles appear in the text followed by a brief indication of gender and age (e.g., "Sensei (M 60)"). At the end of this chapter, a list of these names adds each member's real name and state or country of residence (e.g., "Sensei—Bill Ellis, Maryland, M 60") (see appendix A). At the request of some Betarians, the last name, the entire name, or the place of residence are also withheld. A few asked me to withhold all personal information. Because of this concern for privacy, conclusions about the make up of Anime-Beta members must be based on what participants *choose* to share with the larger public rather than objectively verifiable information. However, the available quantitative data is consistent with the qualitative answers given on threads in survey responses, providing a clear view of how the community presents itself to other collectors and the public.

14. For example, statistics for Otakon, the most important convention for anime fans in the eastern United States, shows that attendance at the annual meetings grew from a start of 350 in 1994 to just over 20,000 in 2004, experiencing double- or triple-digit growth each year. At this point, attendance levels plateaued, possibly due to the limitations of the convention facilities (a city block-sized convention center in downtown Baltimore, Maryland) but continued to expand at a slower rate, reaching a new high of 28,044 in 2010.

15. See Barrier (1999, 15–25, 566–567) for a historical summary of these techniques, which became the standard method used by The Walt Disney Studios and all other major animation firms.

16. As pure celluloid proved very unstable as a backing for animation art, it was replaced first by cellulose nitrate (the medium used in classic Disney movies) and then by cellulose acetate, the plastic used in all recent animated films, including Japanese anime.

17. See "Art of Disney and Sotheby's" (2011).

18. The term, however, has become widely used in a positive sense by non-Japanese fans as a way of referring to someone who is very knowledgeable about anime.

19. Notable among these others is the Japanese Animation Cel Mailing List (JACML), which went live on January 5, 2000, and initially attracted a large number of

members, some of whom remain active in the collecting community. However, the archive of updates shows that activity became much slower when Anime-Beta began growing rapidly, and the network essentially ceased operation after October 2002. Ten years later, the site was still accessible at http://usagis-house.net/jacml/ (accessed 19 January 2012). Rubberslug, the preferred hosting site for online galleries, added a forum to its site about March 2006, but as messages are archived by month and day but not year, the exact date cannot now be pinned down. While still visited, it remains much less active and cohesive than Anime-Beta.

20. The term "newbie" is commonly used in virtual communities for a person who has recently joined the group. Following the folkloric Rule of Three (see Dundes 1980), I coined two other terms to refer to members who had been active for longer periods, using language familiar to anime art collectors. A "key" image is a cel or sketch that is based on a design drawn early in the animating process by a senior artist. So a key member in Anime-Beta has senior experience and group status. Later, junior animators add "in-betweener" images to fill in the action, so an in-betweener member of Anime-Beta is experienced enough to have graduated from newbie status but also not one of the founders. I introduced these terms to the forum while sharing early drafts of my essay and was amused that the latter term was almost immediately shortened to "ibby" to make it more parallel to the already established newbie.

21. 52 percent female, 45 percent male, 2 percent "right in the middle of changing." Source: "Do ladies rule. . .," Anime-Beta v9.1 Forum, started by Wendy on 23 January 2004, accessed 19 March 2011, http://www.anime-beta.com/phpBB/viewtopic.php?t=6798 (N: 40). Because of the ever-changing nature of Internet communications, some cited materials are longer available online.

22. Sources: "I'm curious about the male/female ratio of cel collectors," Anime-Beta v9.1 Forum, started by Sletia on 27 December 2005, accessed 25 March 2011, http://www.anime-beta.com/phpBB/viewtopic.php?t=16332 (N: 71); "Which category do you fall into?," Anime-Beta v9.1 Forum, started by miz ducky on 3 February 2008, accessed 19 March 2011, http://www.anime-beta.com/phpBB/viewtopic.php?t=23397 (N: 84); and "Which gender/marital category would you place yourself into?," Anime-Beta v9.1 Forum, started by Sensei on 25 February 2011, accessed 19 March 2011, http://www.anime-beta.com/phpBB/viewtopic.php?t=28180 (N: 74). By contrast, the female majority was much smaller in two larger communities of anime fans at large, Anipike (56 percent) and AnimeNewsNetwork (51 percent). However, a similar gender bias is also found at sites created for participants writing anime "fan fiction," which attracts a 68 percent female population ("Anime and Manga" 2010).

23. "What do you do for a living?," Anime-Betav9.1 Forum, started by Strictly-Dragonball on 6 March 2010, accessed 25 March 2011, http://www.anime-beta.com/phpBB/viewtopic.php?t=27060.

24. In his influential study of the *hikikomori* phenomenon in Japan (in which many young people exile themselves from society and refuse to leave their homes), journalist Michael Zielenziger (2007) notes that these individuals do not use the Internet as a replacement for social life. In fact, available data from Japanese psychologists suggests that fewer than 10 percent of such sociopathic loners communicate with others using personal computers (Zielenziger 2007, 223).

25. This mirrors Mason's (2007) observation that the proportions of active, occasional, and passive participants were crucial to a virtual community's health. If too many list

members were active, they generated more messages than the others could handle easily; if too few participated, the group grew stagnant.

26. A classic instance of the use of fetish objects in a patriotic context is provided by the widespread dissemination and public display of steel beams salvaged from the wreckage of the World Trade Center after the terrorist attack of September 11, 2001.

27. Although each cel is a unique artwork, some are, in a real sense, "more unique" than others. Especially important scenes often feature one of the characters in a still position, with the camera lingering on the image or panning slowly over it for longer than usual. Such moments require the preparation of an A1 End cel, which means that it is the *only* cel available from that particular moment. As it is designed to stay on the screen for a long time, the animators take special care over its design and make sure that the cel is designed and painted with unusual care. Hence, collectors would consider an A1 End cel to be an especially desirable trophy, especially if it comes from an important scene in a major anime.

28. Similarly, Danet and Katriel note that many of the collectors they surveyed talked about "Hunting for collectibles in antique shops, flea markets, and garbage dumps, or chancing upon them in one's basement or attic" (1994, 30). They also suggest that the prominence of this theme highlights the tension between order (the prominent place of the item in a well-organized collection) and chaos (the trash heap to which society at large consigns them).

29. Since Aztec times, cacao beans have been rumored to contain a natural aphrodisiac, though modern scientific research indicates that its properties are probably psychological rather than biochemical. See O'Conor (2006).

30. Urban Dictionary glosses this term as a portmanteau of "gigantic" and "enormous" and notes that it is "most commonly used in reference to women with large boobies." http://www.urbandictionary.com/define.php?term=gynormous (accessed 19 January 2012).

31. Source: "So you are thinking about making a gyormous purchase," Anime-Beta v9.1 Forum, started by gonzai on 5 January 2012, accessed 19 January 2012, http://www.anime-beta.com/phpBB3/viewtopic.php?f=70&t=28861.

32. "NYT: Urge to Collect Things Linked to Bubonic Plague!," *Anime-Beta v9.1 Forum*, started by Sensei on 9 March 2011, accessed 9 March 2011, http://www.anime-beta.com/phpBB/viewtopic.php?t=28202.

33. Interestingly, nene's comment is paralleled by a quote offered by Danet and Katriel (1994) from a collector: "The most profound enchantment for the collector is the locking of individual items within a magic circle in which they are fixed as the final thrill, the thrill of acquisition, passes over them" (48).

34. In so doing, Milspaw and Evans (2010) consciously extend the work of folklorist Max Lüthi (1976 [1969]) and cultural geographer Yi-Fu Tuan (1998).

35. Source: "How many people have you've [*sic*] shown your Cels and Sketches?," Anime-Beta v9.1 Forum, started by RoboFlonne on 27 February 2008, accessed 19 March 2011, http://www.anime-beta.com/phpBB/viewtopic.php?t=23565 (N: 49).

36. Titled "Hector the Collector," the poem first appeared in Silverstein's 1984 collection *Where the Sidewalk Ends*. The title was suggested by an older nursery rhyme concerning "Hector Protector," first published in the nineteenth century by James O. Halliwell in his *Nursery Rhymes of England* (Historical, No. 21).

37. Similar statements were made on many of the surveys. For instance, JuniorMintKiss (F 26), a member from northern Utah, laments that her physical isolation from

other anime enthusiasts adds to the need for making and maintaining contacts with other collectors via the Internet. animeobsessed (F 52) was even more explicit, saying that he appreciated being able to contact "friends whom I can openly talk to about my obsession with anime and cel collecting. They understand me and have similar interests so I don't have to explain or justify my addiction with this hobby." Joost, a European collector, agreed: "It's the only place that I know where I can talk about a hobby that's very dear to me, and where people are as crazy about collecting as me."

38. The psycholinguistic term "engrossment" is used by Erving Goffman (1974) to mean an mental state in which a spectator is "caught up in" and "carried away by" an experience that is "something he [or she] can claim is really going on and yet claim is not real" (6).

39. This paradox came home when I displayed some of the art I had collected myself from the series *Inuyasha*, which was then being broadcast in English adaptations on the Cartoon Network. A young fan admired the production sketches and then commented, "You draw Inuyasha very well!" I explained to the youngster that I had not actually drawn the sketches myself; rather, they were some of the artwork that the studio had used to create one of the scenes in the show. "They aren't drawings of Inuyasha," I said. "They *are* Inuyasha." The young fan went away, obviously thinking this through.

40. As documented by Foster (2009, 166–169) and Reider (2010, 144 ff.), the series *Dragonball Z* was inspired by the Chinese folk epic *Journey to the West*, itself a compilation of picaresque folktale plots. *Sailor Moon* is based on the basic situation of the Western folktale "Sleeping Beauty," as the protagonist is the victim of a death curse uttered by a magical being left uninvited to the feast celebrating her birth. In this case, her mother softens the curse by allowing her child to be reborn as a human girl who can regain her magical princess identity and save her world by performing a series of difficult tasks. Interestingly, the acclaimed Mexican film *Pan's Labyrinth* (directed by Guillermo del Toro 2006) uses a similar premise.

41. Sakura is the central character of *Cardcaptor Sakura* (1998–2000); she is a young girl whose growth toward maturity is reflected in her quest to recapture a series of magical cards, many of which embody dilemmas she faces in her real life. Once she is able to control these "cards," she then uses them creatively to overcome new challenges. See Ellis (2009).

42. "Grammar," interestingly, is historically related to the word "grimoire," meaning a book explaining how to perform magick.

43. Spacher asked that he be identified by his real name rather than by his screen name. He explained in a private message that the "century's end savior" line comes from the Japanese title of a 1980s anime series best known in English as *Fist Of The North Star*, or more properly, *Seikimatsu Kyuseishu Densetsu—Hokuto no Ken* ("The Legend of the Century's End Savior, Ken, the Fist of *Ursa Major*"). (*Ken* is the main character's name but also the Japanese term for a doubled-up fist used to land a punch in a fight. Similarly, *Hokuto* is literally "great bear" but means the constellation rather than a literal animal). The series is set in a shattered postapocalyptic world at the turn of a century (literally 1999, a decade into the future from when the series was created).

44. "What's your cel collecting pet peeve?" Anime-Beta v9.1 Forum, started by Momo on 9 December 2009, accessed 19 March 2011, http://www.anime-beta.com/phpBB/viewtopic.php?t=26720.

45.   Steiner credits Lévi-Strauss's formative work, *Anthropologie structurale* (1958) but without giving a specific page reference.

46.   One should note that a "fortune" among anime art collectors is still a very modest amount in the collecting world at large. The same post mentions the hoarder's spending $3,000 in a single month as a sign of the enthusiast's "bottomless wallet." From the author's experience, this is indeed an unusually large amount of money to spend on anime art when most top-of-the-line items exchange hands for under $1,250 each (Source: Poll in "How much for one piece of art?," Anime-Beta v9.1 Forum, started by kizu on August 2010, accessed 25 March 2011, http://www.anime-beta. com/phpBB/viewtopic.php?t=27652. Serious collectors in other autographic fields, such as the work of twentieth-century abstract artists, would consider the amounts discussed in this article to be no more than pocket change.

47.   Strictly speaking, "(TM)" should be in superscript, but this typographical option was not available on Anime-Beta's platform.

48.   Within its first year, the Rubberslug website gained over 16,000 images. By January 2005, the site hosted over 100,000 scans of animation art; by July 2007, the total had reached 200,000, and the counter went over 300,000 in January 2010.

49.   On the other hand, Betarian majinuub (F 24) expresses irritation when a much-fought-over cel is put on display in the owner's gallery but "ends up getting slapped in a section with other series and without any description on the character/scene." That implies, she argues, that "the person knows nothing about it." In such a case, restitution is attempted, but the books do not balance.

50.   Emically, the term refers to an item that a collector knows (or suspects) exists and would certainly add to his or her collection. In Rubberslug, there is an option for curators to fill in a page titled "Wishlist," giving descriptions of the items the collector wishes for and the priority with which it is desired. Priorities (set by the creator of the Rubberslug hosting site) range from "Low" to "Would Give Kidney."

51.   Both Beta members named the specific series, but in reviewing the threads still live on the site, I found it easy to search for the series and identify likely candidates for the former members mentioned in this quote. While these persons are no longer active on the forum, some personal information and contact links still are available for a number of them. Therefore, I eliminated the name of the series. Anecdotally, I have heard this same practice associated with several different series and groups of collectors in the early days of Anime-Beta. "Things have definitely appeared to have changed for the better," duotrouble commented in a personal message to me.

52.   "Sniping" means submitting a very high bid during the last seconds of an auction so that the previous bidder does not have time to answer it. The metaphor is valid, as the bidder lies patiently in wait and then fires off a single well-aimed shot intended to win the auction. It is potentially dangerous, as two snipers submitting high bids at the same time can raise the bidding level dramatically without warning, catching each other in a crossfire, so to speak. Japanese auctions do not allow sniping but reset the end clock whenever a bid is lodged during the last five minutes. However, the third-party services who submit bids on behalf of subscribers do allow its customers to attempt to snipe each other internally—up until the final second of the auction— so the practice continues.

53.   I borrowed the language here from Ben-Amos's characterization of a folk group (1971, 13).

Appendix A

Anime-Beta Members Contributing to This Project

Demographic information is limited to what individual members agreed to share in this essay. Ages are, at times, approximate and refer to age on January 1, 2011.

Angelic-Lair—Joel and Valerie Kern, Ottawa, M 34 and F 27
Ashenfairy—Stephanie McKay, Minnesota, F 28
animeobsessed—[name withheld], Nevada, F 52
beatrush—[name and place withheld], M 27
blueheaven—[name and place withheld], M 33
Cordelia—Cordelia [last name withheld], Singapore, F 30
cutiebunny—Amanda [last name withheld], California, F 30
dark-water-dragon—Sean McCallep, Alaska, M 29
Deadly Whispers—[name withheld], Colorado, F 31
duotrouble—[name withheld], Georgia, F 39
eyes0nme19—[name withheld], California, F 25
Goldknight—[name withheld], Colorado, F 36
gonzai—Nida Dieckmann, Iowa, F 48
GuyvarIII—Chris Romano, California, M 29
irmgaard—[name withheld], California, 30 F
jcaliff—Jennifer Califf, Texas, F 36
Joost—Joost Backaert, Belgium, M 31
JuniorMintKiss—Jessica Morris, Utah, F 26
JWR—Joe Ryan, California, M 53
Keropi—Terence Tamashiro, California, M 45
Macron One—Pieter Dijkstra, The Netherlands, M 31
majinuub—Danielle [last name withheld], New York, F 24
Massacrist Manslayer—[name withheld], Australia, M 27
nene—[name withheld], England, 24 F
Quacker—James Duckworth, Australia M 32
pixie_princess—Lori Lancaster, Illinois, F 32

ReiTheJelly—[name and place withheld], F 27
rosesleep—Cecilia [last name withheld], New York, F 21
RatherSilent—[personal information withheld]
Sensei—Bill Ellis, Maryland, M 61 ◀ ◀ ◀
Starfighter—Frank J Polizzi II, New Jersey, M 33
star-phoenix—Jeanie Croshaw, Texas, F 29
Sky Rat—Maryland, F 28
Sui Kune—Samantha Goblirsch, Oregon, F 24
Sylia—[name withheld], England, F 27
teggacat—Kate [last name withheld], Pennsylvania, F 38
theultimatebrucelee—David Ray, California, M 21
Yume Hime—[name withheld], France, F 21
zerospace—Amanda Mizuno, California F 31

Thanks also to: BeautifulAlone, My Baby, Benoit Spacher, Mae Lucier, Patti Nguyen, Sarah Winzenburg, and Brenda Zera for special assistance in becoming acquainted with the Anime-Beta community.

Appendix B

Survey Questions Distributed to Anime-Beta Members

To key members (registered in 2002–2005 and still active):

1. What is one thing that attracts you back to the Anime-Beta website? Why?
2. Name one way that Anime-Beta has changed since you first registered. Is this change good, bad, or indifferent?
3. Give five words that you would use to describe a good "neighbor" in the Anime-Beta community.
4. Describe an action by a member that you would consider beneficial to the AB community. (This should be general without mentioning names.)
5. Describe an action by a member that you would consider an offense to the AB community. (Ditto.)

To newer members (registered in 2006 or later and still active):

1. What was the main thing that drew you to the Anime-Beta website? How was it different from the animation-art-related contacts you'd had before?
2. What is the main reason that you have decided to continue visiting Beta regularly?
3. Give five words that you would use to describe a good "neighbor" in the Anime-Beta community.
4. Describe an action by a member that you would consider beneficial to the AB community. (This should be general, without mentioning names.)
5. Describe an action by a member that you would consider an offense to the AB community. (Ditto.)

9

Face-to-Face with the Digital Folk
The Ethics of Fieldwork on Facebook

Montana Miller

WHAT SETS US APART AS FOLKLORISTS FROM OTHER researchers is that we stand shoulder to shoulder with the people we study (see Ben-Amos 1973b; Dorson 1972, 5–7). Through firsthand fieldwork, with courageous and patient participant observation and naturalistic observation, folklore scholars have stood out in the academic world by respecting and prioritizing the voices and meanings of the insiders who trust them with their memories and their traditions.[1] In the new millennium, the virtual landscape has blurred boundaries between "real" and online identities, relationships, and research methods. This chapter addresses the implications of Internet technologies, communities, and norms for ethical and practical decisions in carrying out folklore fieldwork.

One afternoon in spring 2010, "Dr. Pepper,"[2] a young adjunct professor at a large midwestern university, sat down at her computer and tossed a question out to her hundreds of Facebook friends. She typed into her status-update line:

> I'm looking for anyone who remembers playing hypnosis games when they were kids or teenagers. I know I did, and I'm interested in what you recall of them. Send me a message or an email, and feel free to forward the request to your other friends—good research karma will follow! :)

Dr. Pepper soon received helpful replies from friends, some of them also folklorists. But when her post popped up in my Facebook "news feed," my own response veered away from hypnosis and toward a question that has increasingly preoccupied research ethicists in recent years: Was this an

DOI: 10.7330/9780874218909.c09

appropriate place, and method, for collecting data for what most academic institutions would consider research with human subjects?

I am not only a folklorist and ethnographer but also an institutional review board (IRB) member since 2005 at Bowling Green State University in Ohio; on the national level, I have been working with those who write and interpret the emerging rules for ethical research in online environments. Folklorists' relationships with their institutions' human-subject review boards—which are federally required to monitor the ethical conduct of research involving interviews, surveys, and observations of people—have been inconsistent. These relationships usually are troubled with misunderstandings about how to employ qualitative methods in emerging, often spontaneous fieldwork contexts. The discussion that ensued between Dr. Pepper and me (a friendly and collegial one, which she has kindly permitted me to recount here) underscored many of the tricky issues that arise as folklore research finds its foothold in the Digital Age.

In an e-mail to my friend, I expressed concern about her solicitation of informants on Facebook: she hadn't informed her audience that their immediate responses could be used as research material for publication. "Does your university require folklore people to go through review?" I asked, after ascertaining that her question was for a paper she intended to present at a peer-reviewed conference.

"I've already gotten the one great interview I was waiting on, and I thought I'd fish around to see if I could dredge anything else up on short notice," explained Dr. Pepper. She agreed that it would have been advisable to ask for responses with a more informed consent-like query. "I usually include my informed consent blurb when I start contacting people individually," she wrote me, "and I hadn't thought that the initial net-toss would require it, too."

Her university, she noted as an aside, had "strangely, never mentioned IRB approval to me for specific research projects, though I do have the current certificate that says I've gone through the general training (which I also wasn't told to do—I just did it because I wanted to)." While her department was starting to have graduate students get IRB approval on their theses, it wasn't because the university had demanded it. "It's quite a gray area," she said.

In fact, many folklorists collect information in just the same way that Dr. Pepper did—probably in violation of their institutions' review policies. However, despite the fact that so much of our work clearly involves research with human subjects, many IRBs appear to pay little or no attention to folklorists. It is tempting to rely on our own ethics and principles and simply proceed with Internet-based research; we are drawn by its boundless riches of material from people's stories, jokes, pictures, and living relationships online. Like Dr. Pepper, many folklorists use their own consent statements and follow research procedures that have been taught to them through training under expert professors in our field. But the broadening scope in recent years of IRBs' authority to approve or reject projects requires more careful planning and review of our methods, including our initial recruitment of subjects in digital contexts.

Many folklorists (and especially those from generations when IRBs did not exist or did not yet concern themselves with qualitative studies) may find this an intrusive hindrance to our work. As Dr. Pepper told me, "At this stage, it hadn't occurred to me to get consent." I empathized with her frustration, even with my IRB-member perspective. After all, folklorists are observers of folk culture and tradition, and many of our best ideas come from spontaneous events, interactions, and queries like hers. Moreover, we wondered, might interrupting such online conversations with disclaimers and consent documents deter people from replying? "The casualness of my question about hypnosis games seems to draw out people who don't think their answers are necessarily revolutionary," wrote Dr. Pepper. "I worry that if they felt I were asking an 'official' scholarly question, they wouldn't volunteer responses as easily." She also pointed out that she had asked informants to message her privately with their responses but that they had chosen to share their experiences in "quasi-public comments" anyway. "Folklore is *regularly* shared spontaneously with friends, which is a forum that Facebook allows for," she noted. Would an IRB have expected her to get clearance before tossing out the same question at dinner with a group of friends? Is IRB approval required to simply mention an upcoming project at a social gathering? Where do we draw the line, especially as our social gatherings now increasingly take place in Internet forums such as Facebook?

Ultimately, Dr. Pepper contacted some of those who had responded to her Facebook post to conduct in-depth interviews after obtaining formal consent from them. But I believe that her example highlights an uncomfortable new position for fieldworkers in folklore. Our responsibility is to clarify with our IRBs whether our projects (Internet-based or not) need to be reviewed. Some IRBs will consider our studies exempt—that is their prerogative. (IRBs work with federal regulations for human-research protections, but the institutions of which they are part have the individual flexibility to determine whether their IRBs will review certain types of low-risk research, which often includes humanities and other qualitative fields.[3]) However, if the IRB does require review, then we must submit a protocol before collecting examples. As an IRB member, I would advise my folklorist colleagues this: *if* the university does not have a clear policy regarding their department, they are not in violation, but they really *should* give their informants a consent form. Even at universities where the IRB governs all qualitative research, including folklore, the IRB does not have the manpower to go around making sure everyone is complying—but compliance is to our advantage as a profession.

In any case, we must approach Facebook solicitations with caution. Ideally, Dr. Pepper's hypnosis question was a recruitment post; she asked people to contact her by e-mail, and she intended to interview them *after* obtaining informed consent. But her method got swept up in the galloping pace of Internet dialogue. Recruitment, response, conversation, and self-revelation can happen in the blink of a cursor, and the folklorist may no longer be sure what material is fair game for research. Suddenly, right there on the Facebook wall, the interviews seem to have begun of their own accord; yet none of the respondents is aware of the project's purpose nor the risks and benefits of participating.

ORAL EXPRESSION AND ARCHIVED TEXT, TANGLED IN THE NEW ETHICS OF THE WEB

Folklorists who work with digital informants—with or without regulation by IRBs—often have to rely on their instincts and ethnographic training about ethics, doing the best they can to protect their subjects. What kinds of protections are adequate and necessary? Should our analysis of online texts be classified as "research with human subjects"? From whom do we obtain consent, and how? The emerging field of Internet research ethics has carried on rich and lively debates over these issues during the past decade; since 2002, Charles Ess and his collaborators have revised and published the most valuable guidelines available for Internet researchers (Consalvo and Ess 2011). But most folklorists have not taken an active role in the discourse. In fact, in the absence of IRB regulation over folklore work, many who have ventured into online fieldwork have made these judgment calls on their own, for better or for worse.

Many dilemmas relate to the differing perspectives with which scholars may view Internet expression. A great deal of what goes on in chat rooms, virtual worlds (such as Second Life, World of Warcraft, and other avatar-populated simulations), and even sites like Facebook and Twitter constitutes data that can be conceptualized as oral expression. As we observe the rapid artillery fire of text messages and status updates that now compose the daily narrative of people's lives, we can see these forms of digital communication as a new form of orality or folk speech, complete with slang abbreviations and emoticons (see Danet 2001; Fernback 2003; Kirshenblatt-Gimblett 1995; Mason 1998; Ong 1988). The traditional rules and methods for observing such human interaction are quite different (and for the IRB, in an entirely different realm of research) from the rules and methods for examining data considered to be "published text"—blogs, archives of discussion forums, and again, Facebook and Twitter, can arguably be classified as such texts! No IRB should require review and approval of a study based on already published, publicly available material. But it is not always easy to determine where oral expression (behavior) turns to archive (published text). Observing people interacting in a virtual world or live chat room? This seems to call for informed consent; or, if it is practically impossible to obtain consent (as in some anonymous or constantly changing venues), a waiver of consent bestowed by the IRB. But what if those chats, or events in Second Life, are recorded (by participants or administrators) and archived or posted on video-sharing sites? Do they automatically become a free-for-all database for folklorists to plunder and celebrate?

Answering these questions may be particularly difficult considering the discipline's reluctance to embrace the study of the Internet, let alone acknowledge its validity as a generator and purveyor of genuine folklore. Nevertheless, several intrepid scholars have endeavored to engage and fully document the medium over the years: John Dorst (1990), with his inquiry into the emerging patterns of communication and expression on the comparatively primitive World Wide Web; Barbara Kirshenblatt-Gimblett (1996), in her explorations of the "electronic vernacular"; and Bruce Lionel Mason, in his early research on virtual ethnography (1996, 1998, 2001). In the age of Web 2.0, more folklorists found compelling materials online and distinguished them and/or related them to real-world phenomena: Bill Ellis (2001, 2003) produced an expansive collection and analysis of 9/11 folklore online (see also Frank 2004); Robert Glenn Howard prolifically published numerous studies on folk religion and communities online (1998,

2005a, 2005b, 2008a, 2008b, 2011); Trevor J. Blank examined the ways in which humor and narratives uniquely appear online (2007, 2009c) while also working to expand the profile of folkloristic approaches to the study of the Internet and new media (Blank 2009a); Merrill Kaplan has analyzed epic poetry performances online as well as legends and belief on YouTube (2010, 2013); Kimberly Lau (2010) has studied play in virtual worlds; and Kate Ristau—embodied by her avatar, with a "Second Life Ethnographer" title hovering above her animated head—conducted firsthand observations of sacred rituals *within* Second Life (2009).

Of course, this is not an exhaustive list of scholarship but rather a representation of several works that have made a noticeable impact on folkloristic discourse. Still, the scholarly efforts of these folklorists—once decried as a distraction from "real" folklore—have ironically managed to provide a theoretical foundation for contemporary folklorists to build upon as the Internet becomes increasingly accepted as a locus of vernacular expression. I was among those folklorists who, early on, embraced and reflected upon the study of subjects from the Internet. In the year 2000, when I undertook my first online study (observing the candid discussions of those suffering with eating disorders in an anonymous, real-time chat room), I became the first researcher to successfully submit an Internet-based research protocol to the institutional review board of the Harvard University School of Medicine. At the time, Harvard's board hardly knew what to make of me, a UCLA folklore student doing a summer fellowship in medical anthropology, fervently arguing that the Internet context was an unprecedented window into the daily lives and uncensored stories of those living with stigmatized illnesses and addictions (Miller 2005). Ten years and many online studies later, there is still a considerable amount of ambiguity on how we can and should ethically conduct ourselves as we gather data through virtual conduits.[4]

THE ETHICS OF ONLINE ETHNOGRAPHY

Ethnography, as I have been trained to understand it as a folklorist, is the study of culture in depth over time from multiple perspectives, using multiple methods. The ethnographer immerses herself in the culture; she stays long enough to recognize the patterns and understand the insiders' points of view, including the dissenting voices. Is it even possible do this online? Certainly the things ethnographers research—communication and expressive behavior, relationships, community—all exist online. Whether we can truly understand people's perspectives and experiences without also observing their *offline* lives is a matter of disagreement among online ethnographers. But just as some (anthropologists of education, for example) do undertake ethnographies of specific places, an argument can be made for the value of a study limited to one online space, and the personae and activities observed within its bounds.

The American Folklore Society (AFS) has weighed in on research with human subjects, constructing a formal position statement, initially approved by the AFS Executive Board in 2006 and updated in 2011 (see American Folklore Society 2011 [2006]; Lloyd 2011). While it is admirable that the AFS has devoted time and interest into articulating a cogent framework for ethical fieldwork guidelines and considerations, it is unfortunate that the society's official position statement is nevertheless riddled with flawed arguments and misconceptions of contemporary IRB policies. The following excerpt is a representative example:

> Folklorists do not speak of their collaborators as "human subjects" but tend to consider them rather as knowledgeable partners in dialogue and as resources for exploring cultural forms and performances: these cultural practices, not their practitioners, are typically the object of our research. Human subjects review of qualitative interpretive research commits a category error. OHRP [U.S. Office for Human Research Protections] regulations and individual IRBs have developed their procedures taking the controlled lab experiment as the paradigm of all research, but most humanistic research is framed as documentation, interpretation, or conversation. (American Folklore Society 2011 [2006])

In 2006 the AFS's official position statement described the "people with whom folklorists work" as "artists, performers, hosts, teachers, and often . . . friends." Part of the problem here seems to lie with a fundamental distaste for the label "human subject" and its connotations. After all, it does sound a bit clinical and impersonal, which is an ethos that runs counter to how folklorists envision their relationship with "informants" (a term that, while far more accepted and used by folklorists, is not a particularly collaborative or respectful label either!). There may be a terminological disconnect, but this hardly should translate to divergent valuations on ethically conducting fieldwork with people.[5] (And let us not forget that Robert A. Georges and Michael Owen Jones's [1980] highly influential work on folklore fieldwork methods, the challenges of building rapport, and negotiating relationships is entitled *People Studying People: The Human Element in Fieldwork.*)

While IRB regulation originally concerned itself with controlled lab experiments, IRBs throughout the world of academic research now typically include social scientists and scholars in the humanities as well. The concern that the IRB will not understand an anthropological, ethnographic approach to research with humans, or the perception that all researchers must wait for egregious amounts of time before receiving approval on such a proposal, is simply inaccurate, especially since IRBs have invested in better training for board members to be highly competent in reviewing such research (see Abbott and Grady 2011).[6] Even though we are not doing experiments in a lab, we *are* still making analytical conclusions about human behavior and human culture, and this means we *are* generalizing; therefore, our work falls under the umbrella of research, as the OHRP defines it.

To argue that folklorists are merely studying "cultural practices, not their practitioners," skirts the issue, and worse, serves to only further undermine the scholastic validity of folkloristics. We cannot study the practices without studying the people that engage in them—through observation and/or interviews.[7] When we draw meaning from narratives we have transcribed and show how traditional practices express values, we document and interpret folklore forms as revealing of culture on a larger scale. Folklorists cannot have it both ways—if we want our research to be taken seriously, if we want our published work to have credibility and authority, then we also have to accept that that power comes with responsibility. We must not be afraid to be accountable and responsible to an IRB review of informed consent procedures. We must not be afraid to engage in the conversation necessary with the IRB to help them understand our "emergent process, with its continual negotiation of consent" and to plan an ethical and reasonable approach to obtaining that consent.

Ethnography—research with people—is *always* complicated. Online we are still people, and the dilemmas that arise are both the same and new. The diverse and constantly changing field of Internet research ethics is pushing up against a new frontier, where scholars from many disciplines are working with (and sometimes against) IRB reviewers to forge new understandings and consensus. Folklorists, and especially ethnographers, are well suited to help shape these ideas, as we are trained to deal with the concept of ethical pluralism. That is, people may come to a variety of justifiable ethical judgments, depending on context; these vary from place to place, from individual to individual. Researchers and subjects (and IRBs as well) may come to different ethical conclusions, because there is no standard formula that can work to produce *the* answer. With the limitless opportunities for cross-cultural encounters that Internet research affords, it is crucial that we confront the reality that different people have different codes and standards for privacy.

Ethnographic fieldwork is, undeniably, a human process. As folklorists Robert A. Georges and Michael Owen Jones note, "The ways in which fieldworkers and subjects perceive, conceive, interact with, and react to each other necessarily have precedents in their past experiences as and with human beings" (1980, 154). As qualitative researchers, we must always wrestle with the human dynamics, vulnerabilities, and fallibilities that surface during our research procedures. These unpredictable dynamics come up when one does fieldwork online, just as they do in traditional fieldwork situations. Ethnography is messy; it is hard to know when exactly it begins, and it is also difficult to maintain the boundaries that we may have drawn in our research designs. Whether the IRB plays a role or not, folklorists must take thoughtful and proactive steps to protect the rights of the subjects, minimize risk, weigh risks and benefits, and make sure that research is neither coercive nor has harmful effects on subjects' welfare (be it physical harm, emotional distress, or harm to their reputation).

The next generation of folklorists is growing up in a world where privacy, trust, and confidentiality may mean very different things than they did in the era when ethical codes for researchers were first established. Such standards and guidelines for ethical research have been developed by academic disciplines, both officially and unofficially (and by the federal OHRP and individual IRBs as well). We have become accustomed to thinking about the dilemmas they delineate: whether to participate or intervene in situations; when to reveal our exact purposes in the field and when deception is acceptable or necessary; and what responsibility we bear toward the community we write about with regard to member checks, representing a full range of perspectives, and disguising identities.

With online research, many of these dilemmas hinge on the crucial question: *Are we in a public space or a private one?* This is not only the starting point for a discussion with one's institutional review board but a key to determining appropriate methods and ethical decision making in the fieldwork process. A liberal, but somewhat simplistic, perspective is that the Internet is like a public billboard. This view contends that participants have given up their anonymity by posting on any site whose membership is not strictly controlled; therefore, their posts are public data and fair game for researchers to collect. However, some Internet ethicists have argued that we should base our definitions on participants' experience of what *feels* private (King 1996; Lawson 2003; McKee and Porter 2009; Waskul and Douglass 1996). Even though a website may be publicly accessible, if its users are experiencing it as private, how should we as researchers handle that discrepancy? To complicate matters, any single website hosts countless users with varying perspectives of what's public and private, and different aspects of the site may feature different levels of accessibility or privacy. This is where ethnographic skills are of paramount importance, and they are useful as well in the dialogue with the IRB.

A researcher must demonstrate familiarity with the context in order to gauge participants' expectations of privacy. Getting to know the norms and rhythms of one's field site is a process that simply cannot be rushed. Before we design our formal studies, we should go through the process of discovery (Georges and Jones 1980), which, online, usually means a great deal of time spent "lurking" or simply observing the activity and dynamics of an online community. Often the decision to lurk or to participate is not an easy one, especially if the researcher has chosen a community with interests important to her (which is typically the case). Yet making this decision, and sticking to it, is a significant matter when it comes to IRB review. As the definition of "research with human subjects" includes any sort of intervention with our subjects, participating in a discussion forum or interacting with avatars in a virtual world puts us squarely within that definition, just like interviewing informants in traditional fieldwork. Therefore, if we choose to engage in such interactions, ethically, we should get informed consent from our subjects, or at least make a reasonable attempt to do so given the challenges of the online field site.

Every topic, every field site, and every researcher is unique, and carrying out qualitative research is an ongoing process of ethical decision making. Topic sensitivity, subject vulnerability, and community vulnerability are factors that create higher risks and therefore require us to be even more thoughtful and proactive as we strive to protect and respect the people we study. Vulnerable populations include communities of illness and addiction and those who live with conditions that may be stigmatized in society. When we document people discussing their diseases, drug use, or sexual activities, we have a greater responsibility to consider issues of confidentiality and data identification (How "findable" is this data through a simple web search?) than we do when we record their favorite foods, fashions, or music. Using pseudonyms to protect our subjects' identities is an excellent step, but if anyone can Google a phrase from a quoted informant and find it right away on an archived discussion board, how confidential is that? One must keep in mind that the Internet environment and its rules constantly change: at this writing, Facebook is not searchable through Google, but we cannot guarantee that this won't change.

Anonymizing quotes can be an effective way to protect identities—that is, changing just enough of the subject's words to make it impossible to find the quote through a web search. Researchers who use this tactic, however, must struggle with how much to anonymize in order to minimize risk without overly compromising the data. Folklorists have long pondered these sorts of issues; Bill Ellis (1987), for example, has discussed the reasons why folklorists may choose to favor the integrity of their informants' exact words rather than paraphrasing for clarity of meaning. Once again, every project is a complex interplay among the researcher's human motivations and academic goals, the informants as individuals and community, the field site(s), and the (potentially sensitive) subject matter.

Ethics is often not about what we *can* do but what we *should* do. In decisions about research ethics and methodology, the answer is always "It depends."[8] What we *should* do varies depending on how we evaluate the context, weigh the factors, and come to an ethical stance in our particular case. Ideally, we should be discussing and sharing ethical norms with others in our field and in the field of Internet research ethics in general. Folklorists have a strong tradition of solidarity with our subjects, and we can apply these same principles to our research in online communities.

As we consider the new Internet contexts of our inquiries, and our subjects' experience and expectations, we must ask whether our research has benefits that outweigh the risks to our subjects. What are the potential harms to individuals and the community as a whole? At a recent cultural studies conference I attended, a paper was presented on the psychological motives behind people's Facebook profile pictures. The author made what I regarded as judgmental and insulting assumptions about what it means when people display their children or their pets as their profile photos. Lacking any ethnographic component that might have brought out the perspectives of the subjects of this study, the research was misrepresentative and potentially unethical. Even though these Facebook users' profile pictures were viewable online (and thus freely available to collect as data), I saw the researcher's use of them as exploitative and disrespectful to the people involved, especially as no effort was made to adequately conceal their identities. In addition, she did a disservice to the community in general (i.e., to the many Facebook users who post profile pictures featuring pets or children, for reasons nowhere near as pathological as this researcher proposed). It would not have been so difficult to contact such posters and ask them about their reasons for their behavior; however, it would have required IRB review to proceed with such an interactive study.

ON THE WALL: WHO ARE OUR SUBJECTS?

During the early years of the new millennium, as MySpace was thriving and Facebook first came on the scene, my study of how online profiles are used as sites of mourning and memorialization—largely by young people, at that time—brought to my attention some complex and troubling ethical questions.

After the owner of a profile has died, the conversation there often continues for weeks, months, and even years. These orphaned sites offer nostalgic commemoration and space for the bereaved to commiserate. But the sites also receive surprisingly casual messages to the deceased: updates on the everyday happenings at school, jovial advice about partying in the afterlife, and musings and questions regarding fashion, relationships, diet, and college applications. Through such one-way conversations, archived on the sites of the departed, posters often appear to be acting *as if* they believe their friend still checks the site from beyond, although degrees of belief in the afterlife are too private and tenuous for anyone to measure.[9] Like so much of what happens online, the frame in which these messages are written and interpreted is ambiguous and constantly shifting. The posts of the bereaved have multilayered meanings. And the ethical implications of studying them are ambiguous too.

Many such profiles that I have observed are openly accessible but intimately revealing. Are these profiles always fair game even if their owners were thoughtless, ignorant, or reckless and immature in exposing their lives—and the lives of many of their friends—there? I have long argued that while anything publicly accessible is reasonably fair game, we should still be sensitive to and protective of our subjects' well-being by disguising their identities to some extent. But how to disguise them, and how much, is largely at the discretion of the researcher, depending on the context. To reiterate, the factors we must consider include: How vulnerable is the subject or the population in general? How sensitive is the information? How searchable is the content? Quotes and content *may* be recognizable to friends of the deceased or the posters and who have access to the profile being analyzed.

How does this new context for public or semi-public grieving change the ethical issues that should concern researchers collecting data here? As these posts were publicly accessible (thus visible to me even though I was not "friends" with the deceased whose walls were posted on), I did not need consent in order to view them. But should I have tried to obtain consent from the posters anyway?

People posting on such sites have little consciousness of how wide their invisible audience is; they don't know how loosely or carefully their friends' privacy settings have been set. If they do not know *how* public the page is (especially given the current misunderstandings and confusion over evolving Facebook privacy controls), then can we consider them to be "informed" about the implicit consent they give when posting comments that the public (and researchers) can access? Internet researchers are used to thinking about getting consent from the creators of any restricted profiles that we might use for research purposes; we have been trained to think of the wall's owner as the primary human subject. We have not been trained to think about the vulnerable third parties who unwittingly offer their personal data on their friends' walls.

In my folkloristic analysis of this complex space of quasi-public mourning, I have considered many potential situations, including the following hypothetical examples:

- A student dies in a disturbing way (suicide or murder) and his profile is removed. Can we use material that was there before it was removed? His family may not appreciate it—and perhaps we should be considering the harm to *them*, not just the (now dead, and therefore no longer the IRB's concern) immediate subject of our research.
- A teenager who is my friend on Facebook dies of a heart attack. May I use her wall as a site for observation? Again, the question arises: Who is the research subject? Must I get consent from the deceased girl's friends? Have other Facebook researchers

obtained consent from those who post *on* others profiles? Generally, they have not—but perhaps this needs to change.

- One of my students loses her friend to a car accident and then allows me to see that friend's profile to document the expressions of mourning accumulating on her wall. The dead student has 1,500 friends; if her privacy settings allowed access to "friends of friends," her wall has a potentially huge, invisible audience. Yet technically, that student and I were not friends, so I do not have permission to access her page. However, if my student becomes my research assistant, collaborating on the project with me, does that then give me ethical access to her deceased friend's page? (Remember, once she is dead, the person is no longer a "human subject." Should I be held back by the chance that her friends and family, posting on a wall whose audience they have no clear concept of, may be affected by my research?)
- A high school student loses her sister and posts voluminous content about it on her publicly visible Facebook wall. Should her age matter? She seems to be self-consciously, deliberately performing her grief for a limitless audience—should I consider whether her emotional state makes her capable of making good judgments about that? What is my responsibility? Taking the view that this is a published text accessible to all, technically I can use the material, but how can I be more sensitive and respectful to the text's human author? In highly charged examples such as this one, it has also occurred to me that perhaps I should not use the data. People's perceptions of how their grief will be observed and used could be skewed, especially when they are in a vulnerable state.

I continued to follow the online mourning phenomenon over the years while also observing the increasingly intricate privacy issues arising in the social networking world. My misgivings about potential harms to third-party subjects, and the extreme sensitivity of the personal tragedies being displayed on these sites, often contributed to my hesitance to publish the data I collected. Instead, I have used this research as a learning and teaching experience in the field of research ethics, discussing with scholarly and professional audiences the potential tensions, contradictions, and even heartbreak that this type of online research can generate.

FACEBOOK IN FLUX

Facebook is becoming a source of endless ethical quandaries, and laws and policies regarding its use are in flux, if not nonexistent. The privacy options offered by Facebook have changed repeatedly, evolving from public/networks/ friends to the more recent choices among public, friends, and "customized" abilities to make certain features visible or invisible to selected parties.

As the privacy controls have changed without warning, they have become increasingly complicated and difficult to navigate, and the default settings abruptly implemented by Facebook with each change have often resulted in unpleasant surprises for users. Many adults had not yet joined Facebook back in September 2006, when creator Mark Zuckerberg and his crew of programmers first introduced what is known as "the Feed": a rundown of any recent activity by one's friends. Unheralded, this list of "news" appeared one day on every Facebook user's home page; scrolling down it, one was flooded by reports on friends' status updates; wall posts; the addition of new friends, groups, or photos; comments and tags on photos; notes posted and commented on; and romantic relationships forming and dissolving. Most Facebook users were taken unawares by the appearance of this new feature, which distributed information they had *felt* was somewhat private even though it had always been potentially available to those who were permitted to see their profiles (Miller 2008). Now it seemed to be broadcast over a loudspeaker, and there was no way to shut it off.

With the continuing development of Facebook's interface, those who neglect to religiously update their account settings find themselves revealing far more than they ever intended to. For example, many users are not aware of just how much of what they write on *other* people's profiles, including comments on walls or beneath photos, shows up on their friends' news feeds. Facebook is quite disingenuous in its rhetoric, which reassures users that they are in control of their privacy settings at the same time that it has made more and more of their communications public by default. Even with conservatively adjusted privacy settings, individuals can no longer prevent much of their Facebook activity from showing up on other people's home pages when they log in—an outsize village gossip network reaching across every geographical and temporal boundary. A global, timeless bathroom wall: "virtualatrinalia."[10]

Our best attempts to control our digital profiles may be thwarted, as we cannot escape the human element of Facebook privacy. The norm on

Facebook today is to accumulate hundreds, if not thousands, of friends. Naturally, not all of these friends can be trusted to keep our information confidential (the ethics of friendship are not, as yet, monitored by any regulatory board). As a matter of course, Facebook "friends" download and repost each other's photos, take screenshots of each other's pages, and borrow each other's accounts to spy on people who may have unfriended them or blocked them (ex-lovers, for example). According to every class of college students I have taught since the advent of Facebook, young people (emulated, I suspect, by the older generation who soon followed them into Facebook's clutches) share passwords, steal passwords, find accounts unlocked, and prank each other—sometimes vengefully—on a regular basis.

This reinforces an important lesson for researchers: we cannot assume that what has been written on a social networking profile is authentic. The well-worn cliché that "on the Internet, no one knows you're a dog"—originally the caption of a *New Yorker* cartoon of a dog typing at a computer—has come of age in a social networking world where fake profiles, hacked profiles, and profiles belonging to people's pets are ubiquitous. This may be all the more reason for us to go to the trouble of recruiting informants whose offline personae are known to us, whose consent we can obtain and verify to our best ability, and whose physical presence and voice we can evoke when we endeavor to look deeper than surface interpretations of their performances within the Facebook frame.

The independent website Lamebook.com, launched in April 2009, represents an amplified version of the poaching of supposedly personal Facebook communication for use in a public forum. People submit examples of embarrassing, hilarious, or (as Lamebook puts it) "cringeworthy" Facebook posts and pictures, copied from their friends' profiles. The website blurs the pictures and last names of the people whose foibles are exposed in this forum, but often enough, the material is easily recognizable to anyone connected with the subjects. Of course, Lamebook is not required to hold itself to any ethical principles, and its founders make no claim to be serving anyone's best interest. They do promise to remove any post whose subject requests an end to the humiliation, although if the objection is e-mailed "during the weekend, we may not get around to deleting it until the beginning of the next week" (Lamebook 2011).

Disturbing as it may be to victims of its mockery and to defenders of online privacy, Lamebook.com is one of many sites that folklorists may find appealing as a source of published, conveniently anonymous material.[11] Its archives are rich in examples of romantic and family dramas, pranks and humor, and jargon and folk speech of every variety. Folklorists could thrive on such a treasure trove; but *should* we? This is the sort of muddy ethical field where we can lose our footing unless we ground our work in shared values and respect for the human beings behind the screenshots. Clearly, the Internet has complicated our discipline. Its crisscrossing boundaries in data and personal relationships, and its fluidity of multiple identities and frames, require us to carefully rethink our methods.

NEW GENERATIONS AND PERCEPTIONS OF PRIVACY

One of the major challenges we face as ethnographers is trying to teach Internet research ethics to our own students, many of whom grew up in the Wild West of the web era (see McLure 2000). "Flame wars" break out like gunfights with no provocation, people wantonly post and respond to polls, and many surrender the content of their lives, willy-nilly, to Google, Facebook, and so on—seemingly oblivious to the risks of the increased sharing, selling, and leaking of online data. Further, cultural norms and standards of privacy are changing rapidly. For example, a couple of years ago, few parents were comfortable putting their children's photos on the Internet; today this practice is so acceptable that parents who *don't* post pictures are harangued by relatives eager to see every family milestone documented and displayed for loved ones (and hundreds of others) to view and comment on. The posting of prenatal ultrasound photos and even ultrasound videos is now widespread, as the news feed replaces the birth announcement; some newborns already have Facebook profiles (administered by their parents, I can only assume).

In a time when privacy is becoming essentially unattainable or obsolete, how do we help our students to understand and practice ethical methods when collecting data online? When they find something they like on the web, they may see no reason not to jump on their claim and use it for a paper. Their generation is used to seeing the news media descend on people's web profiles when their tragedies or scandals suddenly hit the headlines, looking for clues to better understand them. Not surprisingly, students may be confused and unprepared when we ask them to think like ethnographers and consider alternative interpretations. It is essential that we understand, and teach, the distinctions between "academic research" (as federal guidelines for human-subject protection define it) and other ways in which people collect, use, and present data about other people (including journalism, memoirs, documentary films, and marketing research). The way institutional review boards see it, "research" refers to systematic inquiry that is *generalizable* (in qualitative fields, this means that we are analyzing it to shed light on human culture and behavior) and contributes to an academic field. If we can help our students to grasp this concept, we may well have accomplished a heroic feat.

With the rise in cyberbullying and the prevalence of anonymous vitriol on discussion forums, many have suggested that this generation lacks empathy. No one can spend much time online without observing how often the Internet brings out the darker, crueler sides of human expression. Some psychologists have attributed this to the "disinhibition effect" (Suler 2004) and the detachment of communicating with a screen presence (text or image) rather than a real, reacting human being. Unfortunately, this disinhibition effect also may interfere with a researcher's ethical decisions and instincts. For example, it is all too easy to design a study based on naturalistic observation of a discussion forum and then find oneself spontaneously compelled to get involved, sometimes redirecting or inflaming the conversation or influencing the community. When this has happened to my students, I have advised them to limit their analysis to discussion threads where they were not involved. To instigate or contribute to a conversation and then use it as data constitutes an intervention with human subjects, and therefore requires consent procedures—*before* the fact, not afterward. This may not be the way that many folklorists went about their firsthand, often serendipitous research in the past, and their resistance to these guidelines is understandable. Yet the bottom line must always be respect for our subjects and concern for their rights and well-being.

The best we can do in situations like those I have described here is represent and practice the ideals we have chosen to subscribe to as folklorists. Our job is to convey to the next generation of researchers the benefits of acting ethically: creating a shared community of values in academia, pride in our work, ethnographic authority, and credibility among our subjects as well as our peers.

CONCLUSION

What expectations do people have about the virtual spaces they visit—whether as participants or as researchers? In public spaces, we can reasonably expect that those present know they may be watched. They realize that they may not know everyone who is watching them or know why others are watching. In closed communities or private interactions, however, people do have a reasonable expectation of some kind of control over their information. At the least, they are usually aware of the risks of revealing themselves to anyone to whom they have chosen to express themselves.

When researchers first began flocking to the Internet to observe chat room discussions, blogs, and the like, it was somewhat easier to distinguish between public and private spaces online. Debates sprang up about communities where public access seemed ambiguous (such as listservs) and topics that were especially sensitive (such as vulnerable or stigmatized groups), but it was easier to determine what a subject's reasonable expectation of privacy would be and then weigh the risks of using that data, the risks to the individual, and the risks to the community being studied.

Folklorists must now consider the risks and ethically navigate the new Internet terrain for our fieldwork because there is so much important cultural behavior occurring in this space. Facebook is no longer a separate phenomenon from real life but a pervasive dimension of everyday life for people of all generations and all demographics. We have a wealth of expressions, narratives and conversations, and images and video to collect at our fingertips. Traditions are emerging—both "Facebook traditions" and traditions that Facebook allows us to access—and the tools of our discipline can be adapted to make sense of these new phenomena. In the Internet Communities classes that I teach, my students and I discuss Facebook's striking influence on a litany of customs and rituals of everyday life. Brainstorming topics for their ethnographic research papers, I ask them: How has Facebook changed the ways we work? eat? travel? express love? break up? work out conflicts? raise children? express sexual identity? act politically? experience depression, anxiety, and loss?

The methodological puzzles presented throughout this essay exemplify the challenges that accompany these new opportunities for exciting research, and the solutions are rarely definitive. Further obscuring our path, our academic field often falls into the gray, half-neglected area of universities' IRB review policies. Folklore is regarded, in some ways, as something of a fringe discipline, and it gets treated as such when it comes to administrative issues like the IRB process. Our sense of ethical research as folklorists is challenged as we make decisions (in the field and off the field) about how closely to stick to official review regulations—restrictions that might in fact be detrimental to the kind of research we do (which is so often spontaneous and informal). Jumping through the bureaucratic hoops of institutional review boards is certainly infuriating, as it seems like there are folklorists all over Facebook (and other social networks and discussion boards) throwing questions out there and reaping abundant harvests. At this writing, increasing numbers of us are Facebook users ourselves, sharing our research and our lives as academics and humans. More than ever before—both online and offline, with the boundaries dissolving all around us—we stand shoulder to shoulder with the folk whose traditions and meanings we explore and interpret.

NOTES

1. The image of "standing shoulder to shoulder" with our informants was powerfully evoked by folklorist John McDowell in his 2008 Archer Taylor Memorial Lecture at the annual meeting of the Western States Folklore Society in Davis, California.
2. As my quotation marks suggest, this is a pseudonym. All pseudonyms are in quotation marks at first reference only.
3. For a relatively concise overview of the historical origins, and current functions, scope, and procedures of institutional review boards, see Smale (2010, 310–314).
4. I have used a range of methods, depending on the nature of the study and the sensitivity of the topic. My studies have included chat rooms and online support groups (Miller 2005, 2007); virtual worlds, such as Webkinz, for children (Miller 2009a); Facebook's influence on college culture and traditional power dynamics in academic culture (Miller 2006a, 2009b); occupational narratives emerging in the comments beneath shared photo albums (Miller 2010b); and mourning and memorialization on social networking sites (Miller 2006b, 2010a), which I discuss later in this chapter.
5. The AFS position statement objects that "it would be absurd to strip individual identifiers" or "suppress individual identities" from the kinds of material we often study as folklorists. This is a misunderstanding of the IRB's guidelines and protocols. IRB regulation does not mean that our informants are turned into anonymous subjects; it simply protects their right to *choose* whether their identities are revealed (and to what extent), and to be fully informed about how their words, images, and interactions will be used by the researcher. It bears noting that IRB protocols usually refer to "participants" in research, not "subjects." The IRB is not only concerned with physical harms but also the profound harms to reputation, privacy and dignity that humans are vulnerable to.
6. It is ironic for folklorists to pride themselves on their "conversational" research with "collaborators" but reject a collaborative conversation with the IRB, whose purpose is one we should support: to advocate for those who can be exploited and harmed by irresponsible research.
7. And without an emphasis on *people*, some of the most compelling and impactful folkloristic research of the last fifty years would be comparatively bland. After all, part of what has made the life work of Henry Glassie, Michael Owen Jones, and

many other prominent folklorists so enriching has been their ability to beautifully focus their studies on an individual *human* and construct a master narrative from the inside-out—not the other way around—en route to sharing keen insights into a community.

8. As noted earlier, even IRBs differ widely, as they use federal guidelines but adapt them, often case by case.

9. For a folkloristic examination of such public mourning and grief rituals on MySpace, see Dobler (2009).

10. This term is my own. For another folklorist's application of similar concepts, see Bronner (2009, 56–61).

11. Similarly, the website LiterallyUnbelievable.org republishes Facebook users' embarrassing wall posts in which they erroneously interpret an outlandish news story published by The Onion.com (a popular, satirical faux news website) as an actual news event. Outside of Facebook, other sites serve a comparably demeaning purpose, such as PeopleOfWalmart.com, which posts "funny" pictures of peculiar-looking Walmart patrons (typically focusing on shoppers' clothing and/or self-presentation); the uploaded images are submitted by fans of the People of Walmart website.

References

"666A The Tenant of the Beast." http://tinyurl.com/42oazda (accessed 3 February 2011).

"668 Neighbor of the Beast" [album]. http://tinyurl.com/3ckumce (accessed 3 February 2011).

"668 Neighbor of the Beast" [lyric]. http://tinyurl.com/3up2nge (accessed 3 February 2011).

"668 Neighbor of the Beast" [beer]. http://tinyurl.com/3f2yy8j (accessed 3 February 2011).

"1474 Small Things." 2006. YouTube. http://www.youtube.com/watch?v=pLT44ZRvFAA (accessed 15 July 2011).

Abbate, Janet. 1999. *Inventing the Internet.* Cambridge, MA: MIT Press.

Abbott, Lura, and Christine Grady. 2011. "A Systematic Review of the Empirical Literature Evaluating IRBs: What We Know and What We Still Need to Learn." *Journal of Empirical Research on Human Research Ethics: An International Journal* 6 (1): 3–20. http://dx.doi.org/10.1525/jer.2011.6.1.3.

Adams, Henry. 1983 [1918]. *Democracy; Esther; Mont Saint Michel and Chartres; and The Education of Henry Adams.* New York: Library of America.

Ali, Amir Hatem. 2011. "The Power of Social Media in Developing Nations: New Tools for Closing the Digital Divide and Beyond." *Harvard Human Rights Journal* 24: 185–220.

Alvin, Julius. 1991. *Gross Jokes.* New York: Zebra Books.

"Alyssa." 2009. The Tapeworm Diet. *Museum of Hoaxes.* http://tinyurl.com/3wg6egq (accessed 22 July 2010).

"Amazing Claude the Hypnotist." 2006. *Jokesy.com.* http://tinyurl.com/6zezu2p (accessed 8 July 2011).

American Folklore Society. 2011 [2006]. "AFS Position Statement on Research With Human Subjects." American Folklore Society website. http://www.afsnet. org/?page=HumanSubjects (accessed 23 February 2012).

Anderson, Benedict. 1991. *Imagined Communities: Reflections on the Origin and Spread of Nationalism.* Revised edition. London: Verso.

"Anime and Manga." 2010. *Fan History Wiki.* http://www.fanhistory.com/wiki/Anime_and_manga#Demographics (accessed 8 March 2011).

Appadurai, Arjun. 1990. "Disjuncture and Difference in the Global Cultural Economy." *Public Culture* 2 (2): 1–24. http://dx.doi.org/10.1215/08992363-2-2-1.

Appadurai, Arjun. 1993. "Patriotism and Its Futures." *Public Culture* 5 (3): 411–29. http://dx.doi.org/10.1215/08992363-5-3-411.

Appadurai, Arjun. 1996. *Modernity at Large: Cultural Dimensions of Globalization.* Minneapolis: University of Minnesota Press.

Appadurai, Arjun, and Carol A. Breckenridge. 1995. "Public Modernity in India." In *Consuming Modernity: Public Culture in a South Asian World,* ed. Carol A. Breckenridge, 1–20. Minneapolis: University of Minnesota Press.

"Apple's 1984 Commercial." 2011. Apple QuickTime Movies. http://www.uriahcarpenter. info/1984.html (accessed 28 February 2011).

Archibugi, Daniele. 2008. *The Global Commonwealth of Citizens: Toward Cosmopolitan Democracy*. Princeton, NJ: Princeton University Press.

"Art of Disney and Sotheby's." 2011. *Gold & Coulson*. Originally published in *Animation Magazine*, January 1995. http://gcjustice.com/Sothebys_Art_Auction.htm (accessed 9 July 2011).

"Ayds Diet Candy." 2003. *Low Carb Diet Support and Eating*. http://tinyurl.com/3k97g2o (accessed 13 November 2010).

Bacon-Smith, Camille. 1992. *Enterprising Women: Television Fandom and the Creation of Popular Myth*. Philadelphia: University of Pennsylvania Press.

Baker, Ronald L. 1982. *Hoosier Folk Legends*. Bloomington: Indiana University Press.

Baker, Ronald L. 1986. *Jokelore: Humorous Folktales from Indiana*. Bloomington: Indiana University Press.

Barabási, Albert-László. 2003. *Linked: How Everything Is Connected to Everything Else and What It Means*. New York: Plume.

Baron, Naomi. 2010. *Always On: Language in an Online and Mobile World*. New York: Oxford University Press.

Barrick, Mac. 1970. "Racial Riddles and the Polack Joke." *Keystone Folklore Quarterly* 15 (1): 3–15.

Barrick, Mac. 1972. "The Typescript Broadside." *Keystone Folklore Quarterly* 15: 27–38.

Barrier, Michael. 1999. *Hollywood Cartoons: American Animation in Its Golden Age*. New York: Oxford University Press.

Barth, John. 1987. *The Tidewater Tales: A Novel*. Baltimore: Johns Hopkins University Press.

Bascom, William R. 1955. "Verbal Art." *Journal of American Folklore* 68 (268): 245–52. http://dx.doi.org/10.2307/536902.

Bascom, William R. 1973. "Folklore, Verbal Art, and Culture." *Journal of American Folklore* 86 (342): 374–81. http://dx.doi.org/10.2307/539361.

Bateson, Gregory. 1955. "A Theory of Play and Fantasy: A Report on Theoretical Aspects of the Project for the Study of the Role of Paradoxes of Abstraction in Communication." In *Approaches to the Study of Human Personality*, American Psychiatric Association. Psychiatric Research Reports, no. 2, 39–51. Reprinted in Bateson (2000), 177–93.

Bateson, Gregory. 1956. "The Message 'This Is Play'." In *Group Processes: Transactions of the Second Conference*, ed. Bertram Schaffner, 145–242. New York: Josiah Macy Jr. Foundation.

Bateson, Gregory. 2000 (1972). *Steps to an Ecology of Mind*. Chicago: University of Chicago Press.

Bauman, Richard. 1971. "Differential Identity and the Social Base of Folklore." *Journal of American Folklore* 84 (331): 31–41. http://dx.doi.org/10.2307/539731.

Bauman, Richard. 1975. "Verbal Art as Performance." *American Anthropologist* 70 (2): 90–311.

Bauman, Richard. 1983. "Folklore and the Forces of Modernity." *Folklore Forum* 16(2): 153–58. https://scholarworks.iu.edu/dspace/handle/2022/1874 (accessed 22 February 2012).

Bauman, Richard. 1984 (1977). *Verbal Art as Performance*. Long Grove, IL: Waveland Press.

Bauman, Richard. 1986. *Story, Performance, and Event: Contextual Studies of Oral Narrative*. Cambridge Studies in Oral Literature and Culture. Cambridge: Cambridge University Press.

Bauman, Richard. 1992. "Performance." In *Folklore, Cultural Performances, and Popular Entertainments: A Communications-Centered Handbook*, ed. Richard Bauman, 41–49. New York: Oxford University Press.

Bauman, Richard. 2004. *A World of Others' Words: Cross-Cultural Perspectives on Intertextuality*. Malden, MA: Blackwell Publishing.

Bauman, Zygmunt. 1998. "Allosemitism: Premodern, Modern, Postmodern." In *Modernity, Culture, and "the Jew"*, ed. Bryan Cheyette and Laura Marcus, 143–56. Palo Alto, CA: Stanford University Press.

Baym, Nancy K. 1993. "Interpreting Soap Operas and Creating Community: Inside a Computer-Mediated Fan Culture." *Journal of Folklore Research* 30 (2/3): 143–177.

Baym, Nancy K. 1994. "The Emergence of Community in Computer-Mediated Communication." In *CyberSociety: Computer-Mediated Communication and Community*, ed. Steve Jones, 138–163. Thousand Oaks, CA: Sage Publications.

Baym, Nancy K. 1995. "The Performance of Humor in Computer-Mediated Communication." *Journal of Computer-Mediated Communication* 1 (2). http://tinyurl.com/Baym1995 (accessed 16 February 2011).

Baym, Nancy K. 2010. *Personal Connections in the Digital Age*. Digital Media and Society Series. Malden, MA: Polity Press.

Belknap, Robert E. 2004. *The List: The Uses and Pleasures of Cataloguing*. New Haven, CT: Yale University Press.

Bell, Louis Michael, Cathy Makin Orr, and Michael James Preston. 1976. *Urban Folklore from Colorado: Photocopy Cartoons*. Ann Arbor, MI: University Microfilms.

Ben-Amos, Dan. 1971. "Toward a Definition of Folklore in Context." *Journal of American Folklore* 84 (331): 3–15. http://dx.doi.org/10.2307/539729.

Ben-Amos, Dan. 1973a. "The 'Myth' of Jewish Humor." *Western Folklore* 32 (2): 112–131. http://dx.doi.org/10.2307/1498323.

Ben-Amos, Dan. 1973b. "A History of Folklore Studies: Why Do We Need It?" *Journal of the Folklore Institute* 10 (1/2): 113–124. http://dx.doi.org/10.2307/3813884.

Benkler, Yochai. 2008. *The Wealth of Networks: How Social Production Transforms Markets and Freedom*. New Haven, CT: Yale University Press. http://yupnet.org/benkler/archives/8 (accessed 8 September 2008).

Bennett, Gillian. 2005. *Bodies: Sex, Violence, Disease and Death in Contemporary Legend*. Jackson: University Press of Mississippi.

Berger, Arthur Asa. 2006. *The Genius of the Jewish Joke*. New Brunswick, NJ: Transaction.

Bhabha, Homi. 1990. "Narrating the Nation." In *Nation and Narration*, ed. Homi Bhabha, 1–7. New York: Routledge Press.

Billig, Michael. 2001. "Humour and Hatred: The Racist Jokes of the Ku Klux Klan." *Discourse & Society* 12 (3): 267–89. http://dx.doi.org/10.1177/0957926501012003001.

Biro, Adam. 2001. *Two Jews on a Train: Stories from the Old Country and the New*. Chicago: University of Chicago Press.

"Bizarro." 2011. *Los Angeles Times*. 4 February, D23.

BLACKberry. 2009. "Blackfolk: Mental Experiment: Live Blogging the Tyra Banks Show." LiveJournal [blog]. http://blackfolk.livejournal.com/7795391.html (accessed 13 November 2010).

Blank, Trevor J. 2007. "Examining the Transmission of Urban Legends: Making the Case for Folklore Fieldwork on the Internet." *Folklore Forum* 37(1): 15–26. https://scholarworks.iu.edu/dspace/handle/2022/3231.

Blank, Trevor J. 2009a. *Folklore and the Internet: Vernacular Expression in a Digital World. Logan.* Logan: Utah State University Press.

Blank, Trevor J. 2009b. "Toward a Conceptual Framework for the Study of Folklore and the Internet." In *Folklore and the Internet: Vernacular Expression in a Digital World*, ed. Trevor J. Blank, 1–20. Logan: Utah State University Press.

Blank, Trevor J. 2009c. "Moonwalking in the Digital Graveyard: Diversions in Oral and Electronic Humor Regarding the Death of Michael Jackson." *Midwestern Folklore* 35 (2): 71–96.

Blank, Trevor J. 2013. "Hybridizing Folk Culture: Toward a Theory of New Media and Vernacular Discourse." *Western Folklore.* Forthcoming.

Blitstein, Ryan. 2006. "More than Zero." *SF Weekly*, May 31. http://www.sfweekly. com/2006-05-31/news/more-than-zero/full (accessed 30 January 2011).

Bloemraad, Irene. 2004. "Who Claims Dual Citizenship? The Limits of Postnational-ism, the Possibilities of Transnationalism, and the Persistence of Traditional Citizenship." *International Migration Review* 38 (2): 389–426. http://dx.doi. org/10.1111/j.1747-7379.2004.tb00203.x.

"Blonde Jokes." Jokeforum. http://www.jokeforum.com/jokes_Blonde-jokes.html (accessed 16 February 2011).

Blumenfeld, Gerry. 1965. *Some of My Best Jokes Are Jewish!* New York: Kanrom.

Boas, Franz. 1902. "The Ethnological Significance of Esoteric Doctrines." *Science* 16 (413): 872–874. http://dx.doi.org/10.1126/science.16.413.872.

Boas, Franz. 1938. "Mythology and Folklore." In *General Anthropology*, ed. Franz Boas, 109–126. Boston: Heath.

Booker, Janice L. 1992. *The Jewish American Princess and Other Myths: The Many Faces of Self-Hatred.* New York: SPI Books.

Boorstin, Daniel. 1987 (1961). *The Image: A Guide to Pseudo-Events in America.* New York: Vintage Books.

boyd, danah. 2006. "Identity Production in a Networked Culture: Why Youth Heart MySpace." Presented at the American Association for the Advancement of Sci-ence Meeting, February 19, St. Louis, Missouri. http://www.danah.org/papers/ AAAS2006.html (accessed 29 June 2011).

Boyer, Jay. 1993. "The *Schlemiezel*: Black Humor and the *Shtetl* Tradition." In *Semites and Stereotypes: Characteristics of Jewish Humor*, ed. Avner Ziv and Anat Zajdman, 3–12. Westport, CT: Greenwood Press.

"Brad." 2008. *Two Jews Three Opinions.* Weblog. http://tinyurl.com/2Jews3OpinionsBlog (accessed 5 July 2011).

Brandes, Stanley. 1983. "Jewish-American Dialect Jokes and Jewish-American Identity." *Jewish Social Studies* 45 (3/4): 233–240.

Briggs, Charles L. 1988. *Competence in Performance: The Creativity of Tradition in Mexicano Verbal Art.* Philadelphia: University of Pennsylvania Press.

Brod, Harry. 1995. "Of Mice and Supermen: Images of Jewish Masculinity." In *Gender and Judaism: The Transformation of Tradition*, ed. T. M. Rudavsky, 279–293. New York: New York University Press.

Bronner, Simon J. 1986. *American Folklore Studies: An Intellectual History.* Lawrence: Uni-versity Press of Kansas.

Bronner, Simon J. 1988. *American Children's Folklore.* Little Rock, AR: August House.

Bronner, Simon J. 2004 (1986). *Grasping Things: Folk Material Culture and Mass Society.* Lexington: University Press of Kentucky.

Bronner, Simon J. 2006. "Dialect Stories." In *The Encyclopedia of American Folklife*, ed. Simon J. Bronner. Armonk, NY: M. E. Sharpe.

Bronner, Simon J. 2009. "Digitizing and Virtualizing Folklore." In *Folklore and the Internet: Vernacular Expression in a Digital World*, ed. Trevor J. Blank, 21–66. Logan: Utah State University Press.

Bronner, Simon J. 2010. "Framing Folklore: An Introduction." *Western Folklore* 69 (3/4): 5–27.

Bronner, Simon J. 2011. "Framing Violence and Play in American Culture." *Journal of Ritsumeikan Social Sciences and Humanities* 3: 145–60.

Brown, Katie, Scott W. Campbell, and Rich Ling. 2011. "Mobile Phones Bridging the Digital Divide for Teens in the US?" *Future Internet* 3 (2): 144–58. http://dx.doi. org/10.3390/fi3020144.

Brunvand, Jan Harold. 1963. "A Classification for Shaggy Dog Stories." *Journal of American Folklore* 76 (299): 42–68. http://dx.doi.org/10.2307/538078.

Brunvand, Jan Harold. 1984. *The Choking Doberman*. New York: W. W. Norton & Co.

Brunvand, Jan Harold. 1988. *The Mexican Pet*. New York: W. W. Norton & Co.

Brunvand, Jan Harold. 1998. *The Study of American Folklore*. 4th edition. New York: W. W. Norton & Co.

Brunvand, Jan Harold. 2004. "The Vanishing 'Urban Legend.'" *Midwestern Folklore* 30 (2): 5–20.

Camporesi, Valeria. 2002. *Mass Culture and National Traditions: The B.B.C. and American Broadcasting, 1922–1954*. Florence, Italy: European Academic Press Publishing.

Caron, Andre H., and Letizia Caronia. 2007. *Moving Cultures: Mobile Communication in Everyday Life*. Montreal: McGill-Queen's Press.

Cashman, Ray. 2008. *Storytelling on the Northern Irish Border: Characters and Community*. Bloomington: Indiana University Press.

Caughey, John L. 1984. *Imaginary Social Worlds*. Lincoln: University of Nebraska Press.

Caverly, David C., Anne R. Ward, and Michael J. Caverly. 2009. "Techtalk: Mobile Learning and Access." *Journal of Developmental Education* 33 (1): 38–39.

CERN (The European Organization for Nuclear Research). 2000. "A CERN Invention You Are Familiar With: The World-Wide-Web." http://stoner.phys.uaic.ro/old/ IDESC/CERN%20and%20WWW.pdf (accessed 1 December 2000).

Ceruzzi, Paul E. 2003. *A History of Modern Computing*. Cambridge, MA: MIT Press.

Charlot, John. 1983. "A Pattern in Three Hawaiian Chants." *Journal of American Folklore* 96 (379): 64–68. http://dx.doi.org/10.2307/539835.

Chernin, Kim. 1994. *The Hungry Self: Women, Eating, and Identity*. New York: Harper Paperbacks.

Chief, Rabbi. 1893. "In Defence of Jewish Wit and Humour." *Review of the Churches* 3: 370–371.

"Children's Answers to Sunday School Questions." http://www.virtualchristiancenter. com/humor/childrensanswers.htm (accessed 1 February 2011).

Christie, Les. 2010. "America's Wealthiest (and Poorest) States." *CNN Money*, September 16. http://tinyurl.com/cnnrichpoor (accessed 26 January 2012).

Clements, William M. 1973. "Unintentional Substitution in Folklore Transmission: A Devolutionary Instance." *New York Folklore Quarterly* 29 (4): 243–273.

"Cocky Tapeworm Diet Expert." 2008. YouTube. http://www.youtube.com/ watch?v=RDWFXWiIq0Y (accessed 4 January 2011).

Coleman, E. Gabriella, and Alex Golub. 2008. "Hacker Practice: Moral Genres and the Cultural Articulation of Liberalism." *Anthropological Theory* 8 (3): 255–277. http://dx.doi.org/10.1177/1463499608093814.

"Colonoscopy Demonstrating a Moving Worm." 2008. YouTube. http://www.youtube.com/watch?v=HOaZCkA8Zvk (accessed 5 January 2011).

Compaine, Benjamin M. 2001. *The Digital Divide: Facing a Crisis or Creating a Myth?* Cambridge, MA: MIT Press.

Consalvo, Mia, and Charles Ess. 2011. *The Handbook of Internet Studies*. Malden, MA: Wiley-Blackwell Publishing. http://dx.doi.org/10.1002/9781444314861.

Correll, Timothy Corrigan. 1997. "Associative Context and Joke Visualization." *Western Folklore* 56 (3/4): 317–30. http://dx.doi.org/10.2307/1500282.

Cray, Ed. 1964. "The Rabbi Trickster." *Journal of American Folklore* 77 (306): 331–345. http://dx.doi.org/10.2307/537381.

Crystal, David. 2006. *Language and the Internet*. 2nd edition. Cambridge: Cambridge University Press. http://dx.doi.org/10.1017/CBO9780511487002.

Crystal, David. 2011. *Internet Linguistics: A Student Guide*. New York: Routledge Press.

Danet, Brenda. 2001. *Cyberpl@y: Communicating Online*. Oxford: Berg Publishers.

Danet, Brenda, and Tamar Katriel. 1994. "Glorious Obsessions, Passionate Lovers, and Hidden Treasures: Collecting, Metaphor, and the Romantic Ethic." In *The Socialness of Things: Essays on the Socio-Semiotics of Objects*, ed. Stephen Harold Riggins, 23–61. New York: Mouton de Gruyter.

Dash, Anil. 2007. "Cats Can Has Grammar." *Wired Magazine (A Blog about Making Culture)*. http://tinyurl.com/2f24wq (accessed 1 July 2011).

Davies, Christie. 1990. *Ethnic Humor around the World: A Comparative Analysis*. Bloomington: Indiana University Press.

Davies, Christie. 2011. *Jokes and Targets*. Bloomington: Indiana University Press.

Dawkins, Richard. 1976. *The Selfish Gene*. New York: Oxford University Press.

de Souza e Silva, Adriana. 2006. "From Cyber to Hybrid: Mobile Technologies as Interfaces of Hybrid Spaces." *Space and Culture* 6 (3): 261–278.

Dégh, Linda. 1994. *American Folklore and the Mass Media*. Bloomington: Indiana University Press.

Dégh, Linda. 2001. *Legend and Belief: Dialectics of a Folk Genre*. Bloomington: Indiana University Press.

Dégh, Linda, and Andrew Vázsonyi. 1994 (1975). "The Hypothesis of Multi-Conduit Transmission in Folklore." In *Narratives in Society: A Performer-Centered Study of Narration*, ed. Linda Dégh, 173–212. Helsinki: Academia Scientiarum Fennica.

Del Negro, Giovanna P. 2010. "From the Nightclub to the Living Room: Party Records of Three Jewish Women Comics." In *Jews at Home: The Domestication of Identity*, ed. Simon J. Bronner, 188–213. Oxford: Littman.

Derby, George Horatio. 1856. *Phoenixiana: or, Sketches and Burlesques*. New York: D. Appleton and Company.

Desser, David. 2001. "Jews in Space: The 'Ordeal of Masculinity' in Contemporary American Film and Television." In *Ladies and Gentlemen, Boys and Girls: Gender in Film at the End of the Twentieth Century*, ed. Murray Pomerance, 267–282. Albany: State University of New York Press.

Devita-Raeburn, Elizabeth. 2008. "If Osama's Only 6 Degrees Away, Why Can't We Find Him?" *Discover* (February): 41–6.

"Die It." 2003. *1,000 Ways to Die*, episode 734. SPIKE TV. Aired 12 June 2003.

"Diet Fads." 2008. *E! Investigates*. Entertainment Network. Aired 5 January 2008. *DietsinReview.com*. http://www.dietsinreview.com (accessed 22 July 2010).

DigiBarn. 2005a. Homebrew Newsletter, Volume 1, Issue 2, page 5. *Homebrew Newsletter Archives*. http://www.digibarn.com/collections/newsletters/homebrew/V1_02/page5.jpg (accessed 28 February 2011).

DigiBarn. 2005b. Homebrew Newsletter, Volume 1, Issue 3, page 1. *Homebrew Newsletter Archives*. http://www.digibarn.com/collections/newsletters/homebrew/V1_03/index.html (accessed 28 February 2011).

DigiBarn. 2005c. Homebrew Newsletter, Volume 1, Issue 4. *Homebrew Newsletter Archives*. http://www.digibarn.com/collections/newsletters/homebrew/V1_04/index.html (accessed 28 February 2011).

DigiBarn. 2005d. Homebrew Newsletter, Volume 1, Issue 5, page 1. *Homebrew Newsletter Archives*. http://www.digibarn.com/collections/newsletters/homebrew/V1_05/homebrew_V1_05_p1.jpg (accessed 28 February 2011).

DigiBarn. 2005e. Homebrew Newsletter, Volume 2, Issue 1, page 1. *Homebrew Newsletter Archives*. http://www.digibarn.com/collections/newsletters/homebrew/V2_05/Homebrew_CC_May76_Page_1.jpg (accessed 28 February 2011).

Dobler, Robert. 2009. "Ghosts in the Machine: Mourning the MySpace Dead." In *Folklore and the Internet: Vernacular Expression in a Digital World*, ed. Trevor J. Blank, 175–193. Logan: Utah State University Press.

Dorson, Richard M. 1968. "What Is Folklore?" *Folklore Forum* 1 (4): 37.

Dorson, Richard M. 1972. *Folklore and Folklife: An Introduction*. Chicago: University of Chicago Press.

Dorst, John. 1990. "Tags and Burners, Cycles and Networks: Folklore in the Telectronic Age." *Journal of Folklore Research* 27 (3): 179–190.

Douglas, Mary. 1968. "The Social Control of Cognition: Some Factors in Joke Perception." *Man* 3 (3): 361. http://dx.doi.org/10.2307/2798875.

Douglas, Mary. 1994. "The Genuine Article." In *The Socialness of Things: Essays on the Socio-Semiotics of Objects*, ed. Stephen Harold Riggins, 9–22. New York: Mouton de Gruyter.

"Downfall." http://www.youtube.com/watch?v=vT2-AuEb7Bc (accessed 15 February 2011).

Dresner, Eli, and Susan C. Herring. 2010. "Functions of the Nonverbal in CMC: Emoticons and Illocutionary Force." *Communication Theory* 20 (3): 249–268. http://dx.doi.org/10.1111/j.1468-2885.2010.01362.x.

Dundes, Alan. 1962. "From Etic to Emic Units in the Structural Study of Folktales." *Journal of American Folklore* 75 (296): 95–105. http://dx.doi.org/10.2307/538171.

Dundes, Alan. 1965. *The Study of Folklore*. Englewood Cliffs, NJ: Prentice-Hall.

Dundes, Alan. 1966. "Metafolklore and Oral Literary Criticism." *Monist* 50 (4): 505–516.

Dundes, Alan, ed. 1980. *Interpreting Folklore*. Bloomington: Indiana University Press.

Dundes, Alan. 1981. "Many Hands Make Light Work or Caught in the Act of Screwing in Light Bulbs." *Western Folklore* 40 (3): 261–266. http://dx.doi.org/10.2307/1499697.

Dundes, Alan. 1985. "The J.A.P. and the J.A.M. in American Jokelore." *Journal of American Folklore* 98 (390): 456–475. http://dx.doi.org/10.2307/540367.

Dundes, Alan. 1989. *Folklore Matters*. Knoxville: University of Tennessee Press.

Dundes, Alan. 1997. *Cracking Jokes: Studies of Sick Humor Cycles and Stereotypes*. Berkeley, CA: Ten Speed Press.

Dundes, Alan, and Carl R. Pagter. 1978 (1975). *Work Hard and You Shall Be Rewarded: Urban Folklore from the Paperwork Empire.* Bloomington: Indiana University Press.

Dundes, Alan, and Carl R. Pagter. 1987. *When You're Up to Your Ass in Alligators: More Urban Folklore from the Paperwork Empire.* Detroit: Wayne State University Press.

Dundes, Alan, and Carl R. Pagter. 1991. *Never Try to Teach a Pig to Sing: Still More Urban Folklore from the Paperwork Empire.* Detroit: Wayne State University Press.

Dundes, Alan, and Carl R. Pagter. 1996. *Sometimes the Dragon Wins: Yet More Urban Folklore from the Paperwork Empire.* Syracuse, NY: Syracuse University Press.

Dundes, Alan, and Carl R. Pagter. 2000. *Why Don't Sheep Shrink When It Rains: A Further Collection of Photocopier Lore.* Syracuse, NY: Syracuse University Press.

Eamon, Mary Keegan. 2004. "Digital Divide in Computer Access and Use between Poor and Non-Poor Youth." *Journal of Sociology and Social Welfare* 31 (2): 91–112.

"eBaum's World Forum." http://forum.ebaumsworld.com/archive/index.php/t-32121.html (accessed 5 February 2011).

Ebo, Bosah. 1998. *Cyberghetto or Cybertopia? Race, Class, and Gender on the Internet.* Westport, CT: Praeger Publishers.

Eco, Umberto. 2009. *The Infinity of Lists,* trans. Alastair McEwen. New York: Rizzoli.

Eilbirt, Henry. 1981. *What Is a Jewish Joke? An Excursion into Jewish Humor.* Northvale, NJ: Jason Aronson.

Ellis, Bill. 1987. "Why Are Verbatim Transcripts of Legends Necessary?" In *Perspectives on Contemporary Legend II,* ed. Gillian Bennett, Paul S. Smith, and J.D.A. Widdowson, 31–60. Sheffield, UK: Sheffield Academic Press.

Ellis, Bill. 2001. "A Model for Collecting and Interpreting World Trade Center Disaster Jokes." *New Directions in Folklore,* October 5. https://scholarworks.iu.edu/dspace/handle/2022/7195.

Ellis, Bill. 2003. "Making a Big Apple Crumble: The Role of Humor in Constructing a Global Response to Disaster." In *Of Corpse: Death and Humor in Folklore and Popular Culture,* ed. Peter Narváez, 35–82. Logan: Utah State University Press. Earlier version published in *New Directions in Folklore,* 6 June 2002. https://scholarworks.iu.edu/dspace/handle/2022/6911.

Ellis, Bill. 2004. *Lucifer Ascending: The Occult in Folklore and Popular Culture.* Lexington: University Press of Kentucky.

Ellis, Bill. 2009. "Sleeping Beauty Awakens Herself: Folklore and Gender Inversion in *Cardcaptor Sakura.*" In *The Japanification of Children's Popular Culture: From Godzilla to Spirited Away,* ed. Mark I. West, 249–266. Lanham, MD: Scarecrow Press.

"Emoticons." *Wikipedia.* http://en.wikipedia.org/wiki/Emoticons (accessed 5 February 2011).

"The Evil Tapeworm." 2008. YouTube. http://www.youtube.com/watch?v=7q4rRRTuDrU (accessed 4 January 2011).

Falk, Avner. 1993. "The Problem of Mourning in Jewish History." In *The Psychoanalytic Study of Society, Volume 18: Essays in Honor of Alan Dundes,* ed. L. Bryce Boyer, Ruth M. Boyer, and Stephen M. Sonnenberg, 299–316. Hillsdale, NJ: Analytic Press.

Farrell, Nicoloe. 2009. "*Inu Yasha*: The Search for the Jewel of Four Souls in America." In *The Japanification of Children's Popular Culture: From Godzilla to Spirited Away,* ed. Mark I. West, 227–248. Lanham, MD: Scarecrow Press.

Fernback, Jan. 2003. "Legends on the Net: An Examination of Computer-Mediated Communication as a Locus of Oral Culture." *New Media & Society* 5 (1): 29–45. http://dx.doi.org/10.1177/1461444803005001902.

Fine, Gary Alan. 1992 [1979]. "Folklore Diffusion through Interactive Social Networks: Conduits in a Preadolescent Community." In *Manufacturing Folklore*, 86–119. Knoxville: University of Tennessee Press.

Fine, Gary Alan, and Bill Ellis. 2010. *The Global Grapevine: Why Rumors of Terrorism, Immigration, and Trade Matter.* New York: Oxford University Press.

Fine, Gary Alan, and Barry O'Neill. 2010. "Policy Legends and Folklists: Traditional Beliefs in the Public Sphere." *Journal of American Folklore* 123 (488): 150–178. http://dx.doi.org/10.1353/jaf.0.0133.

Fine, Gary Alan, and Patricia Turner. 2001. *Whispers on the Color Line: Rumor and Race in America.* Berkeley: University of California Press.

Fischman, Fernando. 2011. "Using Yiddish: Language Ideologies, Verbal Art, and Identity among Argentine Jews." *Journal of Folklore Research* 48 (1): 37–61. http://dx.doi.org/10.2979/jfolkrese.48.1.37.

Foote, Monica. 2007. "Userpicks: Cyber Folk Art in the Early 21st Century." *Folklore Forum* 37 (1): 27–38. https://scholarworks.iu.edu/dspace/handle/2022/3251.

Foster, Michael Dylan. 2009. *Pandemonium and Parade: Japanese Monsters and the Culture of Y kai.* Berkeley: University of California Press.

Fox, William S. 2007 [1983]. "Computerized Creation and Diffusion of Folkloric Materials." *Folklore Forum* 37 (1): 5–14. https://scholarworks.iu.edu/dspace/handle/2022/3235. Originally published in *Folklore Forum* 16 (1): 5–20.

Foxman, Abraham H. 2010. *Jews and Money: The Story of a Stereotype.* New York: Palgrave Macmillan.

Frank, Russell. 2004. "When the Going Gets Tough, the Tough Go Photoshopping: September 11 and the Newslore of Vengeance and Victimization." *New Media & Society* 6 (5): 633–658. http://dx.doi.org/10.1177/146144804047084.

Frank, Russell. 2009. "The *Forward* as Folklore: Studying Emailed Humor." In *Folklore and the Internet: Vernacular Expression in a Digital World*, ed. Trevor J. Blank, 98–122. Logan: Utah State University Press.

Frank, Russell. 2011. *Newslore: Contemporary Folklore on the Internet.* Jackson: University Press of Mississippi.

Freiberger, Paul, and Michael Swaine. 1984. *Fire in the Valley: The Making of the Personal Computer.* New York: McGraw-Hill.

Freud, Sigmund. 1960 (1905). *Jokes and Their Relation to the Unconscious*, trans. James Strachey. New York: W. W. Norton & Co.

Friedlander, Judith. 2011. "Typical Jokes in the Shtetl." *Professor Judith Friedlander's Peopling of New York, Spring 2011* [website]. http://tinyurl.com/6y79vfc/ (accessed 5 July 2011).

Friedman, Rabbi William S. 1912. "Report of Committee on Church and State." In *Yearbook of the Central Conference of American Rabbis*, volume 22, ed. Samuel Schulman and Solomon Foster, 101–18. New York: Central Conference of American Rabbis.

Friedman, Ted. 2005. *Electric Dreams: Computers and American Culture.* New York: New York University Press.

Gagné, Robert M. 1962. "The Acquisition of Knowledge." *Psychological Review* 69 (4): 355–365. http://dx.doi.org/10.1037/h0042650.

Gagné, Robert M. 1985 (1964). *The Conditions of Learning and Theory of Instruction.* 4th edition. New York: Holt, Rinehart, and Winston.

Gagné, Robert M., Leslie J. Briggs, and Walter W. Wager. 1992 (1974). *Principles of Instructional Design.* 4th edition. Belmont, CA: Wadsworth Publishing.

Galambos, Louis, and Eric Abrahamson. 2002. *Anytime, Anywhere: Entrepreneurship and the Creation of a Wireless World*. New York: Cambridge University Press.

Georges, Robert A. 1969. "Toward an Understanding of Storytelling Events." *Journal of American Folklore* 82 (326): 313–328. http://dx.doi.org/10.2307/539777.

Georges, Robert A., and Michael Owen Jones. 1980. *People Studying People: The Human Element in Fieldwork*. Berkeley: University of California Press.

Gilman, Sander L. 1990. *Jewish Self-Hatred: Anti-Semitism and the Hidden Language of the Jews*. Baltimore: Johns Hopkins University Press.

Gilmore, David D. 2009. *Monsters: Evil Beings, Mythical Beasts, and All Manner of Imaginary Terrors*. Philadelphia: University of Pennsylvania Press.

Glassie, Henry. 1968. *Pattern in the Material Folk Culture of the Eastern United States*. Philadelphia: University of Pennsylvania Press.

Glassie, Henry. 1982. *Passing the Time in Ballymenone: Culture and History of an Ulster Community*. Bloomington: Indiana University Press.

Glassie, Henry. 2000. *Vernacular Architecture*. Bloomington: Indiana University Press.

Glassie, Henry. 2006. *The Stars of Ballymenone*. Bloomington: Indiana University Press.

Goffman, Erving. 1974. *Frame Analysis: An Essay on the Organization of Experience*. New York: Harper Colophon.

Golden, Harry. 1965. "Introduction." In *Röyte Pomerantsen: Jewish Folk Humor*, ed. Immanuel Olsvanger, vii–xv. New York: Schocken.

Goldstein, Kenneth S. 1999 (1971). "Strategy in Counting Out: An Ethnographic Folklore Field Study." In *International Folkloristics: Classic Contributions by the Founders of the Field*, ed. Alan Dundes, 231–244. Lanham, MD: Rowman & Littlefield Publishers.

Golomb, Claire. 2011. *The Creation of Imaginary Worlds: The Role of Art, Magic & Dreams in Child Development*. Philadelphia: Jessica Kingsley Publishers.

Goody, Jack. 1977. *The Domestication of the Savage Mind*. Cambridge: Cambridge University Press.

"Grace before Meals." Children's Graces. http://home.pcisys.net/~tbc/mealpryr. htm#prayer11_26 (accessed 2 February 2011).

Grameen Foundation. 2009. "Mobile Phones Empower Ugandans." *Appropriate Technology* 36 (4): 58–60.

Graham, Gordon. 2002. *Genes: A Philosophical Inquiry*. New York: Routledge.

Gray, Jonathan. 2010. *Show Sold Separately: Promos, Spoilers, and Other Media Paratexts*. New York: New York University Press.

Gupta, Akhil, and James Ferguson. 1992. "Beyond 'Culture': Space, Identity, and the Politics of Difference." *Cultural Anthropology* 7 (1): 6–23. http://dx.doi.org/10.1525/can.1992.7.1.02a00020.

GVU. 2001a. GVU's Third WWW User Survey Programming Years Graphs: *GVU WWW User Surveys*. The Graphics, Visualization & Usability Center at Georgia Tech (GVU). http://www.cc.gatech.edu/gvu/user_surveys/survey-04-1995/graphs/info/prog_years.html (accessed 1 April 2001).

GVU. 2001b. GVU's Tenth WWW User Survey Graphs: *GVU WWW User Surveys*. The Graphics, Visualization & Usability Center at Georgia Tech (GVU). http://www.cc.gatech.edu/gvu/user_surveys/survey-1998-10/graphs/graphs.html (accessed 1 April 2001).

GVU. 2001c. GVU's Tenth WWW User Survey Graphs: Graphs and Tables of the Results. *GVU WWW User Surveys*. The Graphics, Visualization & Usability Center at

Georgia Tech (GVU). http://www.cc.gatech.edu/gvu/user_surveys/survey-1998-10/ graphs/graphs.html (accessed 1 April 2001).

Habermaus, Jürgen. 2001. *The Postnational Constellation: Political Essays*, trans. Max Pensky. Cambridge, MA: Polity.

Hafner, Katie, and Matthew Lyon. 1998. *Where Wizards Stay up Late: The Origins of the Internet*. New York: Simon and Schuster.

Hall, Stuart. 1980. "Encoding/Decoding." In *Culture, Media, Language*, ed. Stuart Hall, Dorothy Hobson, Andrew Lowe, and Paul Willis, 128–138. London: Hutchinson.

Halpert, Herbert. 1951. "A Pattern of Proverbial Exaggeration from West Kentucky." *Midwest Folklore* 1 (1): 41–47.

Hampton, Keith N., Oren Livio, and Lauren Sessions Goulet. 2010. "The Social Life of Wireless Urban Spaces: Internet Use, Social Networks, and the Public Realm." *Journal of Communication* 60 (4): 701–722. http://dx.doi.org/10.1111/j.1460-2466.2010.01510.x.

Hanks, Henry. 2010. "Pay Phones: The Search for an Endangered Species." *CNN*, April 2. http://tinyurl.com/cnnpayphones (accessed 23 July 2011).

Hannson, P. O., and Elin Wihlborg. 2011. "Internet Café as a Supportive Educational Arena: A Case Study from the Urban Slum Of Kibera, Nairobi, Kenya." *INTED2011 Proceedings*: 5966–5975.

Hargittai, Eszter, and Eden Litt. 2011. "The Tweet Smell of Celebrity Success: Explaining Variation in Twitter Adoption among a Diverse Group of Young Adults." *New Media & Society* 13 (5): 824–842. http://dx.doi.org/10.1177/1461444811405805.

Hatch, Mary Jo, and Michael Owen Jones. 1997. "Photocopylore at Work: Aesthetics, Collective Creativity and the Social Construction of Organizations." *Studies in Cultures, Organizations and Societies* 3 (2): 263–287. http://dx.doi.org/10.1080/10245289708523498.

Hathaway, Rosemary V. 2005. "'Life in the TV': The Visual Nature of 9/11 Lore and Its Impact on Vernacular Response." *Journal of Folklore Research* 42 (1): 33–56.

Hay, James, and Nick Couldry. 2011. "Rethinking Convergence/Culture: An Introduction." *Cultural Studies* 25 (4/5): 473–486. http://dx.doi.org/10.1080/09502386.2011.600527.

Heilman, Samuel C. 2006. *Sliding to the Right: The Contest for the Future of American Jewish Orthodoxy*. Berkeley: University of California Press.

Hillenbrand, Laura. 2002. *Seabiscuit: An American Legend*. New York: Ballantine Books.

Hilmes, Michele, and Jason Loviglio, eds. 2001. *Radio Reader: Essays in the Cultural History of Radio*. New York: Routledge Press.

"Hitler Emoticons." http://www.buzzfeed.com/expresident/hitler-emoticons (accessed 5 February 2011).

"HK Expats." http://hkexpats.com/showthread.php?p=76099 (accessed 21 May 2011).

Hoffman, Sam. 2010. *Old Jews Telling Jokes*. New York: Villard.

Horrigan, John. 2009. "Wireless Internet Use." *Pew Research Center's Internet and American Life Project*, July 22. http://www.pewinternet.org/Reports/2009/12-Wireless-Internet-Use.aspx (accessed 27 January 2012).

Hou, Weimin, Manpreet Kaur, Anita Komlodi, Wayne G. Lutters, Lee Boot, Shelia R. Cotton, Claudia Morrell, A. Ant Ozok, and Zeynep Tufekci. 2006. "'Girls Don't Waste Time': Pre-Adolescent Attitudes toward ICT." *Proceedings of the CHI Conference on Human Factors in Computing Systems* (CHI 2006). New York: ACM Press.

Howard, Philip N., Laura Busch, and Penelope Sheets. 2010. "Comparing Digital Divides: Internet Access and Social Inequality in Canada and the United States." *Canadian Journal of Communication* 35 (1): 109–125.

Howard, Robert Glenn. 1998. "Researching Folk Rhetoric: The Case of Apocalyptic Techno-Gaianism on the World-Wide Web." *Folklore Forum* 29 (2): 53–73.

Howard, Robert Glenn. 2005a. "A Theory of Vernacular Rhetoric: The Case of the 'Sinner's Prayer' Online." *Folklore* 116 (2): 172–188. http://dx.doi.org/10.1080/00155870500140214.

Howard, Robert Glenn. 2005b. "Toward a Theory of the World Wide Web Vernacular: The Case for Pet Cloning." *Journal of Folklore Research* 42 (3): 323–360. http://dx.doi.org/10.2979/JFR.2005.42.3.323.

Howard, Robert Glenn, and the Robert Glenn Howard. 2008a. "Electronic Hybridity: The Persistent Processes of the Vernacular Web." *Journal of American Folklore* 121 (480): 192–218. http://dx.doi.org/10.1353/jaf.0.0012.

Howard, Robert Glenn. 2008b. "The Vernacular Web of Participatory Media." *Critical Studies in Media Communication* 25 (5): 490–513. http://dx.doi.org/10.1080/15295030802468065.

Howard, Robert Glenn. 2011. *Digital Jesus: The Making of a New Christian Fundamentalist Community on the Internet.* New York: New York University Press.

Hugill, Stan. 1969. *Shanties and Sailor's Songs.* New York: Praeger.

Huizinga, Johan. 1955. *Homo Ludens.* Boston: Beacon.

Humphreys, Lee. 2005. "Cellphones in Public: Social Interactions in a Wireless Era." *New Media & Society* 7 (6): 810–833. http://dx.doi.org/10.1177/1461444805058164.

Hunt, Margaret. 1884. *Grimm's Household Tales with the Author's Notes.* 2 vols. London: George Bell and Sons.

Hymes, Dell H. 1975. "Breakthrough into Performance." In *Folklore: Performance and Communication*, ed. Dan Ben-Amos and Kenneth S. Goldstein, 11–74. The Hague: Mouton.

"'Hypnotist' Thief Hunted in Italy." 2008. FreeRepublic.com, March 22. http://tinyurl.com/3h6leh3 (accessed 8 July 2011).

IBM. 1974. "System/370 Model 115." *IBM Archives.* http://tinyurl.com/6krsa2c (accessed 28 February 2011).

Internet World Statistics, 2010. "United States Internet and Facebook Usage State by State." www.internetworldstats.com/unitedstates.htm (accessed 26 January 2012).

"It's the Links, Stupid!" 2006. *The Economist.* http://tinyurl.com/5s7o4p4 (accessed 19 June 2011).

Jansen, William Hugh. 1959. "The Esoteric-Exoteric Factor in Folklore." *Fabula: Journal of Folktale Studies* 2 (2): 205–211. http://dx.doi.org/10.1515/fabl.1959.2.2.205.

Jansen, William Hugh. 1963 (1959). "The Esoteric-Exoteric Factor in Folklore." In *The Study of Folklore*, ed. Alan Dundes, 43–51. Englewood Cliffs, NJ: Prentice Hall.

Jason, Heda. 1967. "The Jewish Joke: The Problem of Definition." *Southern Folklore Quarterly* 31 (1): 48–54.

Jenkins, Henry. 2008. *Convergence Culture: Where Old and New Media Collide.* New York: New York University Press.

Jennings, Karla. 1990. *The Devouring Fungus: Tales of the Computer Age.* New York: W. W. Norton & Co.

Jenny Craig Weight Loss Program. 2011. http://jennycraig.com (accessed 15 April 2011).

Jones, Michael Owen. 1997. "How Can We Apply Event Analysis to 'Material Behavior,' and Why Should We?" *Western Folklore* 56 (3/4): 199–214. http://dx.doi.org/10.2307/1500274.

Jordan, Scott. 2009. "A Layered United States Universal Service Fund for an Everything-over-IP World." *Telecommunications Policy* 33 (3/4): 111–128. http://dx.doi.org/10.1016/j.telpol.2008.11.007.

Kapchan, Deborah. 1993. "Hybridization and the Marketplace: Emerging Paradigms in Folkloristics." *Western Folklore* 52 (2/4): 303–326. http://dx.doi.org/10.2307/1500092.

Kaplan, Merrill. 2010. "Memorates on YouTube, *or* The Legend Conduit Is a Series of Tubes." Paper presented at the annual meeting of the Western States Folklore Society, April 15–17, Salem, Oregon.

Kaplan, Merrill. 2013. "Curation and Tradition on Web 2.0." In *Tradition in the Twenty-First Century: Locating the Role of the Past in the Present*, ed. Trevor J. Blank and Robert Glenn Howard. Logan: Utah State University Press, forthcoming.

Katz, Naomi, and Eli Katz. 1971. "Tradition and Adaptation in American Jewish Humor." *Journal of American Folklore* 84 (332): 215–220. http://dx.doi.org/10.2307/538991.

Kibby, Marjorie. 2005. "Email Forwardables: Folklore in the Age of the Internet." *New Media & Society* 7 (6): 770–790. http://dx.doi.org/10.1177/1461444805058161.

Kimzey, Anne. 2010. E-mail communication with Elizabeth Tucker. 8 February.

King, Storm A. 1996. "Researching Internet Communities: Proposed Ethical Guidelines for the Reporting of Results." *Information Society* 12 (2): 119–128. http://dx.doi.org/10.1080/713856145.

Kinsella, James (Afro 25). 2009. Anime/Manga fans. Posted in "Average age of Anime Fans," thread on *MyAnimeList*, 10 October. http://myanimelist.net/forum/?topicid=122531&show=0 (accessed 12 March 2011).

Kirshenblatt-Gimblett, Barbara. 1995. "From the Paperwork Empire to the Paperless Office: Testing the Limits of the 'Science of Tradition.'" In *Folklore Interpreted: Essays in Honor of Alan Dundes*, ed. Regina Bendix and Rosemary Levy Zumwalt, 69–92. New York: Garland.

Kirshenblatt-Gimblett, Barbara. 1996. "The Electronic Vernacular." In *Connected: Engagements with Media*, ed. George E. Marcus, 21–66. Chicago: University of Chicago Press.

Kirshenblatt-Gimblett, Barbara. 1998. "Folklore's Crisis." *Journal of American Folklore* 111 (441): 281–327. http://dx.doi.org/10.2307/541312.

Kirshenblatt-Gimblett, Barbara. 2004. "Performance Studies." In *The Performance Studies Reader*, ed. Henry Bial, 43–55. New York: Routledge.

Klaf, Franklin S., and Bernhardt J. Hurwood, eds. 1964 (1887). *A Hundred Merry Tales*. New York: Citadel.

Klein, Amy. 2009. "YouTube Jews." *Jewish Chronicle*. http://thejewishchronicle.net/view/full_story/2210743/article-YouTube-Jews (accessed 14 July 2011).

Knott, Blanche. 1982. *Truly Tasteless Jokes*. New York: Ballantine Books.

Kodish, Debra. 1983. "Fair Young Ladies and Bonny Irish Boys: Pattern in Vernacular Poetics." *Journal of American Folklore* 96 (380): 131–150. http://dx.doi.org/10.2307/540289.

Kristol, Irving. 1951. "Is Jewish Humor Dead? The Rise and Fall of the Jewish Joke." *Commentary* (November). http://tinyurl.com/isjewishhumordead.

Lamebook. 2011. "About." http://www.lamebook.com/about (accessed 20 July 2011).

246

Langlois, Janet L. 2005. "'Celebrating Arabs': Tracing Legend and Rumor Labyrinths in Post-9/11 Detroit." *Journal of American Folklore* 118 (468): 219–236. http://dx.doi.org/10.1353/jaf.2005.0021.

Lardinois, Frederic. 2010. "One Third of U.S. Internet Users Now Post Status Updates Once per Week." *Reading Write Web*, January 19. http://tinyurl.com/yejom2c (accessed 19 March 2010).

Larsen, Jonas, John Urry, and Kay Axhausen. 2008. "Coordinating Face-to-Face Meetings in Mobile Network Societies." *Information Communication and Society* 11 (5): 640–658. http://dx.doi.org/10.1080/13691180802126752.

Lau, Kimberly J. 2010. "The Political Lives of Avatars: Play and Democracy in Virtual Worlds." *Western Folklore* 69 (3/4): 369–394.

"Laugh Break." http://www.laughbreak.com/lists/numbers_of_the_beast.html (accessed 31 January 2011).

Lawson, Danielle. 2003. "Blurring the Boundaries: Ethical Considerations for Online Research Using Synchronous CMC Forums." In *Readings in Virtual Research Ethics: Issues and Controversies*, ed. Elizabeth A. Buchanan, 80–100. Hershey, PA: Information Science Publishing. http://dx.doi.org/10.4018/978-1-59140-152-0.ch005.

Leach, Maria, ed. 1949. *The Standard Dictionary of Folklore, Mythology, and Legend.* 2 vols. New York: Funk and Wagnalls.

Lessig, Lawrence. 2002. *The Future of Ideas: The Fate of the Commons in a Connected World.* New York: Vintage Books.

Leventhal, Nancy C., and Ed Cray. 1963. "Depth Collecting from a Sixth-Grade Class." *Western Folklore* 22 (4): 231–257. http://dx.doi.org/10.2307/1498177.

Levine, Lawrence W. 1988. *Highbrow/Lowbrow: The Emergence of Cultural Hierarchy in America.* Cambridge, MA: Harvard University Press.

Levitan, M. Y. 1911. *Motke Habad, oder Vitse iber Vitse.* New York: Hebrew Publishing.

Lindholm, Charles, and José Pedro Zúquete. 2010. *The Struggle for the World: Liberation Movements for the 21st Century.* Palo Alto, CA: Stanford University Press.

Lloyd, Timothy. 2011. "AFS Issues Comments on Proposed Changes in IRB Regulations and Practices." *AFS Review*, October 25. http://www.afsnet.org/news/77145 (accessed 23 February 2012).

Longenecker, Gregory J. 1977. "Sequential Parody Graffiti." *Western Folklore* 36 (4): 354–364. http://dx.doi.org/10.2307/1499199.

Lowitt, Bruce. 2006. "They're for the Shiva." *Jewish Sightseeing* website, July 4. http://www.jewishsightseeing.com/jewish_humor/punchlines_and_their_jokes/2006-07-04-Number%2093.htm (accessed 6 July 2011).

Lüthi, Max. 1976 [1969]. "Aspects of the Märchen and the Legend." In *Folklore Genres*, ed. Dan Ben-Amos, 17–33. Austin: University of Texas Press. Originally published in *Genre* 2: 162–178.

Lyotard, Jean-François. 1984 [1979]. *The Postmodern Condition: A Report on Knowledge*, trans. Geoff Bennington and Brian Mussumi. Theory and History of Literature Series, Vol. 10. Minneapolis: University of Minnesota Press.

Magliocco, Sabina. 2004. *Witching Culture: Folklore and Neo-Paganism in America.* Philadelphia: University of Pennsylvania Press.

Marchalonis, Shirley. 1979. "Three Medieval Tales and Their Modern American Analogues." In *Readings in American Folklore*, ed. Jan Harold Brunvand, 267–278. New York: W. W. Norton & Co. http://dx.doi.org/10.2307/3813854.

Martin, Steven P., and John P. Robinson. 2007. "The Income Digital Divide: Trends and Predictions for Levels of Internet Use." *Social Problems* 54 (1): 1–22. http://dx.doi.org/10.1525/sp.2007.54.1.1.

Mason, Bruce Lionel. 1996. "Moving toward Virtual Ethnography." *American Folklore Society Newsletter* 25 (2): 4–6.

Mason, Bruce Lionel. 1998. "E-Texts: The Orality and Literacy Issue Revisited." *Oral Tradition* 13 (2): 306–329.

Mason, Bruce Lionel. 2001. "Issues in Virtual Ethnography." *Ethnographic Studies in Real and Virtual Environments: Inhabited Information Spaces and Connected Communities*, ed. Kathy Buckner, 61–69. Proceedings of Espirit 3 Workshop on Ethnographic Studies. Edinburgh, UK: Queen Margaret College, January 1999.

Mason, Bruce Lionel. 2007. "The Creation of Folk Cultures on the Internet: A Proposed Methodology of Investigation with Case Studies." PhD dissertation, Memorial University of Newfoundland, St. John's.

McDowell, John. 2008. "Rethinking Folklorization in Ecuador: Multivocality in the Expressive Contact Zone." Archer Taylor Memorial Lecture, annual meeting of the Western States Folklore Society, April 10–11, Davis, California.

McKee, Heidi A., and James E. Porter. 2009. *The Ethics of Internet Research: A Rhetorical, Case-Based Process*. New York: Peter Lang Publishing.

McLure, Helen. 2000. "The Wild, Wild Web: The Mythic American West and the Electronic Frontier." *Western Historical Quarterly* 31 (4): 457–476. http://dx.doi.org/10.2307/970103.

McMahon, Felicia R. 2007. *Not Just Child's Play: Emerging Tradition and the Lost Boys of Sudan*. Jackson: University Press of Mississippi.

McNeill, Lynne S. 2007. "Portable Places: Serial Collaboration and the Creation of a New Sense of Place." *Western Folklore* 66 (3/4): 281–300.

McNeill, Lynne S. 2009. "The End of the Internet: A Folk Response to the Provision of Infinite Choice." In *Folklore and the Internet: Vernacular Expression in a Digital World*, ed. Trevor J. Blank, 80–97. Logan: Utah State University Press.

McNeill, Lynne S., Trevor J. Blank, John Allen Cicala, Robert Glenn Howard, and Montana Miller. 2010. "Teaching Folklore and Digital Culture." Discussion forum at the annual meeting for the American Folklore Society, October 13–16, Nashville, TN.

Mechling, Jay. 2008. "Gun Play." *American Journal of Play* 1 (2): 192–209.

Mechling, Jay. 2009. "Is Hazing Play?" In *Transactions at Play: Play & Culture Studies*, vol. 9, ed. Cindy Dell Clark, 45–62. Lanham, MD: University Press of America.

"Michael Jackson Dance Tribute." Uploaded 9 July 2009. YouTube. http://vimeo.com/5545871 (accessed 15 July 2011).

Michaels, Ralf. 2006. "Two Economists, Three Opinions? Economic Models for Private International Law—Cross-Border Torts as Example." *Duke Law Faculty Scholarship*. Paper 1234. http://scholarship.law.duke.edu/faculty_scholarship/1234 (accessed 6 January 2012).

Michaelson, Jay. 2006. "Two Lawyers, Three Opinions: On the Jewishness of Law, and Vice Versa." *Jewish Daily Forward*, November 3. http://www.forward.com/articles/7395/ (accessed 6 January 2012).

Mikkelson, Barbara. 2006. As the Worm Squirms. *Urban Legends Reference Pages*. http://www.snopes.com/horrors/vanities/tapeworm.asp (accessed 17 November 2010).

Milgram, Stanley. 1967. "The Small World Problem." *Psychology Today* 1 (1): 60–67.

Miller, Carolyn. 1993. "Are Jews Funnier than Non-Jews?" In *Semites and Stereotypes: Characteristics of Jewish Humor*, ed. Avner Ziv and Anat Zajdman, 13–28. Westport, CT: Greenwood Press.

Miller, Kiri. 2008. "Grove Street Grimm: *Grand Theft Auto* and Digital Folklore." *Journal of American Folklore* 121 (481): 255–285. http://dx.doi.org/10.1353/jaf.0.0017.

Miller, Michael. 2010. "Jokes in Prison." *Old Jews Telling Jokes*, March 10. http://oldjews-tellingjokes.com/post/439016846 (accessed 14 July 2011).

Miller, Montana. 2005. "Candid, Confidential, Contagious? Teenagers and Eating Disorders on the Internet." Paper presented at the annual meeting of the American Folklore Society, October 19–23, Atlanta, Georgia.

Miller, Montana. 2006a. "The Facebook Generation: Negotiating Parallel Campuses, Virtual and Real." Paper presented at the 27th Annual Ethnography in Education Research Forum, February 24–25, Philadelphia, Pennsylvania.

Miller, Montana. 2006b. "Blogging into the Beyond: Emerging Frames of Teenage Death and Immortality." Paper presented at the annual meeting of the American Folklore Society, October 18–22, Milwaukee, Wisconsin.

Miller, Montana. 2007. "Sense, Secrets, and Sanctimommies: Shifting Boundaries in a Women's Chat Room." Western States Folklore Society Annual Conference, April 20–22, Los Angeles, California.

Miller, Montana. 2008. "Private Lives, Public Story: How Facebook's 'Feed' Shattered the Frames." Paper presented at the annual meeting of the Popular Culture Association, March 19–22, San Francisco, California.

Miller, Montana. 2009a. "Ordinary Life, Webkinz Play." Paper presented at the annual meeting of the Western States Folklore Society, April 16–18, Los Angeles, California.

Miller, Montana. 2009b. "Facebook, Faculty-Student 'Friendship,' and the Erosion of Traditional Boundaries in Academic Culture." Paper presented at the annual meeting of the American Folklore Society, October 21–25, Boise, Idaho.

Miller, Montana. 2010a. "Ethical Issues in Researching Internet Mourning and Memorials." Paper presented at the annual meeting of the Popular Culture Association/ American Culture Association, March 31–April 3, St. Louis, Missouri.

Miller, Montana. 2010b. "Breaking the Surface Tension: Professional High Divers' Storytelling Traditions, from Theme Park Survival to Facebook Revival." Paper presented at the annual meeting of the American Folklore Society, October 13–16, Nashville, Tennessee.

Milspaw, Yvonne J., and Wesley K. Evans. 2010. "Variations on Vampires: Live Action Role Playing, Fantasy and the Revival of Traditional Beliefs." *Western Folklore* 69 (2): 211–251.

Minimins. http://www.minimins.com (accessed 23 July 2011).

Minkoff, David. 2005. *Oy! The Ultimate Book of Jewish Jokes.* New York: St. Martin's Press.

Mitchell, Carol A. 1977. "The Sexual Perspective in the Appreciation and Interpretation of Jokes." *Western Folklore* 36 (4): 303–329. http://dx.doi.org/10.2307/1499196.

Mitchell, Carol A. 1985. "Some Differences in Male and Female Joke-Telling." In *Women's Folklore, Women's Culture*, ed. Rosan A. Jordan and Susan J. Kal ik, 163–186. Philadelphia: University of Pennsylvania Press.

"Monsters inside Me: Pork Tapeworm." 2010. YouTube. http://www.youtube.com/ watch?v=bb32g02IIs8 (accessed 27 July 2010).

Museum of Hoaxes. http://www.museumofhoaxes.com (accessed 25 July 2011).

"Nathan." 2009. "Woman Dies from Tapeworm Diet?" *UADDit-Add Something New.* http://uaddit.com/discussions/showthread.php?t=8052 (accessed 30 December 2009).

Nelson, Theodor H. 1974. *Computer Lib: You Can and Must Understand Computers Now/ Dream Machines: New Freedoms Through Computer Screens—A Minority Report.* Chicago: Hugo's Book Service.

Nevo, Ofra, and Jacob Levine. 1994. "Jewish Humor Strikes Again: The Outburst of Humor in Israel during the Gulf War." *Western Folklore* 53 (2): 125–145. http://dx.doi.org/10.2307/1500100.

"New England Brewing Company." http://beeradvocate.com/beer/profile/357/58731 (accessed 11 February 2011).

Nilsen, Alleen Pace, and Don L.F. Nilsen. 2000. *Encyclopedia of 20th-Century Humor.* Phoenix: Oryx.

Norris, Pippa. 2001. *Digital Divide: Engagement, Information Poverty, and the Internet Worldwide.* Cambridge: Cambridge University Press.

"Not Just Talk." 2011. *The Economist,* January 27. http://www.economist.com/node/18008202 (accessed 22 February 2012).

Nowak, Mike. 2005. "One Login to Bind Them All." *Wired.* http://tinyurl.com/3jwomzb (accessed 19 June 2011).

Noyes, Dorothy. 2003. "Group." In *Eight Words for the Study of Expressive Culture,* ed. Burt Feintuch, 7–41. Champaign: University of Illinois Press.

O'Brien, Chris. 2011. "How One Student's Pepper Spray Photo Became an Internet Meme." *San Jose Mercury News,* November 23. http://www.mercurynews.com/chris-obrien/ci_19401731 (accessed 5 February 2012).

O'Conor, Anahad. 2006 "The Claim: Chocolate Is an Aphrodisiac." *New York Times,* July 18. http://www.nytimes.com/2006/07/18/health/18real.html?_r=1 (accessed 19 January 2012).

Olivarez-Giles, Nathan. 2011. "Egyptian Man Names His Baby Girl 'Facebook,' Reports Say." *Los Angeles Times* (Technology), February 21. http://tinyurl.com/3eyosyv (accessed 21 July 2011).

Olrik, Axel. 1965 (1909). "Epic Laws of Folk Narrative." In *The Study of Folklore,* ed. Alan Dundes, 129–141. Englewood Cliffs, NJ: Prentice-Hall.

Olsvanger, Immanuel, ed. 1965. *Röyte Pomerantsen, Or How to Laugh in Yiddish.* New York: Schocken.

Ong, Walter J. 1988 (1982). *Orality and Literacy: The Technologizing of the Word.* London: Methuen.

O'Reilly, Tim. 2005. "What Is Web 2.0: Design Patterns and Business Models for the Next Generation of Software." *O'Reillynet.* http://www.oreillynet.com/lpt/a/6228 (accessed 10 November 2006).

Oring, Elliott. 1983. "The People of the Joke: On the Conceptualization of a Jewish Humor." *Western Folklore* 42 (4): 261–271. http://dx.doi.org/10.2307/1499501.

Oring, Elliott. 1986. "On the Concepts of Folklore." In *Folk Groups and Folklore Genres: An Introduction,* ed. Elliott Oring, 1–22. Logan: Utah State University Press.

Oring, Elliott. 1992. *Jokes and Their Relations.* Lexington: University Press of Kentucky.

Oring, Elliott. 2003. *Engaging Humor.* Champaign: University of Illinois Press.

Paradise, Viola. 1913. "The Jewish Immigrant Girl in Chicago." *Survey* 30, September 6: 700–704.

Paredes, Américo. 1958. "'El Corrido de José Mosqueda' as an Example of Pattern in the Ballad." *Western Folklore* 17 (3): 154–62. http://dx.doi.org/10.2307/1496039.

Paredes, Américo, and Richard Bauman, eds. 1972. *Toward New Perspectives in Folklore.* Publications of the American Folklore Society. Austin: University of Texas Press.

Perelman, Chaim, and L. Olbrechts-Tyteca. 1969. *The New Rhetoric: A Treatise on Argumentation,* trans. John Wilkinson and Purcell Weaver. Notre Dame, IN: Notre Dame University Press.

Perz, Sally Anne. 2009. "Are You Forwarding Folklore?" *Family Times* 2 (2): 1–2.

Pew Research Center's Internet and American Life Project. 2011. "A Closer Look at Generations and Cell Phone Ownership." http://www.pewinternet.org/Infographics/2011/Generations-and-cell-phones.aspx (accessed 23 July 2011).

Pimple, Kenneth. 1996. "The Meme-ing of Folklore." *Journal of Folklore Research* 33 (3): 236–240.

Platt, Roberta. 2011. "Shloime Is Dying." *Old Jews Telling Jokes,* May 4. http://oldjewstellingjokes.com/post/5188581836 (accessed 14 July 2011).

Poster, Mark. 2002. "Digital Networks and Citizenship." *PMLA* 117 (1): 98–103. http://dx.doi.org/10.1632/003081202X63546.

Prensky, Marc. 2001a. "Digital Natives, Digital Immigrants, Part 1." *Horizon* 9 (5): 1–6. http://dx.doi.org/10.1108/10748120110424816.

Prensky, Marc. 2001b. "Digital Natives, Digital Immigrants, Part 2: Do They Really Think Differently?" *Horizon* 9 (6): 1–6. http://dx.doi.org/10.1108/10748120110424843.

Prensky, Marc. 2010. *Teaching Digital Natives: Partnering for Real Learning.* Thousand Oaks, CA: Corwin.

Preston, Michael J. 1974. "Xerox-Lore." *Keystone Quarterly* 19 (1): 11–26.

Preston, Michael J. 1994. "Traditional Humor from the Fax Machine: 'All of a Kind'." *Western Folklore* 53 (2): 147–169. http://dx.doi.org/10.2307/1500101.

Preston, Michael J. 1996. "Computer Folklore." In *American Folklore: An Encyclopedia,* ed. Jan Harold Brunvand, 154–155. New York: Garland.

Rainie, Lee, and Kristin Purcell. 2010. *The Economics of Online News.* Pew Research Center's Internet and American Life Project. http://tinyurl.com/RainiePurcell2010 (accessed 19 March 2010).

Ramos, Katie. 2009. "'You Can Has Prezidency': Patterns of Folk Punditry in Political Image Macros." Presented at the annual meeting for the American Folklore Society, October 21–25, Boise, ID.

Raskin, Richard. 1992. *Life Is Like a Glass of Tea: Studies of Classic Jewish Jokes.* Aarhus, Denmark: Aarhus University Press.

Ravnitzky, J. H. 1922. *Yidishe Vitsn.* Berlin: Moriya.

Raymond, Eric S., ed. 1996. *The New Hacker's Dictionary.* 3rd edition. Cambridge, MA: MIT Press. http://www.outpost9.com/reference/jargon/jargon_toc.html.

Recent Tapeworm Jokes. 2010. *JokeBuddha.com.* http://www.jokebuddha.com/Tapeworm/recent (accessed 11 July 2011).

Reider, Noriko T. 2010. *Japanese Demon Lore: Oni from Ancient Times to the Present.* Logan: Utah State University Press.

Reik, Theodor. 1962. *Jewish Wit.* New York: Gamut Press.

Renwick, Roger deV. 2009 [2001]. *Recentering Anglo/American Folksong.* Jackson: University Press of Mississippi.

Rheingold, Howard. 1992. *Virtual Reality.* New York: Touchstone Books.

Rheingold, Howard. 2000 (1993). *The Virtual Community: Homesteading on the Electronic Frontier.* Cambridge, MA: MIT Press.

Rheingold, Howard. 2001. "Why Can't We Use Technology to Solve Social Problems?" http://www.edge.org/print/res-detail.php?rid=1691 (accessed 1 January 2003).

Rheingold, Howard. 2002. *Smart Mobs: The Next Social Revolution.* Cambridge, MA: Perseus Publishing.

Ristau, Kate. 2009. "'How Will I Ever Go to Confession If I Can't Make My Avatar Stop Dancing?' Logging into the Sacred through Second Life." Paper presented at the annual meeting of the Western States Folklore Society, April 16–18, Los Angeles, California.

Roberts, Warren. 1949. "Children's Games and Game Rhymes." *Hoosier Folklore* 8 (1): 7–34.

"Rock Paper Scissors!! (Let's Play!!)." 2008. YouTube. http://tinyurl.com/3ep5bpu (accessed 8 July 2011).

Roemer, Danielle M. 1994. "Photocopy Lore and the Naturalization of the Corporate Body." *Journal of American Folklore* 107 (423): 121–138. http://dx.doi.org/10.2307/541076.

Rosten, Leo. 1968. *The Joys of Yiddish.* New York: McGraw-Hill.

Rozakis, Laurie. 2007. *The Portable Jewish Mother.* Avon, MA: Adams Media.

Rubin, Rachel, and Jeffrey Melnick. 2006. *Immigration and American Popular Culture: An Introduction.* New York: New York University Press.

Rudy, Jill Terry. 2002. "Toward an Assessment of *Verbal Art as Performance*: A Cross-Disciplinary Citation Study with Rhetorical Analysis." *Journal of American Folklore* 115 (455): 5–27.

Runnel, Pille. 2001. "Conducting Ethnographic Research on the Internet." In *Input & Output: The Process of Fieldwork, Archiving and Research in Folklore,* ed. Ulrika Wolf-Knuts, 167–188. Turku, Sweden: Nordic Network of Folklore Publications.

Ryan, Yasmine. 2011. "Anonymous and the Arab Uprisings." *AlJazeera,* May 19 (18:16). http://www.aljazeera.com/news/middleeast/2011/05/201151917634659824.html (accessed 22 February 2012).

"Rythospital.com (RYTHospital-Dwayne Medical Center)." 2008. http://www.rythospital.com.

Sahlins, Marshall D., and Elman R. Service. 1960. *Evolution and Culture.* Ann Arbor: University of Michigan Press.

"San Francisco Pillow Fight Flash Mob." 2006. YouTube. http://www.youtube.com/watch?v=TNI_6LsExtw (accessed 15 July 2011).

Saper, Bernard. 1993. "Since When Is Jewish Humor Not Anti-Semitic?" In *Semites and Stereotypes: Characteristics of Jewish Humor,* ed. Avner Ziv and Anat Zajdman, 71–86. Westport, CT: Greenwood Press.

"Save the Endangered Pacific Northwest Tree Octopus from Extinction!" http://zapatopi.net/treeoctopus (accessed 8 March 1998).

"Save the Guinea Worm Foundation." 2010. http://deadlysins.com/guineaworm/index.htm.

Sawin, Patricia E. 2002. "Performance at the Nexus of Gender, Power, and Desire: Reconsidering Bauman's *Verbal Art* from the Perspective of Gendered Subjectivity as Performance." *Journal of American Folklore* 115 (455): 28–61.

"Scale Models 1." http://tinyurl.com/3qgkux2. (accessed 2 February 2011).

"Scale Models 2." http://tinyurl.com/3h6cgay (accessed 10 February 2011).

Schachter, Stanley J. 2008. *Laugh for God's Sake: Where Jewish Humor and Jewish Ethics Meet.* Jersey City, NJ: KTAV.

Schmaier, Maurice D. 1963. "The Doll Joke Pattern in Contemporary American Oral Humor." *Midwest Folklore* 13 (4): 205–216.

Segaller, Stephen. 1998. *Nerds 2.0.1: A Brief History of the Internet*. New York: TV Books, LLC.

Selingo, Jeffrey. 2002. "The Bell Is Tolling for the Beeper." *New York Times*, April 11. http://tinyurl.com/selingo2002 (accessed 30 January 2012).

Serracino-Inglott, Peter. 2001. "To Joke or Not to Joke: A Diplomatic Dilemma in the Age of Internet." In *Language and Diplomacy*, ed. Jovan Kurbalija and Hannah Slavik, 21–38. Msida, Malta: DiploProjects.

SFZero. 2011. "1000 Small (Heavy) Things." *SFZero.com*. http://sf0.org/tasks/1000-Small-Heavy-Things/ (accessed 31 January 2011).

Shibutani, Tamotsu. 1966. *Improvised News: A Sociological Study of Rumor*. Indianapolis: Bobbs-Merrill.

Shields, Rob. 2003. *The Virtual*. London: Routledge.

Shifman, Limor, and Mike Thelwall. 2009. "Assessing Global Diffusion with Web Memetics: The Spread and Evolution of a Popular Joke." *Journal of the American Society for Information Science and Technology* 60 (12): 2567–2576. http://dx.doi.org/10.1002/asi.21185.

Shirky, Clay. 2008. *Here Comes Everybody: The Power of Organizing without Organizations*. New York: Penguin Press.

Shirky, Clay. 2010. *Cognitive Surplus: Creativity and Generosity in a Connected Age*. New York: Penguin Press.

Shredd, Travis. 2000. "The Neighbor of the Beast." http://tinyurl.com/3q6lkot (accessed 2 February 2011).

Shuman, Amy. 2005. *Other People's Stories*. Champaign: University of Illinois Press.

"Sick, Sick, Sick." http://tinyurl.com/43b39x3 (accessed 2 February 2011).

Silverman, Dwight. 2007. "AT&T to Hang Up on Pay Phone Business Next Year." Weblog (TechBlog), Chron.com. http://tinyurl.com/attpayphone07 (accessed 23 July 2011).

Singer, Dorothy G., and Jerome L. Singer, eds. 2000. *Handbook of Children and the Media*. Thousand Oaks, CA: Sage Publications.

Smale, Maura A. 2010. "Demystifying the IRB: Human Subjects Research in Academic Libraries." *Libraries and the Academy* 10 (3): 309–321. http://dx.doi.org/10.1353/pla.0.0114.

Smith, Aaron. 2011. "35% of American Adults Own a Smartphone." *Pew Research Center's Internet and American Life Project*, July 11. http://tinyurl.com/pewsmartphoneadoption (accessed 23 July 2011).

Smith, Paul. 1984. *The Complete Book of Office Mis-Practice*. London: Routledge & Kegan Paul.

Smith, Paul. 1986. *Reproduction Is Fun: A Book of Photocopy Joke Sheets*. London: Routledge & Kegan Paul.

Smith, Paul. 1991. "The Joke Machine: Communicating Tradition Humour Using Computers." In *Spoken in Jest*, ed. Gillian Bennett, 257–278. Sheffield, UK: Sheffield Academic Press.

Soffer, Oren. 2010. "'Silent Orality': Toward a Conceptualization of the Digital Oral Features in CMC and SMS Texts." *Communication Theory* 20 (4): 387–404. http://dx.doi.org/10.1111/j.1468-2885.2010.01368.x.

Solomont, E. B. 2005. "Point, Click, Chuckle: Jewish Humor Goes Online." *Jewish Daily Forward*, February 4. http://forward.com/articles/2879/point-click-chuckle-jewish-humor-goes-online/ (accessed 14 July 2011).

Spalding, Henry D. 1969. "Preface." In *Encyclopedia of Jewish Humor: From Biblical Times to the Modern Age*, ed. Henry D. Spalding, xiii–xix. New York: Jonathan David.

Spalding, Henry D. 1976. "Introduction." In *A Treasure-Trove of American Jewish Humor*, ed. Henry D. Spalding, xiii–xvii. Middle Village, NY: Jonathan David.

Steiner, George. 1975. *After Babel: Aspects of Language and Translation*. New York: Oxford University Press.

Stewart, Susan. 1993. *On Longing: Narratives of the Miniature, the Gigantic, the Souvenir, the Collection*. Durham, NC: Duke University Press.

Stirland, Sarah Lai. 2007. "Don't Tase Me, Bro!" Jolts the Web. *Wired Magazine (Threat Level Blog)*. http://tinyurl.com/448gc5g (accessed 29 May 2011).

Suler, John. 2004. "The Online Disinhibition Effect." *Cyberpsychology & Behavior* 7 (3): 321–326. http://dx.doi.org/10.1089/1094931041291295.

"The Tapeworm Diet (EEEWW!!)." 2008. *MiniMins.com-Weight Loss Forum*. http://tinyurl.com/tapewormdieteww (accessed 27 July 2010).

"Tapeworm in My Bathtub." 2007. YouTube. http://www.youtube.com/watch?v=qbkC_RHqT6w (accessed 27 July 2010).

Taylor, Archer. 1964. "The Biographical Pattern in Traditional Narrative." *Journal of the Folklore Institute* 1 (1/2): 114–129. http://dx.doi.org/10.2307/3814034.

"Teamwork." 2009. *House*, Season 6, Episode 7 (accessed 16 November 2010).

Technology Quarterly. 2009. "Serious Fun—Technology and Society: 'Alternate Reality' Games Mixing Puzzles and Plot Lines, Online and Off, Are Becoming More Popular." *The Economist*, March 5. http://www.economist.com/node/13174355 (accessed 30 January 2011).

Telushkin, Rabbi Joseph. 1992. *Jewish Humor: What the Best Jewish Jokes Say about Jews*. New York: William Morrow.

Terdiman, Daniel. 2006. "Collaborative Gaming Takes to the Streets." CNET News, April 14. http://tinyurl.com/6f8n8qj (accessed 31 January 2011).

Thompson, Tok. 2003. "'Ladies and Gentlemen, the North Road Pounders!': An Inquiry into Identity, Aesthetics, and New Authenticities in Rural Alaska." *Journal of Folklore Research* 40 (3): 273–288.

Thompson, Tok. 2011. "Beatboxing, Mashups, and Cyborg Identity: Folk Music for the Twenty-First Century." *Western Folklore* 70 (2): 171–193.

Titon, Jeff Todd. 1995. "Text." *Journal of American Folklore* 108 (430): 432–448. http://dx.doi.org/10.2307/541655.

Toelken, Barre, ed. 1996. *The Dynamics of Folklore*. Logan: Utah State University Press.

Travers, Jeffrey, and Stanley Milgram. 1969. "An Experimental Study of the Small World Problem." *Sociometry* 32 (4): 425–443. http://dx.doi.org/10.2307/2786545.

"Tristan Café." http://www.tristancafe.com/forum/87331 (accessed 21 May 2011).

Tuan, Yi-Fu. 1998. *Escapism*. Baltimore: Johns Hopkins University Press.

Tucker, Elizabeth. 1977. "The Seven-Day Wonder Diet: Magic and Ritual in Diet Folklore." *Indiana Folklore* 11: 141–150.

Turing, Alan. 1950. "Computing Machinery and Intelligence." *Mind* 59 (236): 433–460. http://dx.doi.org/10.1093/mind/LIX.236.433.

Turkle, Sherry. 1995. *Life on the Screen: Identity in the Age of the Internet*. New York: Simon and Schuster.

Turkle, Sherry. 2011. *Alone Together: Why We Expect More from Technology and Less from Each Other*. New York: Basic Books.

Turner, Fred. 2006. *From Counterculture to Cyberculture: Stewart Brand, the Whole Earth Network, and the Rise of Digital Utopianism*. Chicago: University of Chicago Press.

"University of Florida Student Tasered at Kerry Forum." 2007. YouTube. http://www.youtube.com/watch?v=6bVa6jn4rpE (accessed 23 June 2011).

Valkenburg, Patti M. 2004. *Children's Responses to the Screen: A Media Psychological Approach*. New York: Routledge.

Varnelis, Kazys. 2008. *Networked Publics*. Cambridge, MA: MIT Press.

Walker, Jesse. 2004. *Rebels on the Air: An Alternative History of Radio in America*. New York: New York University Press.

Wallace, Patricia. 1999. *The Psychology of the Internet*. Cambridge: Cambridge University Press.

Warnick, Barbara. 2007. *Rhetoric Online: Persuasion and Politics on the World Wide Web*. New York: Peter Lang Publishing.

Wasik, Bill. 2009. *And Then There's This: How Stories Live and Die in Viral Culture*. New York: Viking Press.

Waskul, Dennis, and Mark Douglass. 1996. "Considering the Electronic Participant: Some Polemical Observations on the Ethics of On-Line Research." *Information Society* 12 (2): 129–140. http://dx.doi.org/10.1080/713856142.

Weaver, Simon. 2011. "Jokes, Rhetoric and Embodied Racism: A Rhetorical Discourse Analysis of the Logics of Racist Jokes on the Internet." *Ethnicities* 11 (4): 413–435. http://dx.doi.org/10.1177/1468796811407755.

Weinstein, Simcah. 2008. *Shtick Shift: Jewish Humor in the 21st Century*. Fort Lee, NJ: Barricade.

Weinstein, Valerie. 2005. "Dissolving Boundaries: Assimilation and Allosemitism in E. A. Dupont's *Das alte Gesetz* (1923) and Veit Harlan's *Jud Süss* (1940)." *German Quarterly* 78 (4): 496–516. http://dx.doi.org/10.1111/j.1756-1183.2005.tb00027.x.

Westerman, William. 2009. "Epistemology, the Sociology of Knowledge, and the *Wikipedia* Userbox Controversy." In *Folklore and the Internet: Vernacular Expression in a Digital World*, ed. Trevor J. Blank, 123–158. Logan: Utah State University Press.

Whitfield, Stephen J. 1986. "The Distinctiveness of American Jewish Humor." *Modern Judaism* 6 (3): 245–260. http://dx.doi.org/10.1093/mj/6.3.245.

Wilde, Larry. 1974. *The Official Jewish Joke Book*. New York: Pinnacle.

"World's Biggest Flash Freeze Mob in Paris OFFICIAL VIDEO." 2008. *YouTube*. http://www.youtube.com/watch?v=qtUNj2BNTsU&feature=related (accessed 15 July 2011).

World Wide Web Consortium. 2000. "A Little History of the World-Wide-Web." http://www.w3.org/History.html (accessed 1 December 2000).

"Yahoo Answers." http://tinyurl.com/blondjokeexplained (accessed 2 February 2011).

Yardi, Sarita, and Amy Bruckman. 2012. "Income, Race, and Class: Exploring Socioeconomic Differences in Family Technology Use." *Proceedings of the CHI Conference on Human Factors in Computing Systems* (CHI '12). New York: ACM Press.

Zauderer, Rabbi David. 2011. "Two Jews, Three Opinions." *Torah from Dixie* website. http://www.tfdixie.com/parshat/korach/013.htm (accessed 5 July 2011).

Zeitlin, Steve. 1997. "Introduction." In *Because God Loves Stories: An Anthology of Jewish Storytelling*, ed. Steve Zeitlin, 17–24. New York: Touchstone Books.

Zickuhr, Kathryn. 2011. "Generations and Their Gadgets." *Pew Research Center's Internet and American Life Project*, February 3. http://www.pewinternet.org/Reports/2011/Generations-and-gadgets.aspx (accessed 23 July 2011).